ATTITUDES TOWARD ENGLISH TEACHING

ATTITUDES TOWARD ENGLISH TEACHING

❧

JOSEPH MERSAND

CHILTON COMPANY · BOOK DIVISION
Publishers
PHILADELPHIA AND NEW YORK

Dedicated to the
OFFICERS AND MEMBERS OF NCTE

Preface

To secure the information, which is summarized and analyzed in the following pages, the following individuals were addressed:

Personnel	Number Addressed	Number Replied
Leaders of:		
1. NCTE Affiliates	143	60
2. Heads of State Education Departments	50	36
3. College Presidents	95	79
4. Business Executives	106	63
5. Civil Service Administrators	50	30
6. Newspaper Editors	54	25
7. Magazine Editors	60	35
8. Educational Editors	37	22
9. Members of Congress	51	15
10. U.S. District Judges	25	6
11. Deans of Law Schools	25	12
12. U.S. Attorneys	25	5
13. Public Librarians	228	87
14. Publishers	122	43
15. Managers of College Bookstores	1100	106
16. Managers of Commercial Bookstores	1750	160
17. College Librarians	2011	467

It was presumed that all of these individuals were familiar with either the nature of English teaching or the competence in English of the high school and college graduates of the last 5 or 10 years. The replies were most encouraging both in quantity and in the details with which the respondents supported their opinions. To all who took the time and trouble to reply to the several questions of the writer, our sincere gratitude. What is perhaps more enlightening than the almost 1250 candid expressions of opinion are the many suggestions for strengthening the English program. These represent the considered opinions of highly educated and successful persons in their chosen fields, and hence deserve our most serious consideration. Perhaps out of this exchange of correspondence may come a greater understanding between members of our profession and our successful colleagues in other professions. Their genuine interest in what we are trying to do for the millions of children and youth entrusted to us is heartwarming.

One area for greater communication is that of the knowledge of the efforts and achievements of the Council. Many of the respondents either were entirely unaware of our work or only vaguely aware. Many of them desired more information about the Council. Hence this report will be a kind of exchange of information: from our 1250 respondents to the 60,000 members of the NCTE, and from the Council to our friends in other professions. From such exchange of information and opinion, we trust that many advantages will come.

The compiler of this Report wishes to express his thanks to Mr. Perry Birnbaum, of Jamaica High School, Queens, N.Y.C., Mr. Joseph Maggio, of Walton High School, N.Y.C., and Dr. J. N. Hook, former Executive Secretary, for their generous assistance.

JOSEPH MERSAND

Contents

ATTITUDES TOWARD ENGLISH TEACHING

Activities of
State Affiliates

NATURE OF THE SURVEY

Early in 1958, 143 letters and questionnaires were sent to presidents of the state affiliates of the National Council of Teachers of English. In each letter, the First Vice-President of the NCTE pointed out that he would be required to submit a report on the state of English teaching throughout the country. Any information received, he added, would be of great value in the preparation of the report. The letter contained these four questions:

1. What improvements in the teaching of Language Arts from kindergarten through grade 12 have taken place in your state in the last year and should be included in my report as of November, 1958?
2. What new courses of study in the Language Arts have been adopted during that time or will be adopted by November, 1958?
3. What changes in methodology and content have taken place or will take place by November, 1958?
4. What changes in administration and supervision of the Language Arts have taken place or will take place by November, 1958?

These questions were not intended to produce a scientifically accurate consensus or even a complete picture of curriculum or administrative changes in all the states. Rather, the questions were exploratory in nature, and the answers were expected to give an idea of what is going on in the states. The answers did just that.

Since relatively few affiliate officers are in a position to keep up with all developments in curriculum revision, methodology, and content on a state level, few respondents answered the questions above; but the 19 sets of answers that were received shed a great deal of light upon the progress that is being made in the areas covered by the question. These replies are to be studied *as a part of the entire report* herein presented. No single group of affiliate presidents, or administrators, or teachers, or businessmen, lawyers, or editors could possibly present a complete picture of what is developing in the language arts. The opinions and information supplied by *all* groups will, it is believed, reveal not only the state of English teaching at this time, but also the sentiments of a broad cross-section of people who are directly or indirectly concerned with the language arts.

Little attempt has been made to edit the following replies since to do so would alter the picture that the writer of this report received, and which he wishes to pass on to the reader.

Alabama Council of Teachers of English

1. Sources of teaching aids have been made available to Alabama teachers; one course in English literature and one course in college preparatory English for high school seniors have been offered by TV.
2. English does not have a separate course of study in Alabama.
3. Structural linguistics is being stressed especially through Council newsletters.
4. There is no supervision of the language arts program on the state level; the ACTE is hoping to get some of its membership on a state committee of supervision.

Central California Council of Teachers of English

1. The State Board of Education and the CCCTE are engaged in a study of written composition.
2. In June, 1954, the San Francisco *Framework for Secondary English* replaced the course of study adopted in 1928. In 1952, 70 area teachers produced a booklet dealing with methodology called *Classroom Practices*.

NCTE Junior Affiliate, Teachers College of Connecticut

The State Department has started a revision of the course of study; attention on a state level has been primarily directed toward the teaching of reading.

Kansas

1. Teachers are showing an awareness of the need to teach reading in grades 7 to 12 both in English and in other subjects.
2. Wichita, Kansas—a recent curriculum guide was published; El Dorado, Kansas—curriculum revision is under way.
3. Emphasis is presently on the improvement of writing; there is also an attempt to substitute structural grammar for the more traditional approach.
4. Larger schools are getting full-time supervisors and directors of the language arts:
   Topeka—director of language arts, 7 to 12;
   Wichita—co-ordinator of language arts curriculum;
   In other parts of the state, department heads with time off for supervision are being added.

Hutchinson (Kansas) Council of Teachers of English

"The Hutchinson (Kansas) Public Schools have a form of continuing English curriculum revision. Each two year period the

Hutchinson Council of Teachers of English, working with the Department of Curriculum and Instruction, concentrates upon one phase of English work from kindergarten through college. At the end of the period a bulletin is issued. The last two bulletins have been on the teaching of usage and on general principles of English teaching. The basis for revision is the course of study, kindergarten through college, worked out several years ago under the direction of Robert C. Pooley."

Kentucky

1. There is attention to the improvement of writing.
2. A program of standard-setting for each grade has been worked out.
3. A proposal for revision of certification policy has been submitted to the state certifying agency.

The English Club of Greater Baltimore

1. A committee is now studying the program from kindergarten through grade 14, with the intention of suggesting modifications of the program.
2. Courses of study and curriculum materials are now being revised and supplemented, and in some cases, materials have been deleted.
3. Units are being developed for special work with the slow learner in reading. Considerable attention is being given to the teaching of writing. English-social studies core is being used.
4. Classes in remedial and developmental reading have been formed through the junior and senior high grades. The reading-centered unit is being emphasized. Heads of departments are now in the junior high schools as well as in the senior high schools.

Minneapolis English Teachers Club

A new functional spelling program has been introduced; a reading study program will begin in fall 1958; reading centers have been expanded; advanced placement programs in English are planned.

Missouri Association of Teachers of English

1. NCTE Curriculum has been in practice in most high schools and elementary schools in this state. A committee on the state level is now working on a curriculum for high school that will embrace integration, motivation, and "communication."
2. Methodology and content are left to each school; the state curriculum is a guide only.
3. MATE is trying to get a state director of language arts and better preparation of English teachers.

Trenton, New Jersey

Trenton Central High School now has a humanities program on the sophomore and junior levels that compares favorably with college literature courses.

Nassau English Council, New York

Heads of departments will have meetings in the fall during which syllabi will be shared and discussed.

Ohio

NCTE thinking has influenced the revision of the senior composition course.

Oklahoma Council of Teachers of English

The OCTE has produced a *Teaching Guide for the Language Arts.*

English Club of Philadelphia

1. A course of study is printed in *The English Guide,* which is constantly revised by the curriculum committee.
2. The curriculum committee will send out sample lessons and other information, plus information on linguistics, in which the committee feels teachers are weak.
3. The Committee on the Slow Learner is working on a special guide to be called "A Basic Guide."

Western Pennsylvania Association of English Teachers

1. There are new courses of study in Allegheny County and Pittsburgh.
2. Developmental reading has been added to the junior and senior high school program, with three additional hours of English each week (in certain schools).
3. Classes for the gifted are being added.
4. Revision of the curriculum for grades 7 to 12 is now under way.

Southern Dakota Council of Teachers of English

Attention is being given to the gifted, as shown through a summer institute held in 1958.

Texas State Teachers Association, English Section

1. Most curriculum work is done through district workshops; they have worked out articulation plans for grade one through college.
2. Many new course outlines have been produced throughout

the state; the Texas Education Agency has produced *Suggestions for the Teaching of English*.

3. Emphasis is being placed upon creativity in teaching as well as in learning.
4. Dallas, Houston, San Antonio, Fort Worth, and other cities have added consultants in English.

Texas

1. Texas has a large legislative committee making a survey of conditions in the state.
2. Some high schools will begin special classes for top students.
3. The University of Texas is active in its leadership for better teachers.
4. Conferences are held between high school and college teachers of English.
5. Workshops consisting of high school and college teachers meet by district to study integration of the teaching.
6. Little correlation of the subject disciplines is evident; grammar, however, is now more functional; writing is more expository than creative; there are fewer survey courses.
7. In Houston, reading is taught throughout the grades.
8. San Antonio now has a director of curriculum.

English Association of Greater Milwaukee

1. "If change is meant, then I can report that language arts instruction in this area has not improved materially. It continues to be maintained at an exceptionally high level." Homogeneous grouping is being experimented with; teaching of spelling techniques has been continued through the eighth grade in two schools; developmental reading is being taught in the junior high schools.
2. In one school, a publication called the "Writing Laboratory"

is in use; this is a course of study in writing for both the bright and the dull.

3. A return to the "basic fundamentals" is discernible—grammar, correctness in writing, less tolerance of spelling and other mechanical errors, cultural values of literature for its own sake, traditional selections of literature.

4. In one school, the Board ruled that each teacher *must* have five classes in addition to any extracurricular work.

REPLIES TO THE QUESTIONNAIRE

Enclosed with the letter was a questionnaire containing the following questions:

1. In the seven years since the publication of the *English Language Arts,* have classroom teaching and learning shown any progress? stood still? retrogressed? What evidence can you offer?

2. In workshops, conferences, meetings where teachers come together, have there been questions raised, comments made, attitudes shown which reflect enthusiasm for teaching? discouragement? demonstrated need for some special type of leadership? results in the form of proposals for action by the Council or by some other group?

3. Have research studies or action research projects been carried on in your community or in your institution, to show that children and young people spell or write, and express ideas orally and in writing as well as their fathers and mothers, or as effectively as citizens in a democracy should be able to speak or write? Have there been studies to prove the opposite of the above?

4. If you have personal reactions which you wish to express, please turn over the page and jot them down.

There were 59 questionnaires returned, and these were from affiliate presidents, former presidents, and members to whom the questionnaire was referred for one reason or another. Replies were received from the following states:

Alabama	Illinois	New York
Arizona	Kansas	Ohio
Arkansas	Kentucky	Oklahoma
California	Maryland	Pennsylvania
Colorado	Minnesota	South Dakota
Connecticut	Missouri	Texas
Florida	Nebraska	Virginia
Georgia	New Jersey	Wisconsin

The distribution by level is as follows:

10 questionnaires received from college teachers

42 questionnaires received from junior and senior high school teachers

7 questionnaires received from administrators, especially those involved in consulting and directing on a state level

Before presenting a more detailed treatment of the responses to the individual questions, it might be well to note two generalizations that appear valid after a careful study of the replies:

1. Administrators, bureau workers, consultants, supervisors, and other nonclassroom personnel were, in general, more enthusiastic than were the classroom or college teachers.
2. Geographical area had little or nothing to do with the degree of enthusiasm; the individual system or school, however, had a small but discernible effect upon the degree of optimism or discouragement.

SUMMARY OF REPLIES TO QUESTION 1—
PROGRESS IN TEACHING AND LEARNING

In general, *administrators and state department supervisors and consultants* saw progress reflected in such activities as publishing of teaching materials, workshops, meetings of various kinds, and programs of in-service courses. But one administrator, a president of a large city affiliate, pointed out that newspaper articles have supplied the "immediate incentive," suggesting that English may be getting attention on the "coattails" of mathematics and science. The newer methods, attention to individual needs and differences, and the wider use of resource materials were credited with bringing progress to the field of English teaching. No special credit was given to the volume *English Language Arts,* though several administrators noted that all publications of the NCTE have had some effect upon the progress of the profession.

The *college teachers and college department heads* who replied were not as optimistic in their evaluation of the state of English teaching and learning. Only one college teacher thought there has been progress, while two teachers thought classroom teaching and learning had "stood still," two found "no change" or "retrogression," and three insisted that teaching and learning had definitely "retrogressed." The one college teacher who saw progress pointed out that teachers have become more aware of individual and group needs, of the linguistic approach to language study, and of the need for "integration, motivation, and communication." But this one opinion of progress was assaulted by other claims that students are not as prepared in English skills as they were or as they should be. As one teacher put it:

If there has been change, I haven't noticed it. Nor have any of my colleagues, some of whom think that their students are worse, some of whom see no change. I have not heard anybody say that his students are better than they used to be.

Another teacher noted that "Little progress is discernible as a direct result of NCTE publications" because, presumably, "there are six uninformed, unenthusiastic teachers to every one informed, enthusiastic teacher." Still another college teacher wrote that "A good many of us here . . . think that the book *English Language Arts* has caused the subject of English to lose its identity as a subject matter. The hybrid language arts makes it difficult for the traditional English teacher to define his 'territory.'" Finally, several college teachers felt that new high school English teachers know little or nothing about literature, which is the subject central to the teaching of English.

A large number of *classroom teachers* saw definite progress in the teaching and learning of English, but three indicated that teaching and learning had retrogressed for the following reasons:

> There is no communication between teachers.
> "I'm a pessimist."
> Students accomplished more in the past.

SUMMARIES OF REPLIES TO QUESTION 2—
DEGREE OF ENTHUSIASM

Human nature being what it is, the consensus on this question can easily be surmised. The majority of each group—administrators and supervisors, college teachers, and classroom teachers— saw enthusiasm for teaching reflected in recent meetings of teachers. However, care must be taken in accepting this consensus, since the respondents are, of course, projecting their own feelings for the most part, and we must realize that their enthusiasm may not be shared by less active colleagues or by those who do not attend workshops, conferences, and other meetings of teachers. Putting the same caution in another and more cutting way, we might say with one college teacher that "Obviously, since teachers of English are a pretty vocal lot, all of the enumerated phenomena have been observed."

Four of the seven *administrators, supervisors,* and *consultants* saw enthusiasm for teaching reflected in a growing professional attitude toward English in particular and toward teaching in general. "Teachers are less complacent," remarked one director of curriculum. The other three administrators who saw enthusiasm noted that teachers are now receiving practical suggestions and helpful literature, from professional organizations as well as from local and state systems. The teachers in their turn are willing to experiment with new materials and methods, to accept the new burdens of teaching reading in all grades, to provide for slow and gifted students, and to give attention to the mass media.

The remaining three nonteaching respondents saw discouragement mixed with enthusiasm. Too much is expected of teachers in matters of class load, size of classes, and extracurricular activities. "The English teacher has the same duties as other teachers who have less grading and often fewer pupils." Two of the three who saw mixed attitudes noted that more leadership was needed on a local, state, and national level:

"The National Council might be able to give leadership in these respects:

1. Free English teachers from nonteaching duties.
2. Direct teachers to more and better teaching aids (audio-visual, reading lists, etc.).
3. Lessen the teaching load; consider English a laboratory subject as well as shop and science."

The *college personnel* saw enthusiasm barely outweighing discouragement. They attributed the enthusiasm, in general, to the same stimulants that were cited by the administrators. But discouragement, they noted, was very prevalent because of two factors: (1) the teachers themselves, and (2) teaching conditions. One college teacher wrote: "If students dislike the subject of English, we feel that in a good many cases, it is the fault of the teacher. Sentiment aims for a return to subject matter, away from the four divisions of the language arts." Another charged that the great majority of English teachers are "uninformed, unenthusiastic."

The predominant opinion, however, was that conditions such as the following were hampering teaching and destroying enthusiasm and optimism:

1. Teacher training programs were not requiring enough subject matter courses.
2. "Methods teachers have used the *English Language Arts* and later publications unwisely, we thought."
3. "Pupil load which exceeds 100 students a day is a deterrent to good teaching."
4. "Low economic and egghead status" is affecting teachers' attitudes. Higher salaries for science and mathematics teachers in some areas and reduced programs for them, while English classes grow larger, are also affecting morale. The following statements express the opinions of the officers of one organization:
   a. The secondary school English teacher should have a lighter load than he now has in most schools.
   b. The combining of social studies and English to make a core curriculum is not conducive to effective teaching.
   c. The practice of having no head of the English department may be democratic but it does not contribute to the improvement of teaching.
   d. The Council is to be commended for its action in trying to change requirements for certification.

The *classroom teachers* saw attitudes in the following distribution:

8 teachers noted only discouragement
15 teachers noted only enthusiasm

15 teachers noted both enthusiasm and discouragement, with
the balance going to the side of enthusiasm
4 teachers did not respond to this question

Three of the eight classroom teachers who noted only discouragement gave as the reason unsympathetic administrators who are
unaware of the needs of teachers of English. (Two of these three
teachers teach in the same school.) The belief that "Any teacher
can teach English" was decried by one teacher, and the heavy
class load, clerical duties, and other assignments—curricular and
extracurricular—were deplored by all the others. There was also
sentiment in favor of minimum grade standards in English.
One teacher went so far as to say: "We need some uniformity
in English standards throughout the *whole country*." The de-
emphasis of subject matter was also cited as a reason for discouragement.

The 15 teachers who saw both discouragement and enthusiasm
were almost unanimous in their attack upon the idea that an
English teacher has boundless energy and limitless time at his
disposal. Many cited the need for local supervision and guidance.
But genuine discouragement was seen to be in the minority, since
the recent re-evaluations and changes of curriculum have given
teachers the feeling that they are now at long last moving for-
ward. The 15 teachers who noted only enthusiasm saw the optimism resulting from all of the above-mentioned reasons, but also
from the increased activity of professional and state department
organizations.

The general opinion might be best summarized in the words
of one teacher who wrote:

Teachers seem to rally around the content and worth of their subject area [now]. With current emphasis on science and mathematics,
I detect evidence that many have personally re-evaluated their own
subject and come up with a deep conviction of its worth—In all of

this one may find enthusiasm, discouragement, and certainly an implied demand for leadership.

SUMMARIES OF REPLIES TO QUESTION 3— LANGUAGE SKILLS COMPARED

This question was intended to gauge opinion and optimism more than to produce statistically accurate answers. Certainly it is difficult, if not impossible, to compare conclusively the language effectiveness of children with that of their parents. However, though most teachers responded that they knew of no such studies, many teachers expressed opinions that revealed their optimism and satisfaction in the effectiveness of their teaching. "We like to think," wrote one teacher, "and we do believe that students with equal abilities are learning more today than several years ago." Others admitted that their optimism was based merely upon opinion, but a teacher from Omaha, Nebraska, noted the following:

> Tests in reading, spelling, and writing on the elementary level show much greater proficiency than 30 or 40 years ago. Our college entrants are being excused from Freshman English in increasing numbers. Students are better in English, on the basis of College Boards, than in any other subject.

Professor Oscar M. Haugh of the University of Kansas School of Education was kind enough to enclose a copy of the following tabular summary and synthesis, prepared in 1951, in support of a paper by Dr. Roger M. Shaw of Kent State University entitled: *A Synthesis of Research on Academic Achievement in Our Public Schools, Then and Now.* The tabular summary was also prepared by Dr. Shaw. The seven-year period since the preparation of the summary should have had no adverse effect upon its usefulness in this report.

It would not be fair to omit that several teachers expressed the

A Coded Table for the Purpose of Summary and Synthesis of the 15 Studies

I	II	III	IV	V	VI	VII	VIII	IX	X
	Study: Site, Reporter, Dates	*General Achievement*	*Reading*	*Spelling*	*Arithmetic*	*History*	*Grammar*	*Geography*	*Language Usage*
1	**Boston** Caldwell and Courtis 1945–1919	N		N					
2	**Cleveland** Luther 1848–1947	N			N	O	O	O	
3	**Boston** Fish 1853–1928	N			N		N	T	
4	**Indiana-Indianapolis** 1919–1941	N							
5	**Chicago** Rogers 1923–1946				O				
6	**St. Louis** Boss 1916–1938				O				
7	**Florida** Daughtry 1929–1947			O	T-N				
8	**Houston** Oberholtzer 1937		N	O	T				
9	**Roslyn** Board of Education 1938		O		T				N
10	**Lincoln School** Hopkins and Mendenhall 1934		T		N				N
11	**New York City** Jersild and others 1939		N	N	O				N
12	**Muncie** Pistor 1937		N	N	N				N
13	**Six Metropolitan Communities** Wrightstone 1938		N		N				N
14	**Los Angeles** Woods 1934		N	N	T				
15	**Eight Year Study of Progressive Education** 1932–1940	N							
16	Burke and Anderson 1951	O							
17	Harder and Anderson 1951	O							

Note: Read as follows: Caldwell and Courtis found *newer* practices superior in general achievement and spelling. The Roslyn experiment found *older* practices superior in reading, no marked superiority (TIE) in arithmetic, and *newer* practices superior in language usage.

Code: N—Findings favor newer school practices. O—Findings favor older school practices. T—Findings indicate approximate TIE. T-N—Findings indicate TIE and/or newer superiority.

general opinion that such studies have little or no value "one way or the other." (Indeed, some teachers saw no value in the question.) "It is impossible," wrote one teacher, "to compare the ability of a 13-year-old child with that of an adult." Another asserted, quite correctly, that "Surely we could never say that children and young people speak as 'effectively as citizens in a democracy should be able to.'"

CONTRIBUTORS

Alabama

Association of College Teachers of Alabama — David H. Malone, Former President (Alabama Polytechnic Institute, Auburn)

Alabama Council of Teachers of English — Elizabeth B. Barton, Former President (Chilton County High School, Clanton)

Arizona

Arizona English Teachers Association — Iris Mulvaney, President (Tucson Public Schools)

Arkansas

Arkansas College Teachers of English — William C. Doster, President (Ouachita Baptist College, Arkadelphia)

California

Central California Council of Teachers of English — V. T. Leonard, President (Polytechnic High School, San Francisco)

Colorado

English Section, Eastern Division, Colorado Education Association — Forrest W. Frease, President (Colorado State College, Greeley)

Connecticut

NCTE Junior Affiliate — M. E. Fowler, Advisor (Teachers College of Connecticut, New Britain)

Florida

Leon County Council of Teachers of English — Mrs. Carol Van Assenderp, President (Elizabeth Cobb College, Tallahassee)

Georgia
  Georgia Council of Teachers of   Paul Farmer, Reporter
  English
Illinois
  English Club of Greater Chicago   Olivia M. Cooke, Member
                                          (Curriculum Bureau, Chicago
                                          Board of Education)

Kansas
  Hutchinson Council of Teachers   Ruth Jones, President
  of English   (Lakeview School, Hutchinson)
                                          Oscar M. Haugh, Past President
                                          (University of Kansas, Lawrence)

Kentucky
  Kentucky Council of Teachers of   Gladys D. Marcus, President
  English   (Middleboro High School,
                                          Middleboro)

Maryland
  The English Council of Greater   Josie G. Smith, Liaison Officer
  Baltimore   (Division of Secondary Education
                                          Baltimore Department of
                                          Education)

Minnesota
  St. Paul English Teachers' Club   Kenneth J. Johnson, President
                                          (Highland Park Junior High
                                          School, St. Paul)
  Minneapolis English Teachers'   Robert A. Bennett, Member
  Club   (Consultant in Secondary
                                          Curriculum, Minneapolis Public
                                          Schools)

Missouri
  Missouri Association of Teachers   Frank W. Grube, President
  of English   (Northwest Missouri State College,
                                          Maryville)

Nebraska
  Nebraska Council of Teachers of   Frank M. Rice, President
  English   (Central High School, Omaha)
New Jersey
  New Jersey Association of   Agnell Mathewson, President
  Teachers of English   (Central High School, Trenton)
New York
  Nassau English Council   Muriel M. Paige, Liaison Officer
                                          (West Hempstead Schools)

Ohio

Ohio College English
Association

Don A. Keister, President
(University of Akron)

Summit County Teachers of
English

Edith V. Sherman, Director
(Akron Public Schools)

Oklahoma

Oklahoma Council of Teachers
of English

John M. Murphy, President
(Central State College, Edmond)

Pennsylvania

English Club of Philadelphia

Verda F. Cavallaro, President

Western Pennsylvania Association
of Teachers of English

Stella A. Price, President
(Pittsburgh Public Schools)

English Section—Midwestern
Branch, Pennsylvania Council
of Teachers of English
(PSEA)

Lila Adams, President
(Butler Junior High School)
Dorothy Hahn, Secretary

South Dakota

South Dakota Council of Teachers
of English

Grace Baker, President
(State University of South Dakota,
Vermillion)

Texas

English Section, Texas State
Teachers Association

Ruda P. Pool, Past Chairman
(North Dallas High School)

San Antonio English Club

Mattie Sharp Brewer, President
(Thomas Jefferson High School,
San Antonio)

Virginia

Virginia Association of Teachers
of English

R. C. Simonini, Jr., President
(Longwood College, Farmville)

Wisconsin

English Association of Greater
Milwaukee

Jarvis E. Bush, President
(Wauwatosa High School)

Activities of
State Departments of Education

The officers of 35 state departments of education were kind enough to give their valuable time to answering the following inquiries:

1. What improvements in the teaching of the Language Arts from kindergarten through grade 12 have taken place in your state in the last year and should be included in my report as of November, 1958?

2. What new courses of study in the Language Arts have been adopted during that time or will be adopted by November, 1958?

3. What changes in methodology and content have taken place or will take place by November, 1958?

4. What changes in administration and supervision of the Language Arts program have taken place or will take place by November, 1958?

5. What contributions can the National Council of Teachers of English make to the greater effectiveness of the program?

Replies to these questions were received from the following state departments:

Alabama Department of Education
California Department of Education
*Colorado Department of Education

* Special thanks are due to these respondents for the completeness and usefulness of their replies.

Delaware Department of Public Instruction
*Florida Department of Education
*Georgia State Department of Education
*Idaho Department of Education
Indiana Department of Public Instruction
*Kansas State Department of Public Instruction
Maine Department of Education
*Maryland State Department of Education
*Massachusetts Department of Education
Michigan Department of Public Instruction
Minnesota Department of Education
Mississippi Department of Education
Missouri State Department of Education
Montana State Department of Education
Nevada Department of Education
New Jersey Department of Education
New Mexico Department of Education
*New York State Department of Education
North Carolina Department of Public Instruction
North Dakota Department of Public Instruction
Ohio Department of Education
Oklahoma State Department of Education
Oregon Department of Education
Pennsylvania Department of Public Instruction
South Dakota Department of Public Instruction
*Texas State Department of Education
*Utah Department of Public Instruction
*Vermont Department of Education
*Virginia State Board of Education
Washington State Department of Public Instruction
West Virginia Department of Education
*Wisconsin Department of Public Instruction

* Special thanks are due to these respondents for the completeness and usefulness of their replies.

The following summary presentation of these replies will present a picture of *trends of activity* and *actual work under way* at the state level, of state-initiated or encouraged programs, and of observations of local activity as seen by state administrators. We are confident that the replies herein presented are the result of more than one man's opinion and information; we are confident that the replies represent a collection of opinion and information from colleagues and available state studies and surveys. In any case, no survey of this kind could hope to reflect every facet of activity on the state level. And, significantly, this report offers an analysis of *trends,* not a complete summary of activity.

In some cases, as will be seen, replies are incomplete because many states do not have directors of language arts or state-issued courses of study. In those cases, the state departments reported that the local schools and districts look to the state agency for guidance only.

SUMMARY OF REPLIES TO QUESTION 1— IMPROVEMENTS IN THE TEACHING OF THE LANGUAGE ARTS

By far the greatest improvement in the teaching of the language arts appears to be coming from recent re-evaluations, revisions, rewritings, and reissuings of syllabi and other curriculum materials, with an equally great productivity in the area of *new* courses of study and syllabi in the language arts. Almost every department replying noted some activity in this area, both on the state and on the local level.

Almost as significant as curriculum revision and development is the activity found in the various conferences, workshops, and in-service course programs across the country. Most states reported heavy teacher participation in meetings sponsored or cosponsored by the state agencies and local professional organizations. Probably the most important development is that the local English councils are working hand-in-hand with the state departments of education in curriculum development, revision, and evaluation. Many respondents noted that they have never before seen as much enthusiasm and such good attendance at such gatherings of teachers.

Of course, this activity at meetings of state department officials and teachers cannot in itself be thought of as a direct improvement in the teaching of the language arts, but the activity is certainly indicative of a new vitality, a new sense that there is a job to be done and a goal that can be reached. As W. Morrison McCall of the Alabama Department of Education put it, "There are many in-service groups in the state studying the area of the language arts. I am confident that this procedure contributes to the gradual improvement of the program of education in this area." Phila Humphreys of the Ohio Department of Education adds that about 75% of the schools in her state are engaged in in-service programs.

Other improvements cited in the various states were these:

1. Experimentation with grouping and larger blocks of time (Ohio)
2. Reading at all grade levels (Ohio)
3. "More planning for testing and use of results in planning" (Ohio)
4. Larger, better libraries, especially on the elementary level (Ohio and New Jersey)
5. Provision for the gifted (Ohio and Colorado)
6. Remedial reading programs (Ohio)
7. Ways of clarifying goals to parents (Ohio)
8. Greater integration of subject matter (New Jersey)
9. Individual needs through dramatizations, writing, etc. (New Jersey)
10. Greater articulation between college and high school (New Jersey)

11. Emphasis on communication: listening and speaking especially (Colorado)
12. Minimum grade standards (Alabama)

SUMMARY OF REPLIES TO QUESTION 2—
COURSES OF STUDY

The following work has been recently done or is being carried on presently in the area of curriculum development in the various states. This information supplied to us and which we pass on to the reader makes no claim to inclusiveness; certainly a great deal more is going on than our limited survey was able to determine.

California

The Curriculum Study Commission of the Central California Council of Teachers of English, in co-operation with the Bureau of Secondary Education, State Department of Education, has produced *The English Language Arts in California High Schools; Practices in the Teaching of Composition in California High Schools* was issued this fall.

Colorado

There is local curriculum activity going on, especially on the elementary level.

Delaware

A junior high school curriculum guide for English was issued in September, 1958.

Florida

The State Course of Study Committee has recently revised Bulletin #34, *Experiencing the Language Arts, 1 to 12.* Counties are working on curriculum materials.

Idaho

The State Department is encouraging experimental language programs on the local level, especially in the elementary schools; the State Department also reports continuous curriculum revision.

Indiana

Bulletin #220, *Source Guide for the English Language Arts,* was recently issued.

Kansas

A number of schools are engaged in curriculum study projects. The Wichita school system produced a curriculum guide for junior and senior high schools. The State Department is now working on a curriculum guide for secondary schools that will be ready next year.

Maine

A Guide to Learning in the Primary Grades was recently published.

Maryland

The Division of Instruction has worked with county groups to produce courses of study. A bulletin, *Language Arts* (not a course of study), was issued recently.

Massachusetts

The schools realize a need for vertical and horizontal integration of the language arts. Curriculum development is conducted on the local level.

Michigan

Curriculum development is conducted on the local level.

Minnesota

A new secondary guide was issued in 1956: *A Guide for Instruction in the Language Arts.*

Mississippi

A language arts bulletin was recently distributed.

Missouri

A total revision of curriculum was started in 1950. Guides for junior and elementary levels are already available; the secondary school curriculum materials are being readied now.

Montana

A Tentative Guide for English has been made available.

Nevada

Local districts are working on revisions of curriculum guides; the State Department is currently engaged in a revision of the course of study.

New Mexico

Language arts publications on the elementary level have been recently issued.

New York

A Steering Committee is planning a complete revision of the *Syllabus,* including reorganization of materials, introduction of new sections, and a complete revision of the bibliography. *Audio-Visual Aids for the Teacher of Speech, Fiction for the Superior Student,* and *More Books for the Superior Student* have been issued. *Teaching English Through the Mass Media, So You're Going to Direct a Play,* and two resource units for junior high schools are in preparation. A bibliography for teachers of English as a second language has been distributed.

North Carolina

The State Department is now working on curriculum guides for the secondary schools.

North Dakota

English Language Arts in North Dakota Secondary Schools has recently been published. Other teaching guides are being made available.

Ohio

The State Department encourages local curriculum work.

Oregon

The State Department of Education is in the midst of developing a Scope and Sequence plan that will result in the issuance of guides for elementary and secondary school teachers.

Pennsylvania

A committee is now studying minimal content in English with the purpose of issuing a booklet to be called "How Good Is Your English Program?"

South Dakota

A state-wide committee is studying the entire educational picture in the state.

Texas

A commission to study the language arts has been established. A curriculum bulletin has been issued to superintendents, and local courses of study are being developed.

Utah

The State Department is now revising its general language guides.

Vermont

Mimeographed outlines on college and noncollege English are being prepared. The New England Association of Teachers of English is wrestling with problems concerning curriculum changes.

Virginia

Local schools are encouraged to carry on curriculum development. Three years ago, there was an entire revision of the language arts curriculum.

Washington

Teaching guides through grade six have been issued. Curriculum guides on other levels are being prepared.

West Virginia

Counties work on their own curriculum development and choose their own materials.

Wisconsin

Many curriculum bulletins have been made available.

Aside from the obvious fact that a great deal of curriculum activity is going on, three observations stand forth as important:

1. Very few states have state-wide syllabi or courses of study for the language arts.
2. Much of the curriculum development or revision is still going on on a local level, with little or no state aid or supervision.

3. The state English teachers' councils are taking a growing part in curriculum revision and development, to the credit of the local councils.

SUMMARY OF REPLIES TO QUESTION 3— METHODOLOGY AND CONTENT

Most state department officials pointed out that changes in content and methodology have taken place on the local level as a result of publications and meetings of teachers, but they noted that they were not sufficiently aware of those changes because of their distance from the schools. Enough information was, however, given for an effective picture of recent developments in this area.

Reading, both developmental and remedial, is fast becoming a permanent secondary school area. The addition of reading work to the regular English program has certainly caused changes in content. Some Wisconsin schools report adding reading specialists and conducting reading activities in all subjects and throughout high school. Pennsylvania now requires remedial reading in all junior high schools in grades 7 and 8. Some schools in Massachusetts are adding developmental reading to their programs.

As a result of various workshops and in-service courses in Vermont, teachers are being encouraged to use the unit method of teaching, regardless of school organization. Film and TV demonstrations at last year's conference of the Florida CTE point to changes in methodology in that state, as do the group discussions held at this same meeting on structural linguistics, recreational reading, listening skills, spelling, mass media ("It would help to have a planned sequence of study of the mass media"), discussion techniques in English classes, writing, literature, drama in the classroom, college preparation, and communication skills. "As a result of the Governor's Conference for the Improvement of

Instruction in Pennsylvania, the State Council approved adding
to the requirements for graduation these rather significant ele-
ments—three years of English and developmental reading or
remedial reading in grades 7 and 8!" Utah now requires an additional unit of language arts for graduation. In West Virginia,
many junior high schools are providing an extended period for
language arts. Some schools in Massachusetts are offering special
and optional courses such as the following: an advanced composition course for juniors and seniors with considerable competency; optional classes for those wanting additional work; honor
classes and classes for the gifted both in high school and junior
high school. But in the face of all these advances, Mr. Arthur
Adkins of the Wisconsin State Department of Public Instruction
thinks there may be "some revival of pressure for more emphasis
upon grammar from laymen, college professors, and others equally
misinformed about research on grammar, but we are doing our
best to see that grammar retains its functional place as a means to
effective speaking and writing rather than as an end of teaching."

SUMMARY OF REPLIES TO QUESTION 4—
CHANGES IN ADMINISTRATION
AND SUPERVISION

The great majority of state departments report no significant
changes in administration and supervision of the language arts.
Most state departments remain without directors of language arts,
but there have been some happy additions:

Delaware

The State Department has added a Director of In-Service Training and hopes to add a Director of Curriculum. "Both of these
will enhance our work not only in English but in our total curricular operation."

Idaho

There is no radical change in administration and supervision anticipated, but "We are attempting to encourage local schools to plan the language arts program and the social studies program so that they will complement each other."

Indiana

"Any changes in administration will probably be gradual and normal."

Maryland

In larger counties, general supervisors with special training in language arts have been employed; there is a co-ordinator for remedial reading in one county and a supervisor of a new reading clinic in another.

Minnesota

The State Department will add a Supervisor of Language Arts.

Missouri

No change on the state level; larger cities have supervisors of language arts.

New York

A new Associate in Speech Education has been appointed.

Ohio

Supervisory personnel are being made available.

Utah

"We now have two persons working in general secondary education where we previously had only one."

Vermont

"In two of the larger school systems, capable reading consultants have assumed the wider responsibilities of curriculum consultants."

SUMMARY OF REPLIES TO QUESTION 5— WHAT THE NCTE CAN DO

Most state department officials commended the National Council of Teachers of English for the effectiveness and usefulness of its publications, especially in the planning and conducting of workshops and conferences. The publications were also cited for their "significant value in giving direction to improved programs."

CONTRIBUTORS

Organization	*Officer*
Alabama Department of Education	W. Morrison McCall, Director Division of Elementary Education
California Department of Education	M. E. Mushlitz, Consultant in Secondary Education
Colorado Department of Education	Clifford Bebell, Director Division of Curriculum Services
Delaware Department of Public Instruction	Howard E. Row, Assistant State Superintendent, Secondary Education
Florida Department of Education	John P. McIntyre, Curriculum Specialist, Division of Instructional Field Services
Georgia State Department of Education	Mary Ellen Perkins, Co-ordinator of Teacher Education
Idaho Department of Education	Malcolm Allred, Supervisor, Textbook and Instructional Program
Indiana Department of Public Instruction	I. Owen Foster, State Director of Curriculum
Kansas State Department of Public Instruction	Adel F. Throckmorton, State Superintendent of Public Instruction

Organization	*Officer*
Maine Department of Education	Philip A. Annax, Executive Director, Division of Instruction
Maryland State Department of Education	Thomas G. Pullen, Jr., State Superintendent of Schools
Massachusetts Department of Education	Patrick J. Sullivan, Director, Division of Secondary and Elementary Education
Michigan Department of Public Instruction	Louis Kocsis, Curriculum Consultant
Minnesota Department of Education	Donald L. Clauson, Director of Elementary and Secondary Schools
Mississippi Department of Education	J. M. Tubb, State Superintendent of Education
Missouri State Department of Education	Raymond A. Roberts, Director of Curriculum, Division of Public Schools
Montana State Department of Education	Harriet Miller, State Superintendent of Schools
Nevada Department of Education	R. A. McGuire, Curriculum Director
New Jersey Department of Education	Ablett H. Flury, Assistant Commissioner of Education, Division of Curriculum and Instruction
New Mexico Department of Education	Frances Manzarares, Secretary to Albert N. Valdez, Director of Elementary Education and Supervisor of Spanish
New York State Department of Education	Carl J. Freudenreich, Supervisor of English Education
North Carolina Department of Public Instruction	A. B. Combs, Director, Division of Elementary and Secondary Education
North Dakota Department of Public Instruction	Richard K. Klein, Director of Secondary Education
Ohio Department of Education	Phila Humphreys, Elementary Supervisor, Division of Elementary and Secondary Education
Oklahoma State Department of Education	F. R. Born, Director of Curriculum

Organization	*Officer*
Oregon Department of Education	B. L. Simmons, Supervisor of Curriculum, Division of General Education
Pennsylvania Department of Public Instruction	Sheldon Madeira, Curriculum Planning Specialist, Bureau of Curriculum Development
South Dakota Department of Public Instruction	F. R. Wanek, Secondary School Supervisor
Texas State Department of Education	Dorothy Davidson, Consultant in Secondary Education, Division of Curriculum Development
Utah Department of Public Instruction	Afton Forsgren, Assistant Director of Secondary Education
Vermont Department of Education	A. John Holden, Jr., Commissioner of Education
Virginia State Board of Education	Fred O. Wygal, Associate Director of Instruction
Washington State Department of Public Instruction	John L. Fea, Supervisor of Instructional Materials Lloyd J. Andrews, State Superintendent, Division of Instruction and Curriculum
West Virginia Department of Education	John T. St. Clair, Assistant State Superintendent, Division of Instruction and Curriculum
Wisconsin Department of Public Instruction	Arthur Adkins, State Curriculum Co-ordinator

❧ 3 ❧

Opinions of
Colleges and Universities

So far in this survey, we have been concerned with the changes that have been going on throughout the country in improving the English program, as seen by the affiliates of the Council and the heads of State Departments of Education. The remaining chapters are concerned with the opinions of distinguished leaders in education, business and industry, civil service, journalism, publishing, bookselling, library work, and the law as to the competence of recent graduates from our high schools during the past 5 to 10 years; and their recommendations for improvement. The first group of respondents consisted of presidents of colleges and universities, who were asked the following questions:

1. To what extent are present entrants in your institution better prepared in English than students of 5 to 10 years ago?
2. In what respects are they less prepared?
3. Has the work of the Commission on the English Curriculum of the National Council of Teachers of English influenced the English Department in any significant way?
4. How can the National Council of Teachers of English be of greater service to the cause of better preparation of your students in the field of English instruction?

Ninety-five colleges and institutions were addressed, ranging from the Ivy League colleges to the great state institutions; from the liberal arts colleges to the great engineering colleges; from all sections of the United States and all types of communities. In other words, a fairly complete cross-section was attempted, to give validity and reliability to the opinions expressed.

"Our feeling is that, year in, year out, the teachers of English in the high schools and colleges are engaged in the same campaign."

This comment by David A. Robertson, Jr., of Barnard College, indicated the tenor of the responses received from 79 colleges and universities throughout the nation. Because of their close identification with the problems raised by the questions in the survey, because of feeling that their own labors depended so much on what the high school presented in the way of competency, because of the realization that their own success grew out of the success of the high school teachers, their answers were especially searching and thoughtful. In many instances, entire English departments of colleges and universities were polled, and the ideas expressed represent the consensus of many of our colleagues. They were critical, but at the same time they tried to be fair. What was praiseworthy was accorded praise; what was deplorable was censured.

The spokesmen for 26 institutions of higher learning had favorable responses to Question 1. "There is a general feeling that our entering freshmen are better prepared in English than in the past," writes Earl W. Porter of Duke, "but it is also true that over all preparation and ability of freshmen has improved in recent years."

This opinion is backed by that of the faculty of the University of Idaho. "Within the past 5 to 10 years, the English Department has adopted several measures to improve the quality of student writing. These measures include the use of standardized tests, the sectioning of entering freshmen according to their high school preparation, and the establishing of English and Reading clinics for students needing special help. This has made high school teachers throughout the state increasingly interested in preparing their students in the mechanics of writing and in reading with speed and comprehension. A series of tests given at the beginning and end of the freshman year over several years, revealed steady improvement in the quality of entering freshmen."

A further encouraging note along these lines is sounded by Professor George F. Horner of the University of North Carolina:

"For a number of years we have used a standard test in English as a placement test for incoming freshmen. In the last 10 years the median score on this test made by the entering freshman class has risen 10%, a rise that represents a considerable improvement. Indeed, when this rise is compared with the national norm for various school years, the indicated improvement in preparation represents nearly two years' school work. This rise has been fairly regular through the years, with no extreme retrogression nor progression in any one year."

Writing along similar lines, Gordon B. Carson, Ohio State University, tells us, ". . . we have been observing for some time the scores in the English Placement Tests for the various colleges. An extremely high score on our placement test means that the student receives a proficiency in the first English course, and is permitted to enter the second course. For the last 5 years, the following has been the record of engineering students."

Dates	% Passing Placement Test	% Making Proficiency
1953	83	8
1954	83	10
1955	85	9
1956	89	12
1957	89	12

Certain reservations are expressed by Dean Carson, but these will be gone into in our examination of Questions 3 and 4. Similar reservations are expressed by many of the college leaders who saw improvement in the competence of high graduates. These pertain principally to writing ability.

Typical of these reactions is the response of Robert E. Streeter, Dean of the College, University of Chicago. He declares, "Most of our evidence bears upon our entrants' abilities in reading and writing . . . Much of our instruction in the College is carried on through active discussion classes, and consequently students develop their skills of speaking and listening rather informally in the context of other subjects. We have found that most of our students are well equipped to function in discussion classes. This means, I suppose, that their previous education has given them a satisfactory introduction to these skills."

He continues: "Over the past 10 years there has been improvement in the quality of the reading skills our students bring to college. This improvement has been most marked in reading rate; we encounter few students who read so laboriously, so mechanically, and so slowly that their academic progress is imperiled. There has also been some improvement in the average student's comprehension of difficult material, but this has been less striking than the improvement in reading rate."

A most penetrating discussion of this question comes from Dr. Buell Gallagher, President of the City College of New York:

"How effective has the training been . . . ? Effective enough so that we do not fail notably more students in English 1 nowadays than we did some years ago, nor send notably more into our remedial course.

"But the Devil's advocate will scorn this easy reply. What does it prove? To some instructors it only proves that we have let down our standards. One man claims that a progressive lowering of scores on the Inglis vocabulary tests he gives every semester to his sections of English 1 proves the deterioration. You know, of course, how persistently debates on this question have raged, from grade school through graduate school—whether Johnny can/can't read, spell, write.

"Perhaps the only agreement that can be reached is that the methods and materials have changed. Burke *On Conciliation,* Milton's *Comus,* Addison's *Vision of Mirza* have vanished along with Latin for all but a tiny minority of high school students (or college students for that matter). The history or formal survey of English literature has gone. The names of many writers and periods, the vocabulary of formal grammar, are an unknown tongue to most freshmen. Obviously, the reading, writing, speaking and listening skills that depend on specific information like that listed above have vanished. Whether what has replaced this information—popular linguistics, discussions of usage, readings of contemporary (almost entirely American) materials—can be deemed effective depends in some measure upon the attitude of the respondent."

Avoiding absolute answers, Walter L. Simmons, University of Rhode Island, gives a middle-of-the-road view of improvement: "Recently, we have noticed some improvement in the mechanics of writing—punctuation, sentence structure, etc. There is also some evidence of more self-assurance which leads to freer and bolder treatment of material both in writing and speaking."

A number of high-ranking colleges and universities acknowledge improvement, but are careful to cite the fact that there is a far higher degree of selectivity than existed before. Thus, George F. Sensabaugh, Acting Executive Head of Stanford University: "Stanford students today are better prepared in English than were students of 5 to 10 years ago. This is not surprising, however. Students now coming to Stanford have better grades in all subjects than did their predecessors, and they have received higher grades on achievement and intelligence tests. Competition is now sharper, and only the better applicants get in. Among students now entering Stanford, 88% have a B+ average or better."

A good proportion of the colleges which indicate improvement among the incoming freshmen link that improvement with a distinctly higher degree of selectivity of the applicants.

To quote again from Barnard College, "There was general agreement that Barnard students of this day seem better prepared in English than the students of 5 to 10 years ago, but there was considerable reluctance to account for the impression. We could not determine whether it is simply that Barnard has been in a position to pick better students, nor could we tell how much of our satisfaction was due to the fact that this year's group of Senior majors in English is quite extraordinary."

This point about the importance of selectivity in evaluating the competence in English of recent graduates is one raised by many colleges.

The problem of determining whether there has been a discernible improvement is gone into fully by Professor Paul V. Kreider, of the University of Cincinnati. "The statistics vary amazingly from year to year," he writes. "There is no discernible consistency in the fluctuation. In view of the fact that the same teachers have evaluated all of these students, I can see no explanation other than that the students who have been judged by comparatively unchanging standards have themselves been very unequal in one or more of the following factors: inherent ability, training, earnestness.

"Our highest grade is A," he continues, "and our lowest passing grade is D. Statistics indicate that there has been an actual decline in the percentage of students making A. There has been a very slight increase in the percentage making B, a noticeable increase in the percentage making C, and little if any change in those making D, and a very slight decrease in the percentage receiving unsatisfactory grades. In other words, we apparently have noticeably fewer *excellent* students and slightly fewer *hopelessly weak* ones (italics are Professor Kreider's), and the flat, uncharacterized average students are rather more numerous than they used to be. There is, thus, a tendency to level out, to cause some diminution at both the top and the bottom, and to come up with a greater percentage of mediocre and barely passable students. Whether in the final analysis this can be called actual improvement is debatable."

The Chairman of Freshman English at Northwestern University, Wallace W. Douglas, expresses a similar reservation as to the ability to evaluate improvement. "Our staff seems convinced that students are better prepared for writing than they were 5 years ago. (If we extend the period back to ten years ago, we reach the time of heavy veteran enrollment; no students since then have had the veterans' varied and interesting experience to use in papers, none have been so generally mature if often somewhat uncertainly 'balanced'—as a result no students since then have seemed so well prepared.) Our staff thinks that Northwestern students today can write with some easiness and fairly correctly."

Another minority opinion which sees an improvement is expressed by George J. Becker of Swarthmore College: "Present entrants into Swarthmore are certainly more widely read in modern literature than they were 10 years ago." Muriel J. Hughes, Chairman of the Freshman English Committee at the University of Vermont, states this opinion more strongly: "I believe that our department would say that the students have read more widely in various fields and have a more general breadth of knowledge than students of five or ten years ago."

Where only partial satisfaction with competence is expressed, the area most often given approval is that of speaking. Typical of this view is that expressed by George K. Anderson, Chairman of the English Department of Brown University. "We should say that the present entrants into Brown are perhaps more self-assured and can often talk well, if somewhat glibly, but they are sadly uninformed about general matters of importance in our present-day scene. We would concede that they have a better vocabulary than their predecessors, and often score high on the verbal aptitude tests, but very few of them are able to use this vocabulary in the proper way."

The same ironic note about speaking ability is voiced by Dudley Bailey, Director of Freshman English at the University of Nebraska. "Certainly our students are more at ease in speaking, more self-assured in and out of class, and somewhat more voluble than they used to be. Whether this means they are 'better prepared,' in any serious sense of that phrase, however, I seriously doubt." We shall go into the grounds for Mr. Bailey's doubts in our discussion of Question 2.

In all too many instances, the colleges feel that where a measurable improvement appears, it is attributable to the higher degree of selectivity exercised by the school. Thus, from S. Walter Martin, of Emory University: "Undoubtedly a very important factor in explaining this improvement (in preparation) is the gradual tightening up of requirements for admission of our College. It is quite impossible to determine with any confidence the significance of such a factor as high school or preparatory training because of the great variety of secondary school backgrounds represented by our students."

Admitting that the entrants to the University of Florida are, in general, better prepared than those of 5 or 10 years ago, J. Hooper Wise declares, "We believe that this is accounted for by the principle of selection which the University has followed for the past several years. Formerly we discouraged the bottom third on our state-wide placement tests; now we cut off the bottom forty per cent."

Harvard University's Harold C. Martin has similar reservations about the reasons for improvement among entering Harvard students. "(They) are clearly better prepared than they were 10 years ago, but the standards of admissions have risen so sharply in that time that I cannot say whether the observation is meaningful or not."

There is no gainsaying the impression that where major institutions, such as Northwestern, see an improvement, the tendency is to link it with a higher degree of selectivity, and not with conditions generally prevailing in the country at large. The standards are higher, the competition for admission is keener, and the consequent level of competence among the entrants is inevitably higher.

"Our problems are somewhat different from those of a good many other institutions," states Charles Everett of the College at Columbia University, "in that we are a small college (2,500 students) and on account of the number of applicants we are usually in a position to take the top third. This has been increasingly true during the past five years.

"Present entrants are on the whole better prepared than they were 10 years ago. This is partly due to a better admissions policy. For one thing, we are admitting about 60 students with advanced standing in English, resulting from the new pre-placement work on composition organized by many schools."

However gratifying this judgment may appear, there are many institutions of higher education, particularly the state universities, where this ability to select from the cream of the graduating class is not always feasible.

A typical response comes from William F. Irmscher of the University of Arizona. "I think the educational influences which have molded students during the period (the past 10 years) have not changed significantly. I think we all see indications of a change now, but I would not make any great differentiation between students who were coming to the university 10 years ago and students who are coming today."

"No important change" is the essence of the opinion of some twenty colleges and universities. According to Robert H. Moore, George Washington University, "I don't believe that our present entering freshmen are any better or worse than they were 10 years ago. At least, the percentages on the English placement are about what they were then. Five years ago, however, entering students were decidedly weaker. As many as 40% were failing the placement test and being assigned to a remedial course. That lasted for about two years, and then the failures declined again to the present 27 to 30%. I presume the weakness of the 1953 group can be attributed to the wartime shortage of qualified teachers."

Harry H. Crosby of the State University of Iowa pins down this point of view with a good deal of specificity: "Our placement tests—which include a written theme and extemporaneous speech, and a test on grammar, rhetoric, reading rate and comprehension, and vocabulary—reveal that there is almost no difference (as compared with students of 5 to 10 years ago). A raw score on any of these examinations would give almost exactly the same percentile score on any of the last ten years."

The same opinion is expressed by Dean Cecil G. Taylor of the University of Louisiana. "We have some objective measure of their ability which is identical from the fall of 1951 for each year up to and including the present year. We give to each entering freshman the Cooperative English Test, and have done so since 1951. Though the number of students has been increasing, the percentages placed in the various sections of Freshman English remain constant. We use the same cut-off scores now that were used in 1951. In 1951, 24% of our students placed in the course for those least prepared; in 1956, 23% placed there; and 1957,

25%. The mean score for entering freshmen was in 1951, 55.76; in 1952, 51.65; in 1957, 50.37." Dean Taylor follows this with the observation that the class of 1951 was a definitely superior one.

Robert Estrich, Chairman of the English Department at the Ohio State University, perhaps states the feeling of those who see no discernible improvement over the past 5 to 10 years: "We find our students just about where we have always found them: the great majority come to us with very little controlled and disciplined experience with either reading or writing—as they have for years."

Thus, it may be comforting to realize that 25% of the respondents from colleges and universities, seeing no appreciable improvement in recent graduates, at least see no visible signs of deterioration, either.

QUESTION 2—IN WHAT RESPECTS ARE THEY LESS PREPARED?

The most eloquent group of respondents are those who vote Nay. Thirteen of the 79 colleges answering the survey found that competence was poor, and had, in fact, deteriorated over the past 5 to 10 years. A very searching response comes from Dr. Charles M. Clark, head of the English Department at The American University:

"The members of the English Department at The American University have undertaken a careful study of the questions raised by the National Council of Teachers of English concerning the preparation in English of the students who come to the university. The bases for the conclusions that have been reached are three: (1) scores on tests in English that are given to entering freshmen (2) experience of teachers of English who have taught at The American University over the last five years (3) evaluation by students themselves of their pre-college training in English.

"Between 1952–57, the English Department has used two tests

for evaluating the proficiency in English of entering students, the Iowa Content Test and the Barrett-Ryan Test. Comparing the results of scores made by our students with those representing the national norm, it is apparent that up to 1956, entering students ranked high above the national norm, but that those of the past two years have fallen considerably below this norm. The increase in the number of entering students during the last two years is a factor which should be weighed in estimating the significance of this decrease in proficiency . . .

"Present entrants into The American University are not better prepared than students of 5 years ago. Some students have been made aware of current linguistic attitudes toward such matters as usage and grammar; some few reveal a broader acquaintance with contemporary literature. A few outstanding students might be said to be superior to corresponding students of 5 to 10 years ago. It would, however, be inaccurate to say that the teachers of English have found the average freshman to be better prepared in any respect than his predecessor of five years ago."

Even more severe in judgment of entering freshmen is the opinion of the English Department of DePaul University: "Their feeling for words and phrases is negligible; their knowledge of grammar, deplorable. They read haltingly and with monotony; they write loosely and with indistinctness. Even those who occasionally give the impression of reading well, upon closer analysis betray the superficiality of their faculty, performing as individuals whose voices have been cultivated, but whose intellects and imagination have been allowed to lie fallow."

The writing of recent graduates comes in for the strongest condemnation. "I must say categorically," replies Dean J. Stephen Bloore of the Teaneck division of Fairleigh Dickinson University, "that the English preparation of entering students, far from improving, becomes progressively worse. As far as I can judge, a great many of our students do practically no writing in high school, or, when they do, they rarely get it corrected in any careful manner."

Somewhat mitigating the above opinion is the response of Dr. Robert Gorrell, Chairman of the English Department of the University of Nevada. "Teachers are prone to lament more enthusiastically than they really intend," he writes, "when they view the writing of each new batch of freshmen. Furthermore, we have changed our entrance tests so frequently during the past few years that they are only very dubious evidence about student preparation. The following are the best guesses I can make, but they are only guesses.

"Most instructors, I think, do not feel that entrants are notably better prepared in any aspects of English. There is, however, a suggestion from the entrance tests that students have improved somewhat in their knowledge of standard usage and mechanics. Perhaps our use of the tests has had some influence."

The need for remedial work among entering freshmen is increasing. Particularly significant is this statement from Willard Thorp of Princeton University: "Because Princeton is now taking more students from a greater number of high schools, a fairly large number of freshmen turn up who have been insufficiently trained in English or are weak in the subject, while being very strong in, for instance, science. In the present freshman class, only four high schools are represented by five or more students. The tendency of many high schools to require only three years of English or to permit rather useless electives, such as journalism, is certainly felt here. We estimate that about 200 of our freshmen (in a class of 750) need remedial work in English, yet there is room in our English A (noncredit) for less than half this number. There seems also to be an increasing disparity in the books read in literature courses. In a group of 10 freshmen, if we can count on their having just one play of Shakespeare in common, we think we are lucky."

An attempt to be extremely fair about the competence of current high school graduates is made by Dean Vernon Miller of The Catholic University of America. "It is usual nowadays," he tells us, "for college teachers to depreciate the competence of recent high school graduates in English. I wish the general level of competence were higher, but I do not believe that the deficiencies some of us think we see can be attributed to bad teaching or poor curriculum. I know it is difficult to develop reading habits in children who do not have inducements to read at home. I am guessing that the percentage of high school students like that is greater today than it was when I was in high school 40 years ago. Almost all teen-agers are attending high schools today, and admission standards cannot be high. Considering everything else, English teachers in secondary schools are doing well to give us as many good students as we are getting."

Ability in Written Composition

"Through the verbal ability of our matriculants, as reflected in school grades and College Board tests, is at an all-time high, we do not sense commensurate improvement in the quality of written work as seen in essays and examination papers."

So states Arthur Howe, Jr., the Dean of Admissions at Yale University. He, along with a great majority of the college representatives responding, finds *writing* the chief deficiency of entering freshmen.

To continue, with a joint statement of Louis L. Martz, Chairman, and Frederick W. Hilles, Former Chairman, of the Department of English at Yale: "We have the impression that students now entering Yale appear, on their entrance examinations, to be abler than they really are. Students in the better schools have learned the knack of answering the kind of questions now asked on the College Board Examination in English: they know the fundamentals of grammar and vocabulary, and they do not seem to make frequently the kind of crude errors in their writing that we met quite often 10 years ago. Nevertheless, we feel that this improvement lies only on the surface of their writing; students at Yale now have higher aptitudes as demonstrated on these tests, but in fact they are less competent to write an effective composition than were the students of 10 years ago. There is a grave weakness in their powers of analysis and organization; even the brightest students sometimes show that they lack basic training in the ways of beginning, developing, and concluding an argument or exposition. This is a much more troublesome weakness than any small errors in usage, for it shows a lack of mental discipline in the basic principles of human thought."

Many attribute this "greatest single weakness"—the inability to write—as does Minnie E. Wells of the University of Alaska—to "no experience in composition. Most have had very insufficient experience. They are not able to organize independent ideas logically."

"The inability to write well is, of course, a constant complaint of instructors in freshman composition," says Dr. Clark of The American University. "They agree that there is no sense of responsibility about language, no recognition of the power of words, merely a vague groping accompanied by the hope that the reader or hearer will 'get what I mean.' More specifically, it is apparent that most students arrive at college with little or no training in writing, and in many cases without the basic knowledge of what a sentence is, or what a paragraph is. Even such elementary matters as spelling and punctuation seem to have been neglected, and the poverty of words suggests that little emphasis has been placed on vocabulary-building or the attentive reading that can help build a vocabulary."

In the answers to Question 2, one noticeable recommendation appears over and over: Reduce the teaching hours and number of students which now confront the high school teacher of English. "No teacher," says Robert L. Shurter, Head of the Department of Humanities and Social Studies at the Case Institute of Technology, "with more than 100 students can do justice to paper grading, and the result is that now too few papers are required in high school English courses . . . When such students get to college and are forced to write a paper each week, they are overwhelmed simply because they have had too little practice in high school."

The same condemnation of the high school teacher's load in composition alone, aside from many other duties, emerges strongly in the words of Dean Streeter of the College at the University of Chicago: "My personal impression is that the entrant's weakness in writing arises, not from inherent defects in the secondary school curriculum, but from our general inability to establish conditions which permit teachers of English to have the time needed for thoughtful criticism of student essays. Students who suffer most seriously from lack of detailed criticism are often potentially among the very best writers. In the absence of really precise evaluation, they have fallen into the habit of confusing a burst of verbal energy with responsible statement in writing."

Professor Estrich of Ohio State University expresses his feeling most eloquently, as follows: "The first thing we would like to see in the secondary schools is a system that would have the student writing regularly and often short papers which would be thoroughly criticized for fundamental rhetorical features as well as mechanics—and then rewritten. Our commonest complaint from students is that they have never written a paper of any sort or length. Our commonest complaint from instructors is that when they return papers to new students with detailed explanation for revision, the students come up after class or in conference utterly bewildered, with their papers in their hands, and say, 'But what do I do with it?' It is literally an unheard-of notion that they can rewrite and improve a poor, awkward, wordy, or incoherent sentence or an incoherent paragraph. As they originally wrote it, so it must stand. One expects a good deal of naivete about writing from the average 17-year-old, but not a total lack of experience."

"I think it is safe to say," adds James G. Kelso, of the Massachusetts Institute of Technology, "freshmen have never been well prepared in matters of organization and sustained, coherent, logical thinking. One thing that may be more noticeable now than earlier is an attitude on the part of the student that mistakes in such matters as grammar and spelling are not very important. There seems to be a definite unwillingness to admit that there are certain standards which cannot be violated without serious results in terms of communication."

"The gain (in speaking)," comments Dudley Bailey of the University of Nebraska, "has been made at the cost of a much more serious loss: our students do not read as well, do not write as well, and probably do not hear as well. And we are convinced that the first of these deficiencies is the most serious one, because it is a central and generally debilitating deficiency. Students today in frightening numbers have had no reading at all in British and American literature; an appalling number have apparently never heard such names as Chaucer, Spenser, Bunyan, Dryden, Pope, Johnson, and Wordsworth, Edwards, Hawthorne, Dickinson, Melville, Crane, and Eliot. A fair number have never read a Shakespeare play; and a large number have never read a Victorian novel. Hence in the narrow sense of English, we face the disturbing prospect of students who talk easily and assuredly but have comparatively little to say; and I suspect that this paradox extends far beyond our discipline in the traditional, limited sense of it."

An obverse point of view as to reading is expressed by Northwestern University. "High school teachers," declares Wallace W. Douglas, "too often think that the colleges want students to have a knowledge of the history of literature or a knowledge of a certain body of 'great works' that are valued now because they reflect the culture of the past. In fact, however, many (I would not say 'most') college teachers want their students to know how to read analytically—that is, to be able to understand and describe the structure and effect of a work of literature. This kind of critical reading is not understood by most students we teach. I include here even students who have been in high school honors or advanced standing sections, with whom I have had some experience this last year."

"This inability to express themselves," says C. I. Diehl of Southwestern College at Memphis, "adversely affects the grades they receive in other courses in which essay type tests and examinations are employed. Closely related to their inability to say clearly and concisely what they mean are the facts that their vocabularies are very limited and that they have difficulty in understanding the material that they are assigned to read."

Ability to Read

Thus, reading is the second deficiency to come under strong attack. "Students of 20 to 25 years ago," says George F. Sensabaugh of Stanford University, "could not read as rapidly as students do today. But students of a generation ago could, in the main, read with greater accuracy. The lesson of rapid reading has been well learned; reading for accuracy and precision has apparently not received much emphasis. This holds true for today's students as well as for those of 5 to 10 years ago."

Particularly interesting is the response of Colonel Robert F. McDermott of the United States Air Force Academy. He analyzes his students as follows: *"Reading:* Our average cadet reads at a rapid rate with a high degree of comprehension; however, from the 'blackness' and 'whiteness' of his arguments and his quite limited vocabulary, we believe that he has not read very widely. *Writing:* our average cadet misspells 3 to 5 words in a 500 word theme (frequently misspelling a word in the title), punctuates carelessly, tends to write short paragraphs, and would prefer to be judged on the basis of ideas rather than expression. *Speaking:* our average cadet speaks with a great deal of enthusiasm which often covers up such grammatical faults as lack of subject-verb agreement and such diction faults as colloquialisms and shop talk. *Listening:* the average USAFA cadet listens effectively."

Parallel to these remarks are those of the Air Force ROTC, as voiced by Colonel William E. McEntire, of the Maxwell Air Force Base, Alabama. "Our observations point to deficiencies in three areas: (1) lack of competence with the basic mechanics of the English language stemming from insufficient understanding of its structure and knowledge of its grammatical forms; (2) a fragmented orientation to communication skills which fails to make clear the intimate relation among writing, reading, speaking and listening; (3) an inadequate appreciation of the fundamental importance of English skills and the crucial part they play in the effectiveness of any organized effort."

These comments from the Air Force ROTC might well serve as a summation of the deficiencies touched upon by the responding colleges. It is writing that demands the most attention, reading that needs greater scope and depth with more attention given to comprehension rather than rapidity. There is always an underlying impression that much could be done with the fundamentals—additional training and drill in spelling, punctuation, and vocabulary. Always, however, the complaints come back to "the relatively small amount of writing and rewriting done in high school classes," to quote Dr. Buell Gallagher of the City College of New York. "Either they don't write or they do it somnambulistically and awake with no memory of the act. But the amount of writing that can be done—and carefully examined by a teacher—depends directly upon the size of the teacher's classes. If he is hired primarily to coach a team and do routine chores, he will not have the energy the second job takes . . ."

QUESTION 3—THE INFLUENCE OF THE COUNCIL

Of the 48 respondents who answered this question, only 18 indicated that the publications of the Commission on the Curriculum had any noticeable influence on the department. In individual cases, teachers had changed their methods; some worked with elementary and high school teachers to change curricula. On the whole, however, the influence of the reports of the Commission has to this date remained minor in the colleges whose replies were received.

QUESTION 4—WHAT THE COUNCIL CAN DO

In their discussion of what the profession can do to make training more effective, most respondents tend to overlap into a discussion of deficiencies discovered in the student body. This is hardly surprising, since the two are so closely interrelated, but in this analysis we have tried to separate the recommendations from the detailing of deficiencies.

The Carnegie Institute of Technology has some cogent remarks to make on the score of what the profession can do. "Two things," says President J. C. Warner. "(A) Try to persuade authorities to lighten the burden of English teachers sufficiently to permit the assignment, reading, grading, and discussion of expository papers, and to plan curricula in such a way that the upper years in English in high school are devoted to that kind of activity. (B) Devote themselves as teachers to developing in students the ability to read and understanding and to write simple, straightforward, completely clear, and technically correct English."

While the stress on expository papers may appear a piece of special pleading in the case above cited, the emphasis on reduction of the high school English teacher's burden is not. It is voiced by one educator after another. Thus, J. D. A. Ogilvy of the University of Colorado: "Reduce the size of classes to make a proper amount of training for each student possible." "The problem (the load secondary teachers of English are expected to carry and the size of the classes they are supposed to teach) is as much administrative as anything else. You well know that the establishment of satisfactory conditions for the teaching of writing would eventually be reflected in local tax bills, so the classes remain large and teachers teach literature or put the students through the antics prescribed by workbooks. Who can really blame them for refusing to submit to the drudgery imposed upon them by a society that loves education in the abstract but really doesn't want to pay the price?" So says Dean Bloore of Fairleigh Dickinson University.

The following, from the State University of Iowa, points no finger, but simply cites the information derived from a questionnaire given students "ranking in the top and bottom deciles in the Entrance Placement tests for the Communications Skills Program at the State University in September, 1957.

"Good students—20% of them own six books or less
23% have fewer than six books in the house
40% read two books or less per month

Poor students—53% own six books or less
49% have fewer than six books in their home
16% have read more than one book which would be called a literary classic
90% regularly read no out-of-state newspaper
13% read no newspaper, even occasionally
 8% read no magazine, even occasionally

80% read two books or less a month
23% read no books

"I realize that this information is extremely pessimistic. I realize also that it is said in spite of the fact that there has been tremendous activity by the NCTE members here in this state."

With complete disregard for the fact that their suggestions, if carried out with success, would result in the elimination of a number of college courses and teachers, the colleges have subscribed almost unanimously—and most unselfishly—to the following as expressed by Warner G. Rice, University of Michigan:

"The National Council can be of assistance to the entire profession in the following ways:

"a. By working hard for such improvements of academic standards as will result in the gradual elimination of freshman English and communications courses from college and university curricula. Adequate proficiency in the skills of reading and writing should be a requirement for college admissions. The attention given to the development of these skills at the level of higher education is (like the teaching of elementary foreign languages) proving a burden which it is increasingly hard to justify—and one which is having harmful effects upon the profession. In order to guarantee such improvement, it will be necessary for the Council to establish standards of proficiency which can be appealed to by schools throughout the nation and probably to sponsor proficiency examinations.

"b. By taking the lead in establishing standards which will help to distribute the now intolerable work load and give secondary school teachers of English an opportunity to do their job better. Teachers of English are now called upon to perform many duties which interfere with their professional obligations, and are far too heavily burdened to be efficient.

"c. By bending its efforts to the sponsorship of adequate standards of preparation and proficiency for teachers, and of better methods of certification, the National Council can assist markedly in upgrading the profession."

It is truly surprising how Mr. Rice's three suggestions epitomize and embody the gist of the suggestions that the college people offer.

The individual respondents seem to elaborate upon one or the other of Mr. Rice's ideas, according to their personal impressions and penchants. Thus, Dudley Bailey, University of Nebraska: "I am personally suspicious that the emphasis upon the 'English language arts,' and the 'four aspects of reading, writing, speaking, and listening,' instead of effecting an enriching of high school preparation, has lead to a serious watering down of our students' preparation. In Nebraska we have witnessed a considerable growth of courses in speech and journalism at the high school level, not to supplement, but rather to replace the traditional courses which were reading-centered. Like 'teaching the whole child,' the 'English language arts' has proved a mischievous slogan, which seems to be leading towards courses devoted to peripheral aspects of the language arts. To forget that careful and extensive reading in American and British literature is central and crucial to a command of language is a serious forgetting; to pretend that such reading isn't really as important as speaking and listening, and for that matter, writing, is to encourage a good deal of educational nonsense. And I think we all know it."

Here is where Dr. Bailey embarks on the seas of controversy: what do we all know? All agree that reading is an important deficiency among current college entrants, but whether this deficiency outweighs that in writing is a dubious consideration.

To take these two outstanding weaknesses in turn, the University of Colorado, in the words of J. D. A. Ogilvy, presents both sides of the question: "So far as possible improvements are concerned, I should put better reading at the head of the list with more and better practice in writing—not occasional pretentious big themes, but frequent short ones, with careful correction— a close second. This sort of work, of course, implies a low student-teacher ratio and well-trained and conscientious teachers."

The connection between reading and writing ability is a strong one, as stressed by Charles Everett of Columbia University. He says, "In my opinion, the Council can help most by stressing the ability to write. Little seems to be gained by elaborate courses in World Literature, etc., for students who are seldom mature enough to profit by them. Obviously, a student will not be able to write unless he is able to read, but the nature of the reading is, as you know, a complex matter to which there are no easy answers."

Occasional respondents from the colleges stress the importance of expositional writing, as opposed to the "creative" flights so often stressed in high school English classes. An unusual series of complaints emanates from Barnard College: "Most of our laments—we still have some!—are old familiar ones: not enough grammar, not enough sense of formal organization, not enough inquisitiveness about what is read, not enough awareness of the spoken word. A new lament: some students—just a few—have been subjected in school to *over*doses of Great Books. This is not to say that students in high schools should not read masterpieces, nor is it to complain that the high schools have 'done' books that college teachers cope with; it is merely to suggest that a few students arrive in college with the notion that a masterpiece, once galloped through, has nothing more to offer."

But over and over again, the college teachers return to one "greatest single" weakness—English composition. As J. C. Warner, Carnegie Institute of Technology, states: "The greatest single weakness in the preparation of our students has always been in English composition. Without the ability to read accurately and to write clear, coherent prose, no engineer, scientist, architect or business executive can achieve distinction in his profession. And without this ability no student can expect to do well in his undergraduate studies. Therefore it seems to me that the first order of business of professional organizations such as yours might well be to work for better instruction in these areas."

Professor Paul V. Kreider of Cincinnati University has a number of forceful comments along the same lines: "Put more emphasis on the teaching of composition, with very specific instructions for each assignment and with careful and complete correction of papers. 'Book reviews, undirected and not corrected, seem valueless,' says one teacher. This means reducing the number of students and the amount of supervision of outside activities assigned to teachers of English. There is no virtue in complaining about inadequate instruction in the subject unless there are to be established conditions which make it humanly possible for teachers to find the time required for such a program as we recommend."

This is only the first part of the question. Professor Kreider continues: "Both the statistics and the impressionistic comments raise the question of whether or not teachers' time is strategically distributed: whether possibly, to compensate for an increase in emphasis upon the work which the students with lowest level of attainment clearly badly need, there has been a necessary (or at least a natural) decrease which the best students are capable of doing. If this has occurred, the error should be corrected."

Here, surely, is one of the most important dilemmas facing all teachers of English, as indeed, it faces all teachers: how much time should be taken from the least endowed and given to the most gifted, and vice versa? It is not a question susceptible of a quick or easy answer, but it is certainly one that deserves every teacher's attention, under present conditions.

A further job of the Council, as elucidated by K. H. McFall, Provost of Bowling Green State University, is "to convince the public that more and better teachers of English must be found for the public schools, and to convince the public schools that methods must be brought up to date. Those who are already teaching English should be encouraged to upgrade themselves and influenced to adopt those measures which will improve the teaching of English, at least to the extent that public support can be obtained."

Side by side with this recommendation for reduction of the English teacher's load is the recommendation that the Council champion "better pay for high school teachers, better college training in subject matter, more instruction and practice in composition, and greater freedom from the old, timid anthologies of literature," to quote Leonard F. Dean, University of Connecticut, who voices the opinion of many.

Still another sphere in which the college executives feel there is room for improvement is the field of teacher training. Says David Novarr of Cornell University, "I think the inadequate preparation of our students stems primarily from two things: many teachers in the secondary schools are themselves inadequately prepared, and they carry an impossible teaching load. I hope that the National Council will work to remedy both these situations. Too many teachers are certified for work which does not exceed the level of the college sophomore survey course. Many teachers colleges do not have an adequate offering of genuine high-level period and genre courses, and their students count as work in their specific field courses which are essentially methods courses in Education. We must all work to keep the hours of Education required for permanent certification to a maximum of eighteen and we need to plump increasingly for the M.A. in *English*.

"In addition, we need a fight to reduce the number of students each English teacher is responsible for. Students don't write well because they haven't had enough practice in writing, and they don't get the practice because teachers do not have enough time to grade and comment on papers. If a teacher has 120 or 140 students and spends only 5 minutes on a paper by each of them, he has 10 or 12 hours of work. It is no wonder that not many papers are assigned. A teacher of English ought not to have more than 60 or 65 students a term in classes of 20 or 22, and he ought to read two or three short papers, preferably paragraph-length answers to specific questions, every week. It will be an immense job to persuade Boards of Education that only under these circumstances will students be prepared to write well, but I think we must start propagandizing here, and I think the National Council can help."

In other words, to quote Dean Bloore of Fairleigh Dickinson College, "The National Council might well consider a program of educating, not merely English teachers, but also educational administrators, boards of education, and the general public in the value of adequate instruction in English, particularly in writing, and in the dangers likely to beset a society which neglects its basic heritage by neglecting the only means by which it can be communicated."

But the basic theme developed by most of the respondents goes back to an increased training in English rather than in methodology. Thus, the University of Idaho: ". . . emphasize the necessity of high school English teachers' receiving a strong undergraduate major in English. This should include work in the English language, composition, and British and American literature. Competency in at least one foreign language should be strongly recommended as a related field."

Again and again, we get the emphasis on teachers of English who know what they are teaching. Harry H. Crosby of the State University of Iowa: "English teaching is the football of people who are preparing teachers' loads. Principals in Iowa seem to hire home ec teachers, coaches, foreign language teachers first;

then they spread the English courses among the people they have already hired. Even in a high school as large as Iowa City's—having some 900 students—English last year was taught by a basketball coach. I don't know how we can get at these people, but they certainly are the ones we need to work on. The excellent work of Donald Tuttle and Dick Braddock on teaching certification is helping Iowa greatly. Dr. Wayland Osborn, Iowa Director of the Division of Teacher Certification, has said that English teachers are leading the fight for better standards here."

And, from the University of Kansas, Albert R. Kitzhaber: "I think we would all benefit if the Council were to continue its efforts to secure reduction in load for high school English teachers, higher salaries and improved professional status, increased subject-matter requirements for certification of high school teachers, and increased awareness of the necessity for repeated practice in composition. In addition, I would state as my own personal view that the Council consider whether or not the current practice of speaking of the 'language arts' is really desirable. What I am getting at is that students in Kansas have a language arts requirement to fulfill in Kansas rather than an English requirement. This means that the student can satisfy the entire requirement with work in dramatics or debate or journalism, and not take any systematic work expressly in English composition or English and American literature while he is in high school. This is the kind of student who often has difficulty when he gets to college."

This last statement almost begins to be a summation of the opinions of many of the respondents from the nation's colleges and universities. From all parts of the country—the University of Nebraska, the Massachusetts Institute of Technology, Purdue University, University of Texas, Xavier University, Yale University, come the repeated recommendations:

1. Work for increased recognition of teachers (not forgetting financial recognition).
2. Lighten the work load of the English teacher.
3. Eliminate "gadgetry" and busy work. Concentrate on the fundamentals.
4. Give maximum time and attention to writing—and rewriting.
5. Bring back worth-while reading, especially the classics.
6. Emphasize to the public at large—including the technologists—the vital role of English in every sphere of human activity.

COLLEGES AND UNIVERSITIES RESPONDING TO THE SURVEY

University of Alabama	Harry D. Bonham, Acting Dean of Administration
University of Alaska	Minnie E. Wells, Head of Department of Arts and Letters
The American University	Charles M. Clark, Chairman, English Department
University of Arizona	William F. Irmscher, Chairman, Freshman English
University of Arkansas	Claude W. Faulkner, Chairman, English Department
Barnard College	David A. Robertson, Jr., Chairman, English Department
Baylor University	Edna Haney, Director, Freshman English
Boston University	Donald J. Winslow, Chairman, English Department
Bowling Green State University	K. H. McFall, Provost
Brigham Young University	Leonard W. Rice, Dean, College of Humanities and Social Sciences
Brown University	George K. Anderson, Chairman, English Department
The University of California	George A. Pettitt, Assistant to the President

Carnegie Institute of Technology	Dr. Austin Wright, Head, English Department
Case Institute of Technology	Robert L. Shurter, Head, Department of Humanities and Social Studies
The Catholic University of The University of Chicago	Vernon X. Miller, Dean, School of Law Robert E. Streeter, Dean of the College
University of Cincinnati (McMicken College of Liberal Arts)	Paul V. Kreider, Director of the Freshman Course
The City College of New York	Buell Gallagher, President
University of Colorado	J. D. A. Ogilvy, Chairman, Department of English and Speech
Columbia University	Charles Everett, Department of English and Comparative Literature
The University of Connecticut	Leonard F. Dean, Head, Department of English
Cornell University	David Novarr, Director of Freshman English
University of Delaware	John A. Perkins, President
De Paul University	Phillip H. Vitale, Chairman, Department of English
Drake University	Thomas F. Dunn, Head, Department of English
Duke University	Earl W. Porter, Assistant to the President
Earlham College	David E. Henley, Academic Dean
Emory University	S. Walter Martin, President
University of Florida	J. Hooper Wise, Chairman, Freshman English
Fairleigh Dickinson University	J. Stephen Bloore, Administrative Dean, Teaneck Lloyd Haberly, Chairman of English, Rutherford
Fordham University	Grover Cronin, Jr., Chairman, English Department
The George Washington University	Robert H. Moore, Chairman of Composition
The University of Georgia	O. C. Aderhold, President

Harvard University	Harold C. Martin, Director, Committee on General Education
University of Houston	C. Dwight Dorough, Department of English
University of Idaho	H. Walter Steffens, Executive Dean
State University of Iowa	Harry H. Crosby, Writing Supervisor
The Johns Hopkins University	D. C. Allen, Sir William Osler Professor of English
The University of Kansas	Albert R. Kitzhaber, Director, Freshman-Sophomore English
University of Kentucky	W. S. Ward, Head, Department of English, Speech and Dramatic Arts
Louisiana State University	Cecil G. Taylor, Dean, College of Arts and Sciences
University of Louisville	(Mrs.) Meta Riley Emberger, Director of Composition
University of Maine	John E. Hankins, Head, Department of English
Massachusetts Institute of Technology	James G. Kelso, Executive Assistant
University of Michigan	Warner G. Rice, Chairman, Department of English Language and Literature
University of Minnesota	Theodore Hornberger, Chairman, Department of English
University of Nebraska	Dudley Bailey, Director of Freshman English
University of Nevada	Dr. Robert Gorrell, Chairman, Department of English
University of New Hampshire	Eldon L. Johnson, President
University of North Carolina	George F. Horner, Professor of English
University of North Dakota	George W. Starcher, President
Northwestern University	Wallace W. Douglas, Chairman, Freshman English
Oberlin College	Warren Taylor, Chairman, Department of English
The Ohio State University	Robert M. Estrich, Chairman, Department of English
	Gordon B. Carson, Dean
	R. H. Eckelberry, Editor

The University of Oklahoma	Jack L. Kendall, Chairman, Freshman Committee Department of English
University of Oregon	Gladys Kerlee, Secretary to the President
Princeton University	Willard Thorp, Acting Chairman, Department of English
Purdue University	Frederick L. Hovde, President
Regis College	Rev. Louis G. Mattione, S.J., Dean
University of Rhode Island	Walter L. Simmons, Head, Department of English
Rutgers University	J. Milton French, Chairman, Department of English
University of South Carolina	Havilah Babcock, Head of English Department
State University of South Dakota	I. D. Weeks, President
Southwestern at Memphis	C. I. Diehl, Dean of Men
Stanford University	George F. Sensabaugh, Acting Executive Head, Department of English
Swarthmore College	George J. Becker, Chairman, Department of English Literature
The University of Tennessee	John C. Hodges, Head, Department of English
The University of Vermont	Muriel J. Hughes, Chairman, Freshman English Committee
United States Air Force Academy	Col. Robert F. McDermott, Dean of Faculty
United States Air Force ROTC	Col. William E. McEntire, Chief of Staff
University of Utah	Edwin R. Clapp, Head, Department of English
Vanderbilt University	Randall Stewart, Chairman, Department of English
Villa Madonna College	Rev. John F. Murphy, President
University of Virginia	Frederick L. Gwynn, Associate Professor
University of Washington	Glenn Leggett, Director, Freshman English
University of Wisconsin	Edgar W. Lacy, Director of Freshman English

Xavier University	Very Reverend Paul L. O'Connor, S.J., President
Yale University	Arthur Howe, Jr., Dean of Admissions
	Louis L. Martz, Chairman, Department of English
	Frederick W. Hilles, Former Chairman, Department of English

≫ 4 ≪

Opinions of
Business Executives

Over 100 business executives throughout the nation were asked the following questions pertaining to the competence in English of recent graduates:

1. From your observation and experience, how would you evaluate the competence in English of recent graduates from high school and college?
2. If you have noticed any improvements in the past 5 or 10 years, in which areas did you find improvements?
3. If you have found deficiencies in the past 5 or 10 years, what were these deficiencies?
4. Are you aware of the work that the National Council of Teachers of English has been doing in curriculum revision, in providing better instructional materials, in working for better preparation of English teachers at all levels?
5. What recommendations would you make of ways in which the Council can help to produce students at all levels better equipped in all phases of English?

QUESTION 1—COMPETENCE OF RECENT GRADUATES

"I have often stated to former colleagues that after 9 years in industry I would like very much to be able to return to the classroom and tell the students just how desperately they will need the ability offered them by their English courses . . . Allow me to assure you and your colleagues in the Council that you can, in truth, tell your students that no other part of their training in school will be so vital to them in their careers as their work in English."

These words, by Emil Hubka, Jr., of Motorola, Inc., are typical of the thinking of 63 executives in major business firms throughout the nation, among them some of the "giants" of American industry. Their responses to the survey reveal an awareness of the importance of English in the business careers and personal lives of both high school and college graduates, and a genuine concern to increase competence at all levels.

It is heartening to the work of the Council as a whole to realize that business—as revealed in these responses—does not underestimate the role that competence in English plays in their enterprises, and indeed, values that competence highly. Thus, Mark W. Cresap, Jr., President of Westinghouse Electric Corporation: "Within our organization, we find we must be increasingly mindful of the best means of communication. From a functional point of view, effective communications reduce the amount of time spent in interpreting what a person intends to convey in oral and written form. Because of our constantly changing language, we can never feel that our communications are perfect. Therefore, we must seek from our high school and college students a higher degree of competence than that which presently exists."

The desire for a better school "product" voiced in the last sentence is a very natural one, but where executives express it, it is almost always accompanied by a genuine understanding of the problems faced by teachers. The personnel director of one of our largest corporations expresses it as follows: "Like all other areas of education, the schools turn out some people who are well qualified in the use of English and others less qualified. It is the latter group who are usually commented on and the ones for whom the schools are blamed. All in all, we feel that the schools are doing a good job, considering the large number of students with which they must deal, and considering the wide variety of interests and abilities of these students."

A similar opinion is vividly expressed by Harmon D. Martin of the First National City Bank of New York. "While it appears popular during this post-Sputnik furor about education to criticize everything educational in America, we are quick to say that the educators are doing an adequate piece of work in English despite rather trying and adverse conditions. There seems to be no doubt that the declining calibre of students, the modern social distractions and the general lack of home controls and stimuli, all combine to make the teachers' lives even more difficult than ever.

"My official duties here have taught me—despite masses of critical articles—that many schools and colleges still hold to excellent standards in English, and that many graduates show high competency in the art of self-expression."

Arden E. Firestone, of Goodyear Tire and Rubber Company, responds in a similar vein. "Most of the recent high school graduates now on our payroll have quite a good background in English both written and spoken. The quality of their English depends to some extent on their home environment and the high school they have attended. We select the best available students by means of tests and by checking with the school authorities and the school records.

"The same school, of course, produces good and bad students, so we cannot put all the blame on the teaching or the curriculum. The high school graduating a large number of college preparatory students seems to put more emphasis on the importance of English."

While it is gratifying to find that fully one third of the business executives responding are generally satisfied with the competence of recent graduates, this satisfaction is by no means universally true.

Among the business executives responding, one third disqualify themselves from evaluating the competence of recent graduates, either because there is no statistical information available, or because they have no personal knowledge of the abilities of recent graduates.

Twenty of the business executives who replied took a very dim view of the competence of recent graduates, both at the high school and college levels. Their ratings range from "fair to poor" through "leaves something to be desired," and culminate in "inarticulate," and "this (criticism) applies especially to the high school graduate whose formal studies in grammar, rhetoric and composition, to say nothing of spelling and reading, appear to have stopped at the third or fourth grade."

Fortunately for the conduct of this survey, the dissenters have gone to great lengths to point out the areas in which deficiencies occur, and to back up their criticisms with suggestions for improvements. These will be considered in the discussions of Questions 3 and 5.

The attitude of the dissatisfied business executives is best expressed in this excerpt from the letter of the president of a major manufacturing firm. "I have been distressed by the incompetence of many high school and college graduates. Too often, young people are handicapped by an inability to express themselves, either orally or in writing. Vocabularies are limited and many young people are uncomfortable in the use and understanding of their own language. This is a serious obstacle to adjustment and advancement in industry where communication is so important."

There is some consolation, in an examination of these critical responses, in the fact that the business executives of the country

are far from blind to the importance of competence in English
and that they are deeply concerned and anxious for improvement
where it is necessary.

QUESTION 2—IMPROVEMENTS NOTED IN PAST
5 TO 10 YEARS

"Although we have conducted no studies designed to compare
the competence in English of recent graduates with those of
earlier years," writes L. A. Wetlaufer of the Personnel Division
of E. I. DuPont de Nemours & Co., "we have not observed great
change with respect either to deterioration or significant improvement over a considerable span of time. Perhaps significant
change, if any, has been too gradual to stand out in bold relief.
In any event, we do observe that complaints pertaining to competence in English, which are being expressed today, are of the
same character as those of at least 30 years ago . . . We are inclined to believe that there is opportunity for establishing a better
balance in teacher preparation between method and subject content, which should give us improvement over anything we have
had in the past."

It is comments like the above which hold out hope to the English teacher that there may some day be moderation and understanding in the mind of the public toward the problems of the
teacher.

The business executives who responded to the survey apparently have agreed to disagree, so far as Question 2 is concerned

Of 63 replies received:

18 saw improvement in one phase or another
16 had seen no appreciable improvement
 8 saw deterioration in one phase or another
21 failed to answer this question, or declared their inability
   to judge

Among the encouraging notes is one sounded by an executive of an important manufacturing firm, whose clerical staff runs into the hundreds. "Each year," he says, "there seems to be some improvement in the quality of high school graduates. This is probably due to improved training and perhaps to some degree because most of the present day students expect to work at least during the summer months after high school and therefore prepare themselves to a greater extent."

The same opinion is expressed by another prominent executive about college graduates: "I have concluded from observations and experience that graduates who have been exposed to training in the liberal arts, regardless of their vocational aspirations, are better prepared for careers leading to leadership than most not so trained." This quotation is from the head of a firm as far removed from the liberal arts as any manufacturing firm could be!

This idea is further exemplified in the words of another manufacturing executive: "Our interest in science has definitely increased, but I am glad to see we still stress a broad education for technical students, rather than falling into the pitfall of an imbalanced education."

The role of competence in English is stressed over and over by those whose main interests are scientific or technical: "None of us were conscious of any marked difference between recent graduates and those of 10 years ago or 20 years ago as to their competence in English. In each era it seems to us that we have run into a wide range of competence which has depended largely on such factors as the interests and abilities of the individual, how far he went with his schooling and the course of study he pursued. In the latter connection, however, some of our people who employ young engineers do feel that improvement is observable as a result of the greater emphasis engineering schools have been placing on English and other liberal arts subjects."

When the affirmative responses get down to specifics, it may be significant to note that the improvements cited often involve ability to express oneself orally.

According to the spokesman for the public relations department of one of our most important corporations, "most improvements in the last 5 or 10 years have been in *speaking* either to an individual or to a group or even an audience."

And again, from one of our largest merchandising organizations, "We feel that the recent graduates are able to express themselves verbally in a more poised and self-confident manner." Another manufacturer, in a field completely dissociated from the preceding: "We have noticed some slight improvement in oral English in the past 5 to 10 years; that is, young men that we talk with today coming out of college seem to be required to take more public speaking courses, so they at least have more self-confidence and speak with greater ease."

The spokesman for a chemical manufacturing firm makes a surprising observation. "The most striking improvement is in the lessening of regional differences in speech. For example, the Southerner is beginning to become comprehensible to the New Englander, and vice versa. It would appear that colloquialisms and idiomatic forms are decreasing and more uniform language is emerging."

The awareness of the humanizing effects of English teaching is evidenced by such statements as, "I believe that teaching of English today is more frequently related to living experiences and learning projects—the core curriculum—than in the past." And, even more encouraging, "It would appear that among the better students there has been some increase in reading comprehension, and among all students there is a noticeable broadening of interest fields, particularly in things relating to scientific matters and world affairs."

"Recent graduates," declares another executive, "from both

high school and college, but especially college, are better informed on more subjects than in the past. The ability of recent graduates to communicate, both in writing and verbally, has definitely been improved."

"Verbally" apparently means "out loud." One executive's "feeling is that the recent high school graduate is as competent as the high school graduate of 20 years ago, although the recent graduate is perhaps more skillful in the use of spoken English than the older graduate." The same executive, however, declares that the recent graduate "is not up-to-date on contemporary usage and has some difficulty in the organization of his ideas on paper. Further, his concern for grammatical error and his preoccupation with attempts to be 'literary' or 'businesslike' sometimes impedes effective communication."

The opinion herein expressed is backed by such statements as "Our impression is that the recent graduates are more facile in speech, and that possibly they have a better background in vocabulary and grammar."

The shafts fly thick and fast against this estimate.

The opposition declares, "Regrettably, there have been no appreciable improvements in the past 5 or 10 years. . . . Atrophy of the basic skills for the uses of knowledge began to plague our school systems 25 to 30 years ago, leaving such fine organizations as the NCTE with an almost insurmountable task."

The most representative attitude of the group which sees no improvement over the past 10 years is voiced by the employee relations manager of a major oil company, as follows: "Unfortunately, there seemed to be a lack of unanimity (among various personnel offices in the company and its affiliates) both with respect to adequate preparation, as well as any change over the past 5 or 10 years."

Interestingly enough, some 11 of the answers are stated in

almost identical words: "We have not noticed a particular improvement on the part of either high school or college graduates in competence in English during the past 5 years."

One highly articulate group of respondents declared, in essence, "No improvement in the past 5 or 10 years, the opposite tendency being apparent."

"As a matter of fact," adds the personnel director of a respected insurance company, "in some respects, it has seemed to me that high school graduates and college graduates alike have demonstrated that their reading has lacked depth and breadth and that their interests are extremely narrow and reflect pursuit of interest rather than discipline."

The most gloomy judgment is uttered by a prominent executive who prefers to remain anonymous: "In the past 5 or 10 years, English proficiency has actually gone downhill. This decline is more noticeable in the girl high school graduates whom we hire in large numbers for our stenographic and secretarial jobs. But it is also noticeable in the technical people whom we hire for research and manufacturing positions.

"The one area that has shown some improvement is with management personnel. This may be attributed to the fact that more of these people now have a liberal arts training in college, or perhaps the business schools have increased the amount of training they give in communication skills."

Thus, even the most disapproving of critics mitigates the severity of his remarks with some encouraging notes. Most revelatory in the answers of the business executives is the fact that those who are most severe in their opinions are also the ones who have been most generous and specific in their suggestions. They are the ones most keenly aware that they have a stake in what the schools turn out. They know, better than most, that a high degree of skill in English is a prime factor in the success and prosperity of their enterprises.

QUESTION 3—DEFICIENCIES NOTED IN THE PAST 5 TO 10 YEARS

Because the diagnosis of a weakness carries with it a recommendation for its elimination, the answers to Questions 3 and 5 overlap a good deal.

Overwhelmingly, even in letters where the executives felt there had been an improvement in recent years, they still indicated that they had found deficiencies in spelling, grammar and punctuation.

"We do not test employees or job applicants on their mastery of English," writes the personnel manager of a great oil company. "However, we do test certain job applicants on spelling ability, and you may be interested in our experience in that area.

"In 1955, 69% of job applicants taking our spelling test failed to meet our minimum standards. In 1956, the percentage failing was 53%, and in 1957, 57%. During the first six months of 1958, 56% failed. The applicants taking the spelling test (12th grade level) were primarily high school graduates. However, a limited number of college graduates and secretarial school graduates are included in the total."

"We feel," writes the president of a manufacturing concern, "that many average and below average students look upon entering business as a right rather than a privilege and fail to acquire as a matter of course some of the technical skills of expression. This seems to be particularly true in such matters as sentence structure, spelling and various technical aspects of written expression."

Deficiency in Spelling

This is a comparatively moderate view of the deficiencies in spelling. In all, some 33 of the 63 executives who responded rated spelling as the most glaring deficiency. After some complimentary remarks on improved oral English, one executive complains that at "both the high school and college level we still find a remarkably large percentage of graduates sadly lacking in the ability to spell."

Punctuation

Next to spelling, punctuation is selected as a major deficiency of recent school graduates. This seems to be particularly true in the largest corporations where hundreds of clerical workers are needed.

A banking executive declares, "We are very conscious of the mechanical errors in spelling and punctuation made by female graduates who must fill typing and stenographic positions where these skills are an essential requirement."

In all, 28 of the 63 executives responding cited punctuation as an outstanding deficiency.

Grammar

Next in order of critical notice is grammar. Many of the answers tend to group the term *grammar* with inability to organize thought or to express meaning clearly.

According to an insurance company director, "the most noticeable deficiencies have been in simple grammar and rhetoric. The words are there, frequently in abundance, but they are not put together logically and are not arranged in a manner conducive to rapid and clear comprehension."

Another public relations manager pursues the question from a slightly different angle. "The deficiencies I have noticed are mainly in the lack of a formal grasp of grammar. This could be rectified by a greater emphasis on the fundamentals of our language, both in the written and oral forms and at as early an age as the individual student's capacity permits."

The need for personnel with skill in communications is a very great one in business. In this sphere, apparently, recent graduates are often lacking. In the words of a public relations director, "In business, ability to express one's self either orally, in writing, or both, is of prime importance. If improvements were to be suggested, it would be along both of these lines."

And another similar criticism, from the president of a manufacturing firm: "The majority of these girls (in the secretarial groups) seem woefully inadequate in writing even the simplest piece of correspondence. They are afraid of putting any idea on paper.

"The college graduates have difficulty in writing clearly and concisely. They are not proficient in taking complex material, organizing it, and presenting it simply, directly, emphatically."

A personnel director backs up his very severe criticism by citing "actual cases within our own experience:

"A girl with two years of college failed as a file clerk. She didn't know the alphabet.

"A college graduate employed as a field auditor couldn't write a readable report.

"College graduates promoted to administrative jobs require training in how to write simple business letters. (This is a constant problem.)

"Secretaries don't know how to use the dictionary. Most of them have never heard of Fowler or Roget. (There are, of course, exceptions.)"

In view of the cases cited, it is hardly surprising that this executive's view of deficiencies verges on the caustic: "Recent graduates," he says, "including those with university degrees, seem to have no mastery of the language at all. They cannot construct a simple declarative sentence, either orally or in writing. They cannot spell common, everyday words. Punctuation is apparently no longer taught. Grammar is a complete mystery to almost all recent graduates."

It would be comforting to believe that this particular personnel manager had been very unlucky in his choice of candidates. Unfortunately, there are too many gloomy opinions from other executives which emphasize identical points. "Among deficiencies most often cited by supervisors," another personnel director tells us, "(is) apparent general incapacity to develop in writing a thesis or theme beyond the limits of a few simple paragraphs."

One of the principal difficulties mentioned by the personnel director of a national industrial firm is "no understanding of the basic concept that the form of the writing should reflect the form of the thinking."

In the thinking of many business executives, competence in English grammar goes hand in hand with ability to think clearly.

Thus, the vice president of an important insurance company: "The greatest deficiency seems to be the lack of knowledge of basic sentence structure, spelling and punctuation. This is especially true of many applying for stenographic and typing positions, where such knowledge is essential to successful job performance. On the college level (with the exception of those majoring in English) many graduates seem to have difficulty reporting facts and conclusions clearly and succinctly in reports and other memoranda, where such ability is vital to those aspiring to supervisory and managerial positions."

Next in order, after deficiencies in spelling, punctuation, and grammar, is weakness in vocabulary. Under this deficiency are included such defects as "an increased use of trite words, clichés, and jargon"; "inability to properly use a dictionary, thesaurus, or other similar references"; "lack of knowledge of the meaning of rather commonplace words"; "limited training in the language of the market place—words that are short and to the point."

The vocabulary problem is best expressed by Mr. Wetlaufer of DuPont: "Another complaint pertains to vocabulary, with emphasis on quality rather than quantity. Choice of words, not clearly understood by the reader, may result in confusing or misleading the reader or listener. Many hours are spent in seeking clarification of statements in oral and written reports, for want of good grammar and proper choice of words."

Another deficiency cited by several of the executives has to do with proofreading written work before it can be used. "Failure to assume responsibility" is one cause given for this. Another is that "employees often turn to their employer for assistance in phases of written work they should be able to handle themselves."

Two exceptionally thoughtful responses stress the importance of reading and good literature. The first says, "In addition to my observations in my first answer, too many young people have had little or no touch with the great literature of our language. The habit of reading great books apparently does not get off to a good start with most youngsters. After graduation, either from high school or college, reading seems to be a chore to be avoided, rather than an experience of joy and learning. This is a misfortune, for all of the positive values that reading can give to human beings are lost to our youth."

The second of these advocates of good reading states, "It seems to me the principal deficiency is a sharp reduction in the amount of reading experience of the typical student. Not only is there less required reading in school but there is also less reading in the home. The competition of the complexities of modern community life, television, cartoon books, etc., is most serious and is not being overcome. Reduced reading experience is not only reflected in a lack of background in literature but also in a reduced capacity to understand grammar and to use it properly, to write freely and clearly and to achieve effective oral expression."

QUESTION 4—KNOWLEDGE OF THE COUNCIL
AND ITS ACTIVITIES

The business executives on the whole were not acquainted with the work of the Council, but many of them expressed a desire to know more about that work. Here and there an executive who had formerly been a teacher had heard of the Council or had even been a member. The desire to know more about the work of the Council and the wish to contribute something to the improvement of our program were most encouraging.

QUESTION 5—RECOMMENDATIONS FOR
IMPROVEMENT TO NCTE

Underlying most of the recommendations made by business executives for the improvement of the English curriculum is a strong stress on the importance that English plays in business— both for the student himself and for the business organization involved. "The student must realize," declares the personnel head of a large food-processing firm, "that the personal rewards of work done well may be lost if a report is not well written. Furthermore, he may never have an opportunity to demonstrate his ability if he does not present himself favorably to a prospective employer. Because his first contact is so often by way of his own letter or résumé, his ability to express himself is crucial . . . We believe that the greatest good can be accomplished by a college freshman English course which insures the learning of grammar and develops a consciousness of it and is supported by critical appraisal of the English in the papers and reports presented in all courses in the college curriculum whether literary or technical."

If the emphasis of these executives seems to be mainly on the materialistic, the "practical," the economic uses of English, it is hardly to be wondered at. A glance at the list of these executives

would indicate that they have in their employ hundreds, sometimes even thousands of secretaries, clerks, stenographers, technical writers, etc., and unless they can obtain the best possible
personnel, equipped with skills in English, skills in technology
may well be wasted. What emerges from the responses of business executives is that they appreciate all too well the importance
that good English plays in keeping the wheels of industry running smoothly.

"It is my observation," states the president of a prominent
trust company, "that today's curricula stress the technical and
vocational subjects and that these seem to appeal more to the
young people. If this is truly one of the causes of inferior competence, then I believe that the Council must strenuously work for
curricula that will produce students better equipped in English.
Since the language is the basic tool for development of all intellectual skills, the development of other skills must relate to the
degree of ability that has been developed in the basic skill. Furthermore, I believe that today's students can develop the growth
of mind necessary not only to their vocational employment, but
also to their usefulness as citizens, only by improving the present
unsatisfactory use of English."

First and foremost in the letters of these business executives is
an emphasis on fundamentals—spelling, punctuation, grammar.
Many believe that training in the use of good English must begin
as early as possible. "Our recommendations for improvement
would be that serious instruction must begin far below the high
school level," declares the personnel director of a prominent merchandising company. "If, in some way, students could be made
aware of words as symbols (in the semantic sense), as tools of
communication and as essential components of sentences, perhaps the most onerous disciplines of grammar and spelling could
be better managed."

This opinion was based on responses from various personnel

offices of a major oil company: "Our suggestion would be to have a more thorough and intensive training program commencing early in elementary school and continuing through high school and college on basic written English fundamentals, as well as courses designed to aid students in the art of self-expression."

Over and over, this opinion is repeated: "Make the study of English more interesting and stress it repeatedly from the primary grade up. Continue English grammar, sentence structure, spelling and punctuation on a review basis through high school." And again, "the deficiencies I have noticed are mainly in the lack of a formal grasp of grammar. This could be rectified by a greater emphasis on the fundamentals of our language, both in the written and oral forms and at as early an age as the individual student's capacity permits."

Fully 90% of the recommendations center on the fundamentals—as exemplified in this quotation from one of the largest corporations in the United States: "Further stress on teaching grammar so that it will be understood and remembered; insistence in spelling as well as in grammar and punctuation; more assignments in the writing of letters, reports, surveys, compositions and essays."

Another executive simply urges, "Allow more time for drill, drill, drill!"

A number of writers have recommendations that involve not the work of the students but the training of teachers of English. Says the vice president of a great insurance company: "Unfortunately, meaningless methodology, as prerequisite for license to teach, has precedence over basic knowledge of subject matter as the fundamental qualification for teaching. As a result you find teachers of English, as my associates and I have found, who, in blissful ignorance, use such expressions as 'between you and

I . . .' 'he don't,' and 'If I was you . . .'—completely unaware of grammatical distinction and the wonders of English literature.

"I suggest," he continues, "that educational courses be eliminated and replaced by additional courses in English grammar, literature and composition in the college curriculum as prerequisites for candidates for teachers of English. You might also consider a more intensive program requiring courses in grammar, rhetoric, and composition on the primary and secondary level than is now apparent in the school systems."

This executive is by no means alone in his opinion. Another personnel head tells us, "Majority opinion (within his organization) is that the system of teaching English has turned too far away from fundamentals and probably should again concentrate attention on spelling, word construction, vocabulary building, reading for comprehension and the like."

A most thoughtful view of the qualification of teachers appears in this view of the president of a manufacturing firm: "I think teachers of English must devise ways to instill a lifetime reading habit among students at the earliest possible age. In addition, at an early age students should be inculcated with the knowledge that a love of English and a command of English are prerequisites to success as adults. Wider use, perhaps, of educational television, radio and records should be employed. Teachers themselves should be encouraged to acquire a wider awareness of and facility with the language of contemporary science and technology. These are dominant forces around us. What they mean cannot easily be understood or communicated without the knowledge applying to them. This language is part of contemporary English usage and contemporary literature and journalism. Teachers should be well versed in this field because their students will need it in the world in which they are growing up."

The teacher's problems are also analyzed from an economic

point of view. "Most important," says the director of education of a large insurance firm, "in any teacher-learner situation is the ability of the teacher to inspire in the learner a desire for knowledge and improved skill. Some teachers have this ability but many others do not. Also, sadly enough, many who have it are no longer teaching because they have been driven by necessity or inclination into better paying professions.

"The problem then becomes that of attracting to the teaching profession dedicated persons of outstanding teaching ability. The citizens must regain enough respect for education to induce them to pay more for it. Money may not be the strongest motivating force, but what it can bring (in terms of self-respect and respect of others) makes it one of the strongest controllable motivating forces in attracting people to a given profession.

"I do not believe this problem can be solved by piecemeal contributions from industry, government or individuals. It must come about by a changed attitude on the part of the public at large. Sputnik has done a great deal to start this change by focusing the public's attention upon the importance of education and the acute present need for it. Perhaps this will develop into a permanent change of attitude."

Possibly the most wholesome over-all view is that expressed by the gentleman from DuPont. In wise and reasoned moderation, he makes a number of cogent points. "We have been following the debate for some years as to whether or not pedagogy is being overemphasized at the expense of preparation in the subject to be taught. It is our recollection that there was a time when the argument was in the reverse order. We are inclined to believe that there is opportunity for establishment of a better balance in teacher preparation between method and subject content, which should give us improvement over anything we have had in the past.

"Another broad question about which we hear much these

days is whether or not the energy of the student is so dissipated through the multiplicity of both credit and noncredit kinds that he has too little time for the really basic subjects. We hear about homemaking courses, marriage courses, craft clubs of many kinds, hiking clubs, bird-watching clubs, etc., etc. The usurpation of many of these subjects or activities by the schools which once were considered the responsibility of the family or the church or some other community organization, may not necessarily load more on the student. It may result largely in the transfer of more of the student's energy into the framework of the school system. An aspect of this situation within the context of the subject at hand and about which we feel concerned, is the extent to which it is robbing faculty time that should be devoted to teaching of the basic subjects, of which English is surely one."

Most important in acquiring perspective on current criticism is this comment: "It is our impression that there have been different circumstances from time to time over the years which have prevented or hindered the best possible instruction in English and the best possible student achievement. That the problem is not new is perhaps illustrated by an experiment some time ago when a participant in an industry-education conference read an excerpt from an article which emphasized deficiencies in English competence among people considered to be well-educated. From the nodding of heads and the subsequent discussion, it was apparent that the article was accepted as very timely indeed. It was quite a shock when the participant announced that the article was written in 1835."

CONCLUSIONS

Even a cursory reading of the responses of the business executives reveals a serious interest in the improvement of English, a great desire to know more about the workings of the schools in this field, and a willingness to assist in whatever way they can.

Specific recommendations embrace the following:

1. Increase drills on fundamentals in spelling, syntax, and the essentials of grammar—presumably applied grammar.
2. Stimulate students to read more, including not only current materials and technical subjects, but still more widely in the classics.
3. Give greater emphasis to writing and rewriting, with an approach to self-criticism and evaluation.
4. Improve the techniques of teaching basic English skills, stressing in teacher-training more knowledge of subject matter as opposed to methodology.

Most important of all is the realization that English is not simply a three-year course or a four-year course that terminates in a passing or failing grade. It is an essential part of the life that students must take with them wherever and whenever they go. This leaves a heavy burden of responsibility in the hands of the teacher of English.

BUSINESS EXECUTIVES RESPONDING
TO THE QUESTIONNAIRE

Firm Name	*Executive Responding*
Aluminum Company of America	A. M. Doty, Assistant Manager Personnel Relations
American Machine & Foundry Company	Clark C. Sorenson, Director Public & Industrial Relations
The American Tobacco Company	F. J. Naumann, Personnel
Avco Manufacturing Company	James E. Mitchell, Director Personnel Relations
The Borden Company	E. H. Dare, Manager, Employee Relations
Brown Shoe Company	C. R. Gamble, President
Campbell Soup Company	T. C. Thompson, Personnel Assistant

Firm Name	*Executive Responding*
Carrier Corporation	Allen W. Sherman, Director Personnel Administration
The Chase Manhattan Bank	Robert W. Scofield, Assistant Vice President
Chrysler Corporation	John H. DeCarlo, Manager Educational Services
Chubb & Son	J. J. Schieffelin, Personnel
The Coca-Cola Bottling Company of New York, New York	Edward P. Lewis, President
Commercial Investment Trust, Incorporated	William L. Wilson, Vice President
Continental Can Company, Incorporated	Francis M. Taylor, Manager of Public Relations
Continental Insurance Company	William C. Moore, Vice President and Co-ordinator of Education
America Fire Insurance Group	Co-ordinator of Education
Corn Refining Products Company	W. T. Brady, President
E. I. DuPont de Nemours Company	L. A. Wetlaufer, Assistant Manager, Personnel Division
Eastman Kodak Company	Monroe V. Dill, Director of Industrial Relations
The Equitable Life Assurance Society	Edward A. Robie, Second Vice President and Personnel Director
The Equitable Trust Company	Robert G. Merrick, President
The First National City Bank of New York	Harmon C. Martin, Assistant Cashier
Ford Motor Company	Henry Ford II, President
General Mills	Annette Grosse, Women's Personnel Adviser
General Motors	George A. Jacoby, Director of Personnel Relations
The Goodyear Tire and Rubber Company	Arden E. Firestone, Secretary
Gulf Oil Corporation	George L. Scott, Secretary Education Committee
Hartford National Bank and Trust Company	Robert D. Filon, Vice President
International Business Machines Corporation	R. C. Warren, Director of Education
International Harvester Company	E. H. Reed, Manager

Firm Name	*Executive Responding*
International Paper Company Foundation	William A. Hanway, President
John Hancock Mutual Life Insurance Company	William H. Eastman, Personnel Director
Johnson and Johnson	George F. Smith, President
Kellogg Company	L. C. Roll, President
Koppers Company, Incorporated	Fred C. Foy, President
Libbey Owens Ford Glass Company	George P. MacNichol, Jr., President
Liberty Mutual	W. Moorman, Director of Education
Manufacturers Trust Company	Frederick W. Oswald, Vice President
Merck & Company, Incorporated	John T. Connor, President
Metropolitan Life Insurance Company	Karl H. Kreder, Second Vice President
Motorola Incorporated	Emil F. Hubka, Jr., Public Relations Department
National Gypsum Company	W. S. Corrie, Treasurer
Philco Corporation	Robert M. Jones, Director of Public Relations
Chas. Pfizer and Company, Incorporated	William A. Thompson, Personnel Supervisor, Chairman of the Committee
Rexall Drug Company	Robert K. Young, Personnel Director
Scott Paper Company	Miss H. M. Smith, Personnel Manager for Women
Sears, Roebuck and Company	R. E. Barmeier, Director of Personnel Planning and Research
Shell Oil Company	H. D. Kammerlohr, Manager Head Office Staff Division Personnel Department
Southern Pacific Company	D. J. Russell, President
Standard Oil Company	A. W. Brown, Manager Employee Relations Department
Socony Mobil Oil Company	Herbert Willetts, Vice President and Director in charge of Employee Relations
Sunshine Biscuits, Incorporated	Hanford Main, Chairman of the Board

Firm Name	*Executive Responding*
Swift and Company	Herman W. Seinwerth, Industrial Relations Department
The Texas Company	J. W. Foley, President
The Travelers Insurance Companies	Fred A. Ruoff, Employee Relations Assistant
United States Steel Corporation	Earl O. Ewan, Public Relations Dept.
Western Electric Company	P. S. Shannon, Director of Training Programs
Westinghouse Electric Corporation	Mark W. Cresap, Jr., President
The Yale and Towne Manufacturing Company	Gilbert W. Chapman, President

❧ 5 ❧

Opinions of
U.S. Civil Service
Administrators

NATURE OF THE SURVEY

If there is any *single* organization in our country that is more vitally concerned with the ability of its personnel to communicate effectively than the United States Government, we have not as yet discovered it.

The U.S. Civil Service administrators were asked the questions which were also asked of the business executives, the educational and general magazine editors, the newspaper editors, the attorneys, legislators, judges, and law school deans.

The 30 responses were both gratifying and discouraging. They were gratifying because 60% of those administrators queried responded to our single-page letter with carefully prepared letters of their own. No questionnaire or check list was enclosed, nor was a return envelope supplied. The interest, the great willingness to co-operate, the frankness of the answers, and the thoughtfulness were apparent in almost every reply. "I am delighted to answer your letter of September 2, 1958," wrote W. Richard Lomax, Director of Personnel for the Federal Housing Administration, "because your letter strikes at the heart of something which has concerned me for many years." This expression of vital interest appeared in almost every letter.

Equally apparent was the appreciation for and understanding

of the work of the National Council of Teachers of English and of the profession as a whole. Harry C. Kelly, Assistant Director for Scientific Personnel and Education, National Science Foundation, expressed this appreciation and understanding when he noted: "We have no question but that the better work you do in your curricular and teacher programs, the better will be the training of our scientists and engineers."

The discouragement arises from the overwhelming opinion that the people entering government service, in clerical, administrative, and scientific fields, are in general not effectively equipped in the communication skills. It must be added, however, that the civil service administrators were by no means unanimous in attaching blame to English instruction. Many expressed the opinion that there are many factors involved in this question of competence in English. After noting that the United States Civil Service Commission has had to lower standards on at least one of its tests in certain areas of the country, O. Glenn Stahl, Director, Bureau of Programs and Standards, expressed the following qualifying idea:

"Whether this is because of faulty instruction, lack of application on the part of the students, or a lower segment of the labor market we are attracting, we are unable to say; but the deficiency is there, and it is a marked one."

Replies were received from the following offices of the United States Government (see list of contributors for names and positions of respondents):

*Federal Housing Administration
 Federal Trade Commission
*The Librarian of Congress
 National Science Foundation

* Special appreciation is due for the helpfulness and thoroughness of these replies.

*Office of Civil and Defense Mobilization
*United States Civil Service Commission
*United States Department of Agriculture (2)
*Department of the Air Force (2)
*Department of the Army
 Department of the Navy
*United States Department of Commerce (2)
 United States Department of the Interior
*United States Department of Labor (2)
 United States General Accounting Office
*United States Information Agency (2)
*United States Interstate Commerce Commission
 United States Post Office Department
 Selective Service Commission
*Tennessee Valley Authority
 United States Treasury Department
*Veterans Administration
*General Accounting Office

One extremely valuable answer to the questions came from the United States General Accounting Office, whose Director of Accounting and Auditing Policy Staff, E. H. Morse, duplicated our letter and sent it to 100 members of the staff in 19 regional offices. The replies, arranged and tabulated, were compiled into a 55-page booklet entitled *Observations on the Competence in English of Recent College Graduates and Suggestions for Improvement* (United States General Accounting Office, December, 1958). It is the most comprehensive of all the replies received in this survey.

These preliminary remarks would not be complete without

---

* Special appreciation is due for the helpfulness and thoroughness of these replies.

commenting upon the qualifications of the respondents and the validity of the replies. These might best be given by citing two examples:

1. W. Richard Lomax of the Federal Housing Administration was Director of the Institute of Training for Public Service at Indiana University and Professor of Government in the College of Arts and Sciences and in the Graduate School, before entering government service.

2. Ernest C. Betts points out that his response is based upon consultation with his colleagues, a survey made about 5 years ago, and "our general impressions." This broad base of reference was repeated time and time again in the expressions of opinion, and often actual comparative studies were made of examination results over the years.

SUMMARY OF ANSWERS TO QUESTION 1— COMPETENCE OF RECENT GRADUATES

The distribution of replies is as follows:

13 respondents did not answer this question
 1 respondent found recent graduates proficient in the fundamentals of English
 5 respondents expressed mixed reactions
10 respondents noted that recent graduates, in effect, "leave much to be desired."

Those who failed to answer the first question dealing with evaluations of recent high school and college graduates gave the following reasons variously: "not qualified," "no information," "lack of knowledge," "personal bias," "no opportunity to gather information," etc. Some respondents assumed erroneously that the question (and Questions 2 and 3) called for statistical evidence.

The respondent who replied that the people his organization

engages "show sound learning in fundamentals of English" headed a college trainees program. It must be noted, however, that one criterion for admission to the program is demonstrated proficiency with the English language, since the trainees will work in a public relations writing field.

Two out of the five who expressed mixed reactions noted that their organizations found it necessary to carry on remedial programs for a number of their employees and personnel. For instance, one of our Air Force respondents reported that about 20% of the college graduates attending Squadron Officer School are required to take remedial instruction in communication. On the other hand, this same individual reports that the majority show satisfactory command of the English language, and many show exceptional ability.

The same picture is repeated in the replies of the other three respondents. "In general we have noted that our applicants vary widely in their knowledge." One of the replies from the United States Information Agency states that there is a "wide range" of ability apparent, from the English majors and top-level students who write well, to the "illiterates" among exchange teacher grantees, many of whom are English teachers.

The majority of those who replied to this question expressed the general opinion that "One of the greatest single obstacles to the effective operation of government is the astounding inability of intelligent persons to write clearly and forcefully." Some of the comments received are these: "Generally mediocre," "deplorably low," "relatively low," "considerably below what is required on the job," "general feeling" among many is that technical personnel "are insufficiently equipped to handle the English requirements," etc.

Lest the reader assume the worst too quickly, we quote O. Glenn Stahl's statement again:

Whether this is because of faulty instruction, a lack of application on the part of the students, or a lower segment of the labor market we are attracting we are unable to say . . .

SUMMARY OF ANSWERS TO QUESTION 2—IMPROVEMENTS NOTED IN THE PAST 5 OR 10 YEARS

The distribution of opinions for this question resembles the distribution for Question 1:

12 respondents did not answer this question for the reasons given above.

1 respondent felt that there has been little change or improvement.

1 respondent noted that there has been little, if any, change.

1 respondent wrote that there is no appreciable change to note in his organization since the program is still in its infancy.

1 respondent noted that "One area of improvement is a changing point of view toward writing—an increasingly apparent attitude that written matter is purposeful, that knowledge of rules and usage is a tool rather than an end, and that simplicity in writing can be an effective management tool."

13 respondents found no improvement. One gentleman added that "As a matter of fact, in many regions of the country, we have had to lower standards on our verbal abilities test for typists and stenographers." But this same gentleman noted that "It may be simply a necessary adaptation to changes in the general level of persons in the labor market who apply for jobs with the Federal Government."

SUMMARY OF ANSWERS TO QUESTION 3—
DEFICIENCIES NOTED IN THE PAST 5 OR 10 YEARS

Government Agency	Spelling	Punctuation	Rules of Grammar	Vocabulary	Reading Comprehension	Reading Literature	Sentence Structure	Forceful Writing	Jargon Wordiness	Organization of Ideas	Simplicity	Clarity	Brevity	Oral Expression
Federal Housing Administration	x	x				x	x	x		x	x	x		
The Librarian of Congress	Basic elements													
Civil Service Commission			x		x		x	x		x	x	x		x
Civil Service Commission		x	x		Fundamentals x			x		x	x	x		
Department of Agriculture	x		x	x	Fundamentals x			x		x				
Department of Agriculture	x							x	x	x	x	x		
Department of the Air Force	x							x	x	x	x	x		x
Department of the Army				x						x	x	x		
Department of Commerce			x			x				x	x	x		
Department of Labor				x		x		x	x			x	x	
U.S. Information Agency	All aspects			x			x							x
Interstate Commerce Commission	x				x	x	Fundamentals			x		x		x
Post Office Department	x		x				x	x		x	x	x		
Selective Service	x													
Tennessee Valley Authority	x		x	x			x	Fundamentals						
Veterans Administration	x	x	x				x							

SUMMARY OF ANSWERS TO QUESTION 4—
AWARENESS OF THE NCTE

19 respondents noted that they were unaware of the work of the National Council of Teachers of English.

4 respondents noted that they were cognizant of the organization in name only.

3 respondents pointed out that they were aware of some aspects of the program.

3 respondents noted awareness of the program of the NCTE.

SUMMARY OF ANSWERS TO QUESTION 5— RECOMMENDATIONS FOR THE NCTE

Most replies to the question of ways in which the NCTE can help to produce better equipped students stressed the emphasis upon the fundamentals of spelling, grammar, usage, sentence structure, and vocabulary study. Many mentioned that more writing should be required from high school and college students in all subjects, suggesting the return to "straight" composition courses and the essay question. The requirement of "better performance" was a frequently mentioned suggestion.

The other side of the argument was taken by O. Glenn Stahl of the Civil Service Commission who wrote, "I know there is wide currency to the idea that more emphasis needs to be placed on drilling in grammar, spelling, and vocabulary. I'm a little inclined to think that while some of this may be necessary, more benefit will be gained by simple increase in the total impact of English within the entire curriculum . . ." He recommends wide reading, expository writing, and a broad, liberal, cultural education, which would lead to better communication. Miss Anna Sandvos of the United States Information Agency advances this idea by saying, "Perhaps we fail to some extent . . . because we still give courses in 'rules' throughout elementary school, secondary school, and first year of college, but we seldom fail students because they cannot write coherent English."

Three respondents attributed some of the difficulties to faults in the college and university requirements and programs. One reply states that many engineering and science schools are without sufficient programs in composition. Another states that ". . . there is a bad gap between training received in the high schools and the type of training received in the liberal arts colleges. The liberal arts colleges as well as the graduate schools are essentially medievalistic institutions." Still another states that ". . . I believe that every effort should be made to develop close working relationships between university and high school scholars, and teachers should be given more opportunity for intellectual refreshment, especially during their free summer months." It must be noted that none of these letters minimizes the importance of the lower schools in fixing the basis of later college work. In this area might be added the suggestion that there be homogeneous classes and accelerated groups in elementary and high schools.

Ernest C. Betts offers the following interesting and perceptive recommendations for ways in which the Council can help to produce better equipped students of English.

The following recommendations are made from suggestions which were received primarily from the training officers:

In recent years there has been an emphasis on the training of scientists and engineers. The neglect of training in English may be a natural consequence of this emphasis. We do recommend that the curriculum for both high school and college be adjusted to meet the complete needs of the student regardless of the field for which he is being trained. One means of doing this would be to get the professors and teachers who teach science and related fields to also recognize the need for and emphasize the use of good English.

De-emphasize objective tests. Go back to the essay test in examinations which requires the student to organize and prepare written material.

Require a proficiency examination at the Junior level in college so that the student may make up deficiencies in his senior year.

High schools have generally reduced the required amount of English for a high school diploma. It is recommended that at least three credits be required for high school graduation. Consideration should also be given to the needs of the student in developing English course content.

Screen college freshmen for needs in English and expression and provide a remedial approach to correcting their deficiencies.

Give special training and orientation to those who grade papers emphasizing the importance of effective writing.

Provide each college graduate with a publication which would be a constant reminder to him of the need for proper expression and serve as a guide to him in his work.

Many feel that more emphasis should be placed on home assignments of high school students. Also that the home and community environment has much to do with the expression of the student. Perhaps more should be done in the field of adult education to help parents and others with this problem.

U.S. GENERAL ACCOUNTING OFFICE SURVEY

Our letter to Joseph Campbell, Comptroller General of the United States, was forwarded to E. H. Morse, Jr., Director, Accounting and Policy Staff. Mr. Morse replied to our letter with the advice that several members of the Accounting Office staff would be called upon to offer answers to the questions posed.

The survey was summarized into a report titled *Observations on Competence in English of Recent College Graduates and Suggestions for Improvements.* This 55-page report was forwarded together with a cover letter dated December 29, 1958. A few paragraphs from Mr. Morse's letter will summarize the nature of the Accounting Office survey.

Our Government constitutes the biggest and most complex business in the world, and to discharge our audit responsibilities adequately, we must develop a competent professional accounting, auditing, and investigating staff. Our basic policy is to build a top quality staff based primarily upon selective recruitment of college graduates and upon career development which includes continuous and intensive training and diversified assignments of varying difficulty and complexity. The staff engaged in our audit activities is composed of more than 1,600 professional accountants and auditors, and includes about 400 certified public accountants. Our staff is located in our headquarters office in Washington, in 19 regional offices located in major cities in the United States and in our foreign offices in Europe and the Far East.

The preparation of written reports on our audits and investigations is a very important phase of our work. Such reports are the primary means by which we communicate our findings, conclusions, and recommendations . . . to the Congress . . . its committees, (and other) Government agency managements. Because of the significance of our reporting responsibility, we are vitally interested in the competence of our employees to use English properly and effectively.

We have obtained comments on (the) four questions from our staff throughout the United States. These comments have been classified and compiled in the following pages essentially as received with a minimum of editing or rearrangement. The comments were obtained from 100 different individuals, 30 of whom work in Washington and 70 in our 19 regional offices. Of the 100 people who submitted comments, 75 are supervisors of recent college graduates; the other 25 are mostly regional office managers, but also include training officers and other officials who have had opportunities to observe the work of our new employees.

Mr. Morse also noted that "Since we are not well informed at all on the activities of your organization," comments were not requested on Question 4 dealing with awareness of NCTE programs. He also pointed out that the comments received are based almost exclusively upon observation of college graduates in business administration and accounting curricula.

Summary of the General Accounting Office Survey

QUESTION 1—Competence in English of Recent College Graduates

Competence	Replies Received
Fair to good	5
Competent or average	24
Oral English better than written	12
Inadequate	42
Unclassified	5
	88*

* These figures are taken directly from the report.

The above tabulation was followed by 37 representative comments, none of which expressed unmixed praise for the competence of recent graduates.

In the *fair to good* group, one respondent noted that writing is correct in simple constructions, but that writing, in general, lacks "expressiveness," a deficiency which was attributed to inadequate writing experience in school and college.

The comments in the *competent or average* group stressed the adequacy of oral expression and language mechanics, while noting the inadequacy of written expression. The apparent inability of many accountants to express themselves in writing in a clear, concise manner was mentioned by many respondents. The seriousness of this disparity between ability to speak and ability to write effectively is underscored by the significant number who found *oral expression better than written*. One respondent wrote:

"Most graduates have attained what could be considered an adequate command of the spoken word. However, a higher degree of writing proficiency would enhance their value to us and would be a benefit to them in their future development."

The larger number of staff members who rated recent graduates as *inadequate* in English skills emphasized "insufficient training," "lack of interest," and "failure of the schools to emphasize the importance" of English, rather than poor English teaching. A staff member wrote that, on the average, those with the B.A. degree use English "barely at the level required of high school juniors." The failure of many college-trained men to express themselves adequately was attributed to insufficient training in writing during the college years.

The few comments in the *unclassified* area echoed essentially the comments in the competent or average group:

"The above-average student is competent in spelling and grammar. However, he does not seem competent in such matters as organization of ideas and thoughts."

QUESTION 2—Improvements Observed Within Recent Years

We received comments on this question from 83 supervisors. Of this number, 11 indicated that they had no valid basis for comparison; in most cases this was because the respondents have been in supervisory positions for relatively short periods. Among those who did reply, a large number (47) reported that no improvements had been observed. The other 25 comments are quoted below; they are grouped as follows:

General deterioration	5 responses
Some improvement noted, but not defined	4 responses
Specific areas of improvement observed	16 responses

From among the comments of those who saw some improvement, this one summarizes the general opinion:

"It is my feeling that the graduates of today can do all three (reading, writing, and speaking) as well as the graduates of a generation ago, and perhaps somewhat better."

Practically all areas of written and spoken English were seen as having improved in the past 5 or 10 years. "Imaginative and warmer writing, rather than stereotyped, formal, and cold writing," was cited as a praiseworthy area of improvement, as were organization of thought and sentence structure, though improvements in these areas were attributed to better students, not better instruction.

QUESTION 3—Deficiencies Observed

We received 92 replies to this question. Many of these included examples, which have been deleted from the following quotations. For the sake of brevity many introductory remarks have also been deleted; mostly these remarks indicated that lists of deficiencies are presented in order of significance.

The compilers of the report made no attempt to tabulate the specific areas of weakness which were mentioned in the replies. It was thought, however, that a list of areas of weakness, in order of frequency of mention, would be of significance to the readers of this report on the state of English. The figures below are necessarily approximate since it was often impossible to classify specific areas because of the variety of terminology used.

Area of Weakness	Times Mentioned
Spelling	45
Sentence structure	41
Grammar	33
Choice and use of words	22
Organization of ideas and material	20
Punctuation	19
Vocabulary	15
Conciseness	15
Paragraph structure	13
Clarity	13
Unity and coherence	10
Verbiage	8
Simplicity	6
Jargon and clichés	5
Ability to think	4
Forceful writing	4
Ability to summarize	2
Ability to express ideas	2
Ability of self-criticism	2
Sense of craftsmanship	2

U.S. CIVIL SERVICE ADMINISTRATORS

Federal Housing Administration	W. Richard Lomax, Director of Personnel
Federal Trade Commission	S. F. Stowe, Director of Public Information
General Accounting Office	E. H. Morse, Jr., Director Accounting and Auditing Policy Staff
The Librarian of Congress	Rutherford D. Rogers, Acting Librarian of Congress
National Science Foundation	Harry C. Kelly, Assistant Director for Scientific Personnel and Education
Office of Civil and Defense Mobilization	Paul F. Wagner, Assistant Administrator for Education
United States Civil Service Commission	O. Glenn Stahl, Director Bureau of Programs and Standards
United States Civil Service Commission	Philip W. Schulte, Public Information Officer
United States Civil Service Commission	William A. Hammill, Director of Personnel
United States Department of Agriculture	R. Lyle Webster, Director of Information
United States Department of Agriculture	Ernest C. Betts, Jr., Director of Personnel
Department of the Air Force	Lloyd P. Hopwood, Major General, USAF, Director Personnel Procurement and Training, DSC/ Personnel
Department of the Air Force	James P. Goode, Deputy for Manpower Personnel and Organization
Department of the Army	E. G. Witting, Deputy Director of Research and Development
Department of the Navy	L. Eugene Wolfe, Special Assistant to the Assistant Secretary of the Navy (Personnel and Reserve Forces)
United States Department of Commerce	Carlton Hayward, Director of Personnel

United States Department of Commerce	Henry Scharer, Deputy Director of Information
United States Department of the Interior	Newell B. Terry, Director of Personnel
United States Department of Labor	Edward J. McVeigh, Director of Personnel
United States Department of Labor	George G. Lodge, Director of Information, Publications and Reports
United States General Accounting Office	E. H. Morse, Jr., Director Accounting and Auditing Policy Staff
United States Information Agency	Benjamin B. Warfield, Chief of Training
United States Information Agency	Joseph L. Newman, Assistant Director, Office of Public Information
United States Information Agency	Annis Sandvos, Chief, English Teaching Branch Information Center Service
United States Interstate Commerce Commission	Curtis F. Adams, Director of Personnel
United States Post Office Department	A. E. Weatherbee, Deputy Assistant Postmaster General
Selective Service Commission	Dee Ingold, Colonel, QMC, Chief, Manpower Division
Tennessee Valley Authority	John E. Massey, Chief, Employment Branch, Division of Personnel
United States Treasury Department	Philip M. Light, Regional Director Northwest Region
Veterans Administration	Edward R. Silberman, Assistant Administrator for Personnel

❧ 6 ❦

Opinions of
Magazine Editors

QUESTION 1—COMPETENCE IN ENGLISH
OF RECENT GRADUATES

"The young people with whom I have come in contact have been, I suppose, the cream of the classes—young girls and boys who have prepared themselves for editorial work. They are well read, speak and write fluently, and work with enthusiasm."

This statement from Maurine Halliburton, editor of the *American Mercury,* is unfortunately the exception rather than the rule. Even such divided judgments as this of Karl K. Krueger, editor of the *Rotarian,* are rare: "The competence of recent high school graduates is low; that of recent college graduates is good to excellent." These sentiments are repeated by Ben Hibbs of the *Saturday Evening Post.* "Generally speaking, most high school graduates are very deficient in English—particularly in their use of the written word. Many college graduates are also deficient. On the other hand, English and Journalism majors from the better colleges and universities usually write reasonably well. (We have a number of the latter working for us.)"

And again, from Richard C. Davids of the *Farm Journal:* "It seems to us that our recent graduates are pretty well equipped in English. We can't evaluate high school graduates, since we don't employ them directly from high school."

Since most of the top bracket magazines are in a position to select from the top bracket students, the reply of Kenneth M.

Gould of *Scholastic Magazines* is most revealing: "Naturally, we employ people with varied educational backgrounds and levels of experience. When we are hiring personnel for the editorial department, naturally we are likely to seek English majors, who have at least had experience in college student publications, and possibly some general experience in journalism. We have to evaluate candidates for editorial jobs on the basis of their school and college records, their job experience, their interests, and samples of written work already published or done on assignment, as a test. If any of these methods of evaluation show evidence of inadequate grasp of English fundamentals, naturally such candidates are quickly eliminated. But through classified advertising, high grade employment agencies, and placement services of the leading colleges, we receive an abundant supply of well qualified applicants for the editorial level. We would hardly, therefore, be in any useful position to detect whether competence in English is growing or declining among the graduates of the better colleges.

"At the clerical level, which is more likely to be filled by persons with high school and commercial education, the problem is different. Of course we need good secretaries, good typists and good clerical workers in various departments of the company, and I may say that the supply of them is never equal to the demand from the standpoint of quality. Whether this is something that has gone up or down in the past five years is very difficult to say, but we are now getting large numbers of applicants for the simplest clerical jobs in our subscription service right out of New York commercial high schools. The qualifications of these young people are not high as a rule. At this level, we would expect no more than a reasonable degree of competence in ordinary typing and computing skills, spelling, etc. But even these are hard to find."

To summarize where the difficulties lie, we cite the opinions of

John Fischer of *Harper's Magazine.* "Most recent high school and college graduates of my acquaintance have very little competence in English; many of the high school graduates, in particular, cannot write a decent paragraph, and regard any reading above the comic book level as a painful labor. To my astonishment, many of them have gained admittance to colleges, although I don't think they ought to have been permitted to pass the eighth grade."

Harsh? Possibly. But Mr. Fischer's sentiments are echoed by one after another of the respondents from national magazines, even though they have not gone into so great detail or voiced their opinions so strongly. Thus, Marjorie L. Burns, copy editor of *Cosmopolitan:* "Editing is a task which requires not only intelligence and good taste but also highly developed technical skills. Although many of the job applicants whom I interview appear to possess the first two qualities to some degree, they fall down on the technical skills. They don't know the parts of speech; they don't know the correct use of the semicolon and the single quotation mark; they confuse 'imply' and 'infer'; they have never heard of the dangling participle. They edit a manuscript intuitively, 'just fixing it up so it sounds right.' The result is that the employer who wants them to turn out work worth paying for must first turn teacher and instruct them in these niceties."

Eileen O'Hayer, Managing Editor of *Extension,* takes a more tolerant view. "Unfortunately," she writes, "we are quick to discover and stress shortcomings, and less anxious to acknowledge advancements. Perhaps it is because errors glare so, while proper English usage, taken for granted, bears a gray hue.

"If I must criticize, I would blame haste for grammatical errors, and the young are in a great hurry. If and when they stop to think, the written or spoken sentence, content and construction improve. I believe they know the rules, but everyday corruption and idioms, widely used and accepted, stilt the application and appreciation of these rules."

Such diverse publications as *Good Housekeeping* and *Harper's Bazaar* see no improvement in recent years. "It is my experience," declares Herbert R. Mayes of *Good Housekeeping,* "that most recent graduates are woefully lacking in the ability to write and speak the English language correctly." "Only rarely," says the literary editor of *Harper's Bazaar,* "does the student seem to have grasped the marvelous power and significance of the language when it is used with knowledge, respect and sensitivity." Bruce Gould, editor of the *Ladies' Home Journal,* agrees with these judgments. He finds "the standard of many girls employed surprisingly low." He adds: "I am always surprised that students can be graduated from some of our colleges and have so little ability to speak or write good English."

The condemnation of the competence of recent high school graduates is universal among magazine editors. "From my experience," reports Joseph Gies, copy chief of *This Week,* "it is no very easy matter today to hire a fresh-out-of-college boy or girl with an impeccable knowledge of grammar, punctuation, and especially spelling."

QUESTIONS 2 AND 3

"If there is a deficiency," writes Sey Chassler, executive editor of *Pageant,* "it is concerned with the lack of prestige which seems to be attached to being articulate. It seems to me that Americans in general have always been ashamed to express themselves fully in conversation."

This expression of disapproval is widespread among magazine editors. It is condemnation of the competence, not only of high school and college graduates, but of the abilities of teachers themselves. "We frequently get manuscripts dealing with education, and the writers invariably identify themselves as teachers," declares one editor. "Generally speaking, these particular teachers do the profession little credit. Most of their literary efforts are poorly executed, with an amazing disregard for the rules of English usage."

"Deficiencies," says Marjorie L. Burns of *Cosmopolitan,* "are not confined to editorial assistants. Read the manuscripts of many professional writers, listen to Sunday sermons, hear radio news broadcasts, glance over a few lawyers' briefs, and you cannot help noticing how ineptly language is often handled even in those professions in which it is the stock in trade.

"Of course, we all realize that a cultural machine that grinds out millions of words daily cannot grind them all very fine."

The same opinion is expressed eloquently by Wade H. Nichols of *Redbook Magazine:* "The distressing lack among educated Americans of any 'feel' for their language has been widely—and I think, justly—criticized. This lack has been accompanied by ignorance of, and disinterest in, English and American literature. Responsibility for improving this situation probably lies as much with those of us who work in the popular media as it does with educators."

When it comes to specific deficiencies, the editors of magazines are unanimous: "Among high school graduates I have worked with," says Kay Thomas of *Charm,* "the greatest weaknesses seem to be spelling, inability to express themselves clearly and bad enunciation. Most of them would rather ask an associate the spelling of a word than use the dictionary—a very dangerous procedure, I have found, especially when the associate herself cannot spell.

"College graduates, who do most of the writing I edit, are guilty of sloppy construction. Dangling modifiers and general lack of clarity, especially in relating pronouns to their antecedents, seem to be the greatest faults in writing. Also, I find that among the younger and often brighter girls there is a lack of simplicity in choice of words, too many clichés and trite expressions."

In publications far removed from the sphere of *Charm,* such as the *Farm Journal,* the strictures are similar. "The biggest deficiencies," according to Richard C. Davids, "are in spelling and in sentence structure, especially in a knowledge of the 'why' of grammar. We wonder if there might not be broader reading to encourage both skills and perhaps more drill in parsing or whatever that art is now called."

Ben Hibbs of the *Saturday Evening Post* is even more sweeping in his criticism. "The deficiencies are of almost every variety possible. The two greatest faults are awkward sentence structure and lack of clarity." Backing this impression of Mr. Hibbs is that of Hedley Donovan of *Fortune.* "My general impression is that relatively few 'educated' Americans express themselves with any precision, let alone any distinction. I'm afraid this situation extends even into your profession and mine."

Over and over again, the editors stress the weaknesses in fundamentals. "The deficiencies I have observed most often," says John Fischer of *Harper's Magazine,* "are in spelling, grammar, vocabulary, and the elementary ability to organize thoughts on paper in a coherent and logical fashion."

Spelling, in particular, comes in for severe criticism. *Seventeen, Popular Science, This Week,* and *The American Mercury* stress the weakness here, while other magazines add deficiencies in punctuation and vocabulary. Among these are the *Ladies' Home Journal, Mademoiselle,* and *The Rotarian,* to name but a few.

Possibly the most understanding view comes from Clifford B. Hicks, associate editor of *Popular Mechanics.* "We have noticed very little in the way of improvement in the past 5 or 10 years," he tells us. "Also we find no more deficiencies in that period of time. We might add a footnote here that we feel the cultural background, including home and school of the student, is all-important in determining his competence in English. Individuals with a strong intellectual background in their homes tend to speak and write excellent English. This is also true of students who have the benefit of good schools."

QUESTION 5

Recommendations

"On the score of recommendations, *Life*'s copy editor is frank to admit that as he doesn't know what English teachers are doing, perhaps he shouldn't try to say what you should be doing." So writes Mabel H. Schubert on behalf of the editors of *Life* magazine. "But he feels strongly that you can never put too much emphasis on the fundamentals and the logic of writing. 'If I were a teacher, I would make my English pupils rewrite and rewrite their compositions. It is in self-editing that clear and emphatic writing is learned, not in just having a teacher (or editor) point out errors. This, of course, sounds like an editor's prescription.'"

Perhaps it is natural that magazine editors should put the major stress on the ability to write. Thus, Sey Chassler, of *Pageant:* "I'd recommend that the Council put its major effort into seeing that students are taught to write, and that they are made to write as much as possible in all forms. Benjamin Franklin learned to write by writing and by copying. Can you think of anyone who wrote better prose? He had very little of what used to be called methodology."

In accord with this opinion of Franklin, it is interesting to note that the *Saturday Evening Post*'s Ben Hibbs' remarks closely parallel Mr. Chassler's. "Insist upon more actual writing of compositions in both high school and college. The only way to learn to write is to write and write and write—with, of course, proper supervision and correction. I am constantly dismayed when I find how little actual writing is required in many high school and college English courses."

The editor-in-chief of *Mademoiselle*, Betsy Talbot Blackwell, goes along with the two previous recommendations. She says, "All (not just the work in English classes) written work (should) be marked for errors and graded for competence in English, and teachers should require that work not competent be rewritten with errors corrected."

Joseph Gies of *This Week* has a slightly different suggestion for increasing writing ability. "The best training in use of English that I know of is a good college publication. People who have worked on such college dailies as the *Michigan Daily,* the *Daily Iowan,* etc., have a pretty good grounding in sound writing practices. In short, I think the best way to learn English is to write it."

A novel recommendation comes from Richard C. Davids of the *Farm Journal*. "Why don't you recommend that teachers ask their pupils to get hold of current reading matter—especially the pamphlets, instruction sheets, etc., emanating from government bureaus—and put that material into readable, quick language. Perhaps classes might send in their revised drafts to the originating body. It might even start some long overdue reforms."

Sumner Blossom of the Crowell-Collier Publishing Company suggests "that they be given more instruction in what I would call Applied English—such things as business correspondence, report and speech writing. Supplementing this, the grade schools should offer more intensive training in the fundamentals of grammar and in spelling."

Marjorie L. Burns of *Cosmopolitan* has a number of cogent recommendations: "(1) I would make the students work very hard and I would keep the standards high. Students of English would be disabused of the idea that inheritance of their native language automatically includes its mastery. (2) I would never allow a student to believe that he had made an achievement that he hadn't. Education should help him not only to discover his talents but also acknowledge his deficiencies. It should screen out the incompetents in any field and direct them elsewhere. (3) I would teach students to be critical readers by instructing them in elementary logic and helping them develop sensitivity to diction, tone, and intent in writing. We need shrewd and wary language consumers as much as we need skilled producers. (4) I would make students learn to spell, diagram sentences, decline nouns and adjectives, conjugate verbs, etc. Some of the worst failures in this business are the so-called creative, but undisciplined minds."

It is interesting to note in passing that Mrs. Burns was herself a teacher before becoming a magazine editor, and has unusual sympathy with the teacher's problem. "Unfortunately," she concludes, "the harder the students work, the harder the already heavily burdened teacher must work. I'm sorry I can't offer any solution to that problem."

Some of the editors are most energetic in their insistence upon a return to fundamentals. Howard Allaway, editor of *Popular Science,* says forthrightly: "I favor drilling the young in grammar, punctuation and spelling, and in the practice of clear, simple communication rather than encouraging them too soon in flights of what's called creative writing."

Kay Thomas of *Charm* agrees with Mr. Allaway. "I think spelling could be improved if the old-fashioned drill work and spelling bees were revived. If high school students are found not to spell well, then spelling should be continued into high school.

"In teaching construction, I am a great believer in diagramming of sentences. I found my own children learned the parts of speech and the relations of phrases to main clauses much more readily after I had taught them how to diagram.

"Also, I think all students of English should be encouraged to read more—good books, classics as well as the best modern works.

I believe in long reading lists, during the school year and summer vacation, with mandatory reports, both oral and written. Perhaps some system of credit could be inaugurated to encourage more reading—for those students who settle for minimum work."

Maurine Halliburton of the *American Mercury* also feels strongly about the importance of reading, but her approach is different. She recommends "that reading in the grades be taught in a way to give the child the same control of language that is given in mathematics for the control of numbers (addition, subtraction and multiplication are learned first; then the more involved problems). I feel that a child should know the syllables of the word as well as the sound and meaning of the word; and how to spell the word as a whole. This, in my opinion, will widen the reading range by providing in most cases a means of recognizing by sight, sound and meaning a new word made up of familiar syllables and of being able to incorporate it into the stock of words the student knows."

Clifford B. Hicks of *Popular Mechanics* feels "that the more good literature a child reads, the better will be his English. Most writers, of course, have read a great deal all their lives. Perhaps greater emphasis on reading would tend in the long run to improve the use of English."

"The problem," as seen by Wade H. Nichols of *Redbook,* "seems to be largely a matter of finding teachers who themselves respect our language and literature, and who can convey enthusiasm about them to their students. Developments outside the classrooms, such as inexpensive reprints of good books and TV lectures on the classics, are encouraging."

Herbert R. Mayes, editor of *Good Housekeeping,* declares, "My recommendation, if any, would be to teach English to our teachers in order that they might better be able to teach it to their students." More hopefully, Karl K. Krueger of the *Rotarian* suggests "that the Council urge English teachers to find ways to make the study of English so exciting that students break down doors to get into the classrooms."

In summation, we can do little better than to present the very thoughtful observations of John Fischer of *Harper's Magazine:*

1. Much greater concentration in grade school on solid grounding in spelling, grammar, and English composition.
2. Refusal to admit any child into high school who cannot demonstrate reasonable competence in reading and writing.
3. The appointment of English teachers who have some skill in, and affection for, the English language—whether or not they have taken all the technical courses in education required by most teachers colleges.
4. Adoption of curricula which will demonstrate to high school students that books can be exciting, interesting, and useful rather than deadly bores. A first step might be to eliminate from the required reading lists such old chestnuts as *Ivanhoe* —a third-rate historical novel which is still required (or so I understand) in many American high schools today, in spite of the fact that it probably has alienated more children from reading than any work in history.
5. Require students at all levels to do much more written work than is now demanded in most American schools. I would like to see every student required to produce at least one paper of one thousand words or more each week, these papers to be rigidly graded and criticized by teachers who have both the competence and time for such work. In addition, it might help considerably if written examinations were substituted for the present true-false tests.
6. Refuse admission to college to any student who cannot demonstrate that he is truly literate.

MAGAZINE EDITORS RESPONDING TO THE QUESTIONNAIRE

Magazines	*Editors*
The American Legion Magazine	James C. Keeley, Editor
The American Mercury	Maurine Halliburton, Editor
The American Scholar	Hiram Haydn, Editor
The American Weekly	Ernest V. Heyn, Editor
Argosy Magazine	Henry Steeger, President Popular Publications, Inc.
Charm	Kay Thomas, Managing Editor
Cosmopolitan	Marjorie L. Burns, Copy Editor
The Crowell-Collier Publishing Co.	Sumner Blossom, President
Extension	Eileen O'Hayer, Managing Editor
Farm Journal	Richard C. Davids, Associate Editor
Fortune	Hedley Donovan, Managing Editor
Good Housekeeping	Herbert Mayes, Editor
Harper's Bazaar	Elin V. Morris, Literary Editor
Harper's Magazine	John Fischer, Editor
Holiday	Ted Patrick, Editor
Ladies' Home Journal	Bruce Gould, Editor
Life	Mabel H. Schubert, for the Editors
Mademoiselle	Betsy Talbot Blackwell, Editor-in-Chief
The New Republic	Helen Fuller, Managing Editor
The New Yorker	Louis Forster, Jr., Assistant to the Editor
Pageant	Sey Chassler, Executive Editor
Popular Mechanics Magazine	Clifford B. Hicks, Associate Editor
Popular Science Monthly	Howard Allaway, Editor
The Reader's Digest	Dewitt Wallace, Editor
Redbook Magazine	Wade H. Nichols, Editor and Publisher
The Rotarian	Karl K. Krueger, Editor
The Saturday Evening Post	Ben Hibbs, Editor
Scholastic Magazines	Kenneth M. Gould, Editor-in-Chief
Seventeen	Ruth Whitney, Associate Editor
This Week	Joseph Gies, Copy Chief
Town and Country	Henry B. Sell, Editor
TV Guide	Alex Joseph, Assistant Managing Editor
V.F.W. Magazine	Barney Yanofsky

≥ 7 ≤

Opinions of
Educational Magazine Editors

NATURE OF THE SURVEY

Late in the summer of 1958, letters were sent to 37 editors of educational magazines and journals. The letters were similar in content to those sent to the other editors, business executives, civil service administrators, and the questions asked were the same.

A total of 22 replies were received, some containing detailed answers to all the questions, some containing only a single comment. Contributions were received from editors of the following magazines:

Adult Education
Child Development
*Child Study
Educational Leadership
Educational Research Bulletin
The Education Digest
The Education Forum
*Educational Horizons
Exceptional Children
Grade Teacher Magazine
The Instructor

* Special appreciation is due the editors of these publications for especially thoughtful replies.

*Journal of Developmental Reading
Journal of Educational Research
Journal of Teacher Education
*Bulletin of the National Association of Secondary School
Principals
*New York State Education
North Central Association Quarterly
*School and Community
School and Society
School Life
School Review
*School Science and Mathematics

Before going on to the actual summaries of the answers to the questions, it must be stressed that while a few editors answered the questions, on the basis of the manuscripts that pass their desks, most of the editors expressed opinions based upon broad qualifications that extend beyond their editorial work, into the colleges, universities, and public school administration offices. Of course, the opinions expressed by the editors are their very own and are *not* to be taken as editorial policy of the magazines they head.

SUMMARY OF ANSWERS TO QUESTION 1— COMPETENCE OF RECENT GRADUATES

The distribution of opinions shows a small but significant margin of belief in the growing competence of recent graduates from high school and college.

1 editor noted that there has probably been no change in competence in English over the past 10 or 15 years.

3 editors expressed the opinion that competence in English has decreased in recent years.

---

* Special appreciation is due the editors of these publications for especially thoughtful replies.

1 editor felt that there has been a growth in competence combined with some setbacks.

8 editors noted that the competence in English of recent graduates has considerably increased.

9 editors felt that they were not qualified to express an opinion on this question.

Those editors who did not see any significant change in competence or who saw a decrease in competence expressed the general opinion that "Many are reasonably adequate but hardly outstanding." Another editor went a little further with his opinion: "I am sorry to say that only in exceptional instances have I found the applicants properly equipped with the essential tool of ability in English." An editor adds, "I do know that the level of educational writing as exemplified in articles that are sent to (our publication) is not high."

The other side of the argument was presented by at least five editors, one of whom wrote: "The college graduates we contact are usually journalism students. Their induction course in our manual of style usually takes care of any deficiency." Another editor, M. Virginia Biggy of *Educational Horizons,* wrote a most interesting, complete and inspiring answer:

> My feeling about recent graduates from high school and college and their capacity and competence in using the English language is that by and large they have considerably more to say and this is entirely worth saying. They sometimes are not as eloquent in their description as one might hope, but by and large, they are direct and to the point . . . I am . . . concerned with the student's ability to present his ideas logically, defend them wisely and summarize the case without writing a novel. In large measure I am pleased with what I see. My only complaint comes when I find students who have so little appreciation of the power of the lan-

guage that they do not recognize the tremendous opportunities it affords to capture an audience whether that audience is a reading or a listening audience . . . In my judgment, in the last few years I have noticed an improvement in the students' willingness to write.

SUMMARY OF ANSWERS TO QUESTION 2— AREAS OF IMPROVEMENTS

Six editors noted improvements in the following areas variously:

1. "I presently find students more eager to write."
2. There is an improved relationship between college and high school teachers of English and there is more appreciation of English on the part of administrators and the public.
3. Most students read better.
4. High school graduates and upper classmen in college "show greater recognition of the desirability of competence in English within the years since 1945 perhaps."
5. Writing as a means of communication is better than before.
6. Students have improved in their oral abilities, especially since schools have been using the mass media. "I think we can point out further that many high schools in Michigan have de-emphasized the teaching of classical literature and are now doing more with communications."

SUMMARY OF ANSWERS TO QUESTION 3— DEFICIENCIES IN ABILITY IN ENGLISH

Before listing the areas of deficiency, it might be well to note the admonition implicit in the following quotation: ". . . the college professor never loses an opportunity to condemn the total group with what he sees in one or two students in his class."

1. "I have a sneaky suspicion that the bland and barren writing

emerges from those students whose secondary school English teachers were devoted to teaching rules and regulations and who neglected to point out, perhaps because they didn't know, how exciting the use of the English language can be and how it changes regularly and what a decided part we play in these alterations."

2. More time and effort must be spent with written and oral aspects of English. Students do not have sufficient writing practice to express themselves clearly and adequately. Another editor wrote:

> Perhaps we have gone somewhat too far in emphasizing the pleasure that can be had in writing rather than acceptability in form, spelling, and grammatical structure. In other words we should not take enthusiasm for skill.

3. Several editors cited lack of sentence sense, poor sentence structure, and unclearness of expression as deficiencies.

4. Poor spelling, vocabulary, and agreement were also indicated as deficiencies.

This section might be summarized with this quotation: "If I had any observation to make it would be that a great deal of the material submitted to me is woefully lacking in editorial essentials—spelling, grammar, and correct information." Students must be taught to write clearly, concisely, and forcefully if their communications are to "command attention and interest."

SUMMARY OF ANSWERS TO QUESTION 4— AWARENESS OF THE WORK OF THE NCTE

Only one editor noted that he was not aware of the work of the National Council; the others mentioned awareness in varying degrees, and all expressed interest in and approval of the NCTE's programs.

SUMMARY OF ANSWERS TO QUESTION 5— RECOMMENDATIONS TO THE NATIONAL COUNCIL

M. Virginia Biggy, editor of *Educational Horizons,* notes that she could "detect that though the impact of the Council's program is still small, I am hopeful that it will continue to be as steady as it seems to have been in my observations." This quotation points to an implicit suggestion that was voiced in several letters, namely that the NCTE should make its programs better known to English teachers, other professional groups, and the general public. M. Virginia Biggy suggests one way in which this recommendation and many others can be implemented:

. . . Let me say that it is my feeling that one of the more profitable undertakings which the National Council might consider would be to plan one-day workshops or institutes in several parts of each state where either members of the National Council already in those states or members of the executive board of the National Council might appear to lend some inspiration and stimulation, to listen to teachers' suggestions and in turn to make suggestions to those teachers.

Other recommendations for ways in which the National Council can help to produce students at all levels better equipped in all phases of English fall into three categories:

1. teacher preparation and certification
2. school and class organization
3. curriculum revision and emphasis.

TEACHER PREPARATION AND CERTIFICATION

An opinion (often expressed) was that preparation and certification of English teachers would be revised in many states and colleges, and that the NCTE seems to be the logical agent for encouraging the revisions. As one editor put it, ". . . We need to step up the depth of preparation of English teachers in our high schools." "Other things being equal, better students are produced by better teachers," stated another editor. This opinion was echoed in the statement: "I believe that the interest of children reflects the character and quality of the teacher."

George B. Schick, editor of the *Journal of Developmental Reading,* concludes this way,

> So it seems that we shall have to get down to the level of the PTA, room-mothers, and interested parents and provide these groups with solid facts, cogent arguments, and inspiration to enable them to *demand* that certifying agencies recognize *fully* the requirement of adequate preparation in his own area for every qualified teacher.

Inks Franklin, editor of *School and Community,* suggests that there be careful screening of those who want to take courses leading to a certificate to teach English *and* well-selected education courses for future college English teachers.

SCHOOL AND CLASS ORGANIZATION

The NCTE should, according to two editors, "cease catering to the small high school to the detriment of real competence in teaching." The NCTE should also encourage homogeneous class organization according to vocational aim, native ability, and academic achievement.

CURRICULUM REVISION AND EMPHASIS

1. Attention still must be given to the teaching of reading on the high school and college levels: "In reading, most high school and college graduates still *study* nearly everything they read."

2. Encourage schools to "continue to require written and oral presentations of topics, issues, subjects, with a special emphasis on the clarity and skill of effective presentations."

3. Encourage school boards to adjust teacher-load or provide assistance to English teachers, so that these teachers can supervise and criticize more original and expository writing.

4. "Criticism (of English papers) should reflect to some extent views of modern scholars . . . rather than rigid insistence upon adherence to formal rules of grammar and rhetoric." Of course, the approximately opposite suggestion was also made.

5. "In my own judgment," writes one editor, "much of the classical literature perused by students both in high school and in college is a waste of time." Again, the approximate opposite comes from another editor: "So far as the age group allows I think it would improve our English teaching were the subject matter in literature selected on the basis of enduring rather than ephemeral values."

EDUCATION MAGAZINE EDITORS

Adult Education	Thurman White, Editor
	The University of Oklahoma
Child Development	William E. Martin, Editor
	Purdue University
Child Study	Mrs. Margaret C. Dawson, Editor
	The Child Study Association of America, New York City
The Education Digest	Lawrence W. Prakken, Editor
	Ann Arbor, Michigan
The Education Forum	E. I. F. Williams, Editor
	Heidelberg College
Educational Horizons	M. Virginia Biggy, Editor
	Superintendent of Schools Concord, Massachusetts
Educational Leadership	Ropert R. Leeper, Editor
Educational Research Bulletin	R. H. Eckelberry, Editor
	Ohio State University
Exceptional Children	John McCormick, Editor
Grade Teacher Magazine	Miss Toni Taylor
	Darien, Connecticut
The Instructor	Mary E. Owen, Editor
	Dansville, New York

Journal of Developmental Reading	George B. Schick, Editor
	Purdue University
Journal of Educational Research	A. S. Barr, Editor
	The University of Wisconsin
Bulletin of the National Association of Secondary School Principals	Paul E. Elicker, Executive Secretary
Journal of Teacher Education	T. M. Stinnett, Executive Secretary
New York State Education	A. Ranger Tyler, Associate Editor
	New York State Teachers Association
North Central Association Quarterly	Harlan C. Koch, Editor
	Ann Arbor, Michigan
School and Community	Inks Franklin, Editor
	Missouri State Teachers Association
School and Society	William W. Brickman, Editor
	New York 23, New York
School Life	Theodore E. Carlson, Editor
	Washington, D. C.
School Review	Maurice L. Hartung, Chairman
	Board of Editors
	The University of Chicago
Social Science and Mathematics	George G. Mallinson, Editor
	School of Graduate Studies
	Western Michigan University

8

Opinions of
Newspaper Editors

NATURE OF THE SURVEY

Copies of the questionnaire were sent to 54 editors and publishers throughout the country.

Twenty-five replies were received, representing:

18 different states
19 different cities

Those who answered the questions were in the following categories:

Editor	10 replies
Executive editor	1 reply
Associate editor	1 reply
Managing editor	2 replies
Education editor	2 replies
Publisher	3 replies
City editor	1 reply
News editor	1 reply
Personnel staff	3 replies
Staff member	1 reply
Total	25 replies received

In almost all the instances, the person queried held the title of "editor" or "editor and publisher"; in several instances, however, as can be seen from the listing above, the letter was routed to another staff member for answering.

It was felt that this group—the newspaper editors—constituted a rather reliable measure of fact and opinion, since (1) the newspapers represent most geographical areas of the country; (2)

newspaper staffs are made up of men and women from varied
college "majors," from many colleges of different types and sizes;
and (3) the newspaper editors' very vital concern is the recruitment of men and women who can express themselves clearly,
correctly, and accurately.

Replies were received from representatives of the following
newspapers:

The Baltimore Sun	Maryland
Birmingham News	Alabama
*Buffalo Evening News	New York
Cincinnati Post	Ohio
The Christian Science Monitor (Boston)	Massachusetts
Cleveland Plain Dealer	Ohio
Denver Post	Colorado
*The Detroit Free Press	Michigan
Fort Worth Star-Telegram	Texas
The Houston Chronicle	Texas
*Los Angeles Evening Herald Express	California
*Los Angeles Examiner	California
Memphis Press-Scimitar	Tennessee
*The Milwaukee Journal	Wisconsin
*The Minneapolis Tribune and Star	Minnesota
*New York Herald Tribune	New York
*New York Journal American	New York
The New York Times (2 replies)	New York
The Omaha World-Herald	Nebraska
The Philadelphia Inquirer	Pennsylvania
*Portland Press Herald-Evening Express	Maine
Scripps-Howard Newspapers (New York)	Nationwide
Seattle Post-Intelligencer	Washington
*The Wall Street Journal (New York)	New York

* Special appreciation is extended to the respondents for these newspapers for
their thoughtful and helpful replies.

For the names and positions of all respondents, see the complete list of contributors.

SUMMARY OF ANSWERS TO QUESTION 1—
COMPETENCE OF RECENT GRADUATES

The distribution of answers is as follows:

6 noted *proficiency* in English
6 expressed *mixed reactions*
5 found competence in English to be *lacking*
6 found competence in English to be *grossly lacking*
2 did not answer this question

Among those who were at least satisfied with the competence of recent graduates were three editors who noted "definite improvement." One of these editors wrote that graduates from high school and college express themselves "rather well," while another noted "Test scores (on a general intelligence test with an English word-analogies section) were significantly higher than test scores of five years ago," especially among news and feature department applicants.

Another editor wrote suggestively, "I do not agree with some of the things I have heard at editors' meetings; personally I think young reporters now are turning out as good English as they ever have." This reaction was seconded by the remaining two editors in this group, one of whom, D. F. Caswell, Education Editor for the *Los Angeles Examiner,* included this rather provocative remark:

It seems to me that letters and other writings of younger people are better than those of older people. Whether this proves that competence in English is improving, or that older people forget their schooling, I cannot say. Youngsters of my acquaintance seem to have a little less knowledge of formal mechanics of grammar, but their use of the language is good, and that is the main thing.

The replies classified above as expressing *mixed reactions* do not subject themselves to any simple generalizations. One respondent noted that while "graduates of today are not as well prepared in the formal rules and structure of the English language as they used to be . . . today's graduate can express himself verbally, that is, communicate in an understandable and intelligent manner, better than ever." A similar comment was made by another editor who reported deficiency in the "basic tools of journalism," with the balancing, perhaps redeeming, remark that today's graduates are better educated *generally* and more serious about their work than they were some years ago.

Two editors noted that graduates, especially college graduates, were "decidedly uneven" in competence or that competence is "very spotty." Royce Howes, Associate Editor, the *Detroit Free Press,* wrote that

> . . . the individual who is suitably competent in English either has a special appreciation of the subject which surmounts indifferent teaching, or has had the good fortune to encounter a truly able teacher of English.

Palmer Hoyt, Editor and Publisher of the *Denver Post,* expressed a similar reaction. After stating that the percentage of graduates proficient in English is "not as high as it was, say, 20 years ago," Mr. Hoyt went on to note:

> I am convinced, however, that those who make up the proficient minority are more expert than ever. It is my impression that those who recognize English as a primary tool for success . . . can find rich and rewarding opportunities for this phase of their education.

The question of quality of reading being done was raised by David Peugeot, a member of editor A. H. Kirchhofer's staff on the *Buffalo Evening News:*

> Recent graduates do not seem as competent in English as those of 25 years ago, although there seems to have been a slight improve-

ment in the past ten years . . . despite the attention-consuming demands of television, young people are reading more today than a few years ago, but there is some question about the quality of their reading material.

Finally, two editors expressed opposing opinions on the same question of relationship between the size of a school and the quality of its product. One editor felt that there is "greater variance" in what small-town and large-city high schools accomplish, just as there is great variance in the accomplishments of colleges. Small-town graduates, he notes, are "rather poorly prepared," while his "main complaint (about the colleges) is that it is possible to slip through some college programs without much attention to English." The other editor wrote as follows:

> Graduates of small schools, both high schools and colleges, appear to be better prepared than graduates of larger schools. Products of so-called "progressive" schools show the poorest training.

It might be well to begin this summary of letters which rated competence in English as *lacking* with an excerpt from the letter from Wright Bryan, editor of the *Cleveland Plain Dealer:*

> I do think it is a fair generalization to say that recent high school and college graduates, on the average, are not as well trained in spelling, handwriting, grammar, and general ability to express themselves as were those of 15 or 20 years ago.
>
> Having made this statement, I must now qualify it by adding that I . . . was probably making the same comments when I first went on the newspaper desks in the early 1930s.

Mr. Bryan's surmise, however valid ultimately, does not still the voices of the editors who charge that outside of the "young people who are personally interested in writing careers," there are many graduates who show numerous deficiencies in language competence. Deficiencies in grammar and lack of extensive rhetorical practice have led to an "inability to communicate easily and effectively in writing."

One of the editors in the final group (those finding English competence *grossly lacking*) reminded us that the

> University of Illinois threw up its hands in despair and said it would no longer give such a course (in remedial English for freshmen), demanding that the high schools do what should properly be their function.

Other remarks were rather more concise, as, perhaps, coming from editors, they should be:

> I find it incredible that a college graduate cannot spell or construct grammatically correct sentences.

> Competence is rare.

> I have been appalled at the unfitness of high school and college graduates for newspaper work.

> Graduates have little knowledge of English and care less.

> Pathetically inadequate.

> All I can offer is a distinct impression that the quality of the writing which I see . . . is depressingly low.

SUMMARY OF ANSWERS TO QUESTION 2— IMPROVEMENTS NOTED

The distribution of replies is as follows:

8 replies noted *some improvement*
3 replies noted *no marked improvement*
4 replies noted *no improvement*
2 replies noted *"worsening"*
8 replies contained *no answer* to this question

Improvement was seen by at least one editor in each of the areas here listed:

Writing in "the simplest, most economical style"
The greatest improvement in ten years—grammar
Some improvement in oral communication
Slight improvement in grammar and usage
Spelling, grammar, composition
Less restriction by rules
Improvement mainly in the field of self-expression
Graduates "write more clearly than they speak"
"Simply stated, English is being taught very well, but not to
enough people"

SUMMARY OF ANSWERS TO QUESTION 3—DEFICIENCIES NOTED

Deficiency Area	Noted By
Grammar	9 editors
Spelling	17 editors
Punctuation	2 editors
Word sense	1 editor
Vocabulary	2 editors
Speech skills	1 editor
Reading comprehension	1 editor
Reading literature	4 editors
Lack of ideas	2 editors
Writing skills	
Organization of ideas	7 editors
Coherence	2 editors
Accuracy	4 editors
Clarity	3 editors
Sentence structure	1 editor

One journalist asked a few composing room veterans for their opinion of the competence of recent graduates. Wrote the journalist, "They claim that you can't hardly find good proofreaders no more!"

SUMMARY OF ANSWERS TO QUESTION 4— AWARENESS OF NCTE WORK

7 editors were *familiar* with NCTE work (and among these were four who are now or had been education editors)

2 editors expressed *vague* familiarity

7 editors were *unaware* of NCTE work

9 editors *did not answer* this question

SUMMARY OF ANSWERS TO QUESTION 5— RECOMMENDATIONS TO THE NCTE

15 editors *offered* recommendations

2 editors noted that they were "not competent" enough

8 editors *did not answer* this question

Royce Howes, Associate Editor of the *Detroit Free Press,* appears to have summarized an idea hinted at by many respondents, that schools must give students "better equipment than was formerly necessary." The ever-increasing variety, however, of activities, skills, attitudes and appreciations now included in the teaching of English makes further upgrading a difficult, if not impossible, task. At least two editors recognized this problem and suggested the curtailment of certain activities in favor of higher standards in others. One editor wrote that "Extracurricular activities . . . (should be) in addition to . . . not at the expense of, regular courses of study." Coupled with the recommendation that schools provide "better equipment" is a suggestion by Palmer Hoyt, Editor and Publisher of the *Denver Post,* that schools and the Council

> look for ways to impress upon the whole body of education—students and teachers alike—the fact that learning is strengthened by a solid foundation in English.

The general theme, then, of these letters seems to be "tighten

up," "require more," "upgrade," etc. The recommendations may
be categorized as follows:

Fundamentals

The Council is admonished by one editor to

lend support . . . to those who believe that there should be more
stress on fundamentals and fewer trimmings in secondary schools.

A slightly different slant is taken by another editor who advises
the profession to "Abandon short cuts and return to thorough
instruction in basic matters." The basic matters are presumably
spelling, grammar, vocabulary, and usage. Two recommendations
deserve some special attention.

Some of the weakness in grammar and vocabulary might be
traced to a lack of instruction in foreign languages. (*Buffalo Evening News*)

Spelling: I understand there has been little progress in the teaching of this subject for many years and it is almost entirely a "drill"
subject. I wonder if this subject hasn't been neglected by the inventors of audio-visual devices. (*Los Angeles Examiner*)

Composition

Three editors offered recommendations specifically in the area
of composition. Each recommendation expresses a different approach to improving writing.

Impress upon them (the students) that the true sign of intelligence is the ability to make the complex simple—not the ability
to make the simple complex. (*The Minneapolis Star and Tribune*)

It seems to me that the Council should stress editing on the
part of teachers and students. Editing is of basic importance in
clear exposition and the English class should be the laboratory
for such training. (*Los Angeles Evening Herald Express*)

I feel the Council should concentrate on enlisting the efforts of teachers of other subjects in high school in placing more emphasis on written composition. (*Portland* [Maine] *Press Herald-Evening Express*)

Literature

At least six editors cited lack of sufficient familiarity with "great literature," "good books," or "the classics," as a cause of deficiencies in spelling, grammar, sentence structure, vocabulary, and punctuation. The Council should encourage parents and teachers to develop in their charges "at the earliest possible age . . . sound reading habits." "Reacquaint young people," writes another editor, "with the joys of reading," which will lead to a "decent respect" for the language. Still another editor notes that the "greatest weakness lies in the matter of accuracy and lucidity." He continues, "The exposure to good literature is insufficiently coupled with a requirement that (the student) analyze good writing."

Preparation of Teachers

Three editors called for a change in the preparation of English teachers. Two of these emphasized "better preparation of English teachers—as English teachers." One editor went on to comment that "In a country that communicates in English, I can think of no teaching field in which special qualification is more important." Only one editor called for the profession to "Give up the requirement that a teacher study 'education'—which none of my own excellent high school teachers have studied—but require them to know their subjects."

Unclassified

Showmanship always was the main tool of the teacher of English, long before TV, whether he would admit it or not. (*Los Angeles Examiner*)

Much good work could be done by a joint committee of newspaper copy editors and collegiate grammarians toward a universal newspaper style book that would bring further order.

NEWSPAPER EDITORS RESPONDING TO
THE QUESTIONNAIRE

Newspaper	Editor
The Baltimore Sun	Philip M. Wagner, Editor
Birmingham News	Charles A. Fell, Editor
Buffalo Evening News	A. H. Kirchhofer, Editor
Cincinnati Post	Dick Thornburg, Editor
Christian Science Monitor	Erwin D. Canham, Editor
Cleveland Plain Dealer	Wright Bryan, Editor
Denver Post	Palmer Hoyt, Editor and Publisher
Detroit Free Press	Royce Howes, Associate Editor
Fort Worth Star-Telegram	John Ellis, Editor
Houston Chronicle	Roderick J. Watts, Managing Editor
Los Angeles Examiner	Donald F. Caswell, Education Editor
Minneapolis Star and *Minneapolis Tribune*	Richard P. Kleeman, Minneapolis Tribune News Editor
Los Angeles Herald Express	David W. Hearst, Publisher
Memphis Press-Scimitar	Edward J. Meeman, Editor
Milwaukee Journal	Wallace Lomoe, Managing Editor
New York Herald Tribune	Terry Ferrer, Education Editor
New York Journal American	Seymour Berkson, Publisher
Portland (Maine) *Sunday Telegram*	Richard H. Woodbury, Editor
New York Times	Lester Markel, Sunday Editor; Loren B. Pope, Education Editor
Philadelphia Inquirer	F. Z. Dimitman, Administrative Assistant
Omaha World-Herald	W. E. Christenson, President and Publisher
Scripps-Howard Newspapers	Ben Foster, Jr., Executive Assistant to Mr. Howard
Seattle Post Intelligencer	C. B. Lindeman, Publisher
Wall Street Journal	Robert Bottorff, Executive Editor

9

Opinions of
Legislators, U.S. Attorneys,
U.S. District Judges,
and Deans of Law Schools

NATURE OF THE SURVEY

During recent years, several public officials and law school deans have expressed their opinions, both in the press and in speeches, of the competence in English of high school and college students. It was thought that a sampling of opinion from these and various groups under the general heading of "law profession" might help in our nationwide survey of the state of English teaching and learning.

The survey letter contained the same questions asked of the other groups represented in this report.

Letters were sent in the following numbers:

Legislators	51
U.S. Attorneys	25
U.S. District Judges	25
Law School Deans	25

Replies were received from the following individuals:

Legislators

Lister Hill, United States Senate, Alabama
E. L. Bartlett, House of Representatives, Delegate from Alaska
John J. Rhodes, House of Representatives, Arizona
Fred Schwengel, House of Representatives, Iowa

Wm. H. Avery, House of Representatives, Kansas
F. Edward Hebert, House of Representatives, Louisiana
Robert Hale, House of Representatives, Maine
*Lee Metcalf, House of Representatives, Montana
*Phil Weaver, House of Representatives, Nebraska
 Charles A. Wolverton, House of Representatives, New Jersey
 Stuyvesant Wainwright, House of Representatives, New York
*George McGovern, House of Representatives, South Dakota
 Henry Aldous Dixon, House of Representatives, Utah
 Don Magnuson, House of Representatives, Washington at Large

U.S. Attorneys

*James W. Dorsey, Georgia
*Phil M. McNagny, Jr., Indiana
*Charles R. LeMaster, Indiana (Assistant U.S. Attorney)
*M. Hepburn Many, Louisiana
*Thomas R. Ethridge, Mississippi
*(Mrs. Theodore F. Bowes), New York (For her husband, U.S. Attorney Theodore F. Bowes.)

Law School Deans

Jacob D. Hyman, University of Buffalo
*William L. Prosser, University of California
 Edward H. Levi, The University of Chicago
 Wilber G. Katz, Professor of Law, The University of Chicago
 Roscoe L. Barrow, University of Cincinnati
 Daniel P. Ward, De Paul University
 David C. Bayne, S.J., University of Detroit
*Martin Tollefson, Drake University
*William Hughes Mulligan, Fordham University
*Erwin N. Griswold, Harvard University
 Leon H. Wallace, Indiana University

* Special appreciation is extended to these respondents for their detailed and useful replies.

This is not the place for an analysis of why replies were not forthcoming in greater numbers. It might be noted, however, that many Congressmen were engaged in election campaigns at the time the letters were dispatched in late summer, and several legislators were good enough to notify us that they were too busy to write replies that would be valuable to us. Then, too, the attorneys and judges may have felt unqualified to answer the questions because their work necessarily takes them out of the broad streams of communication. The law school deans answered in sufficient numbers, but more might have responded if our letter had stressed the student entering law school instead of the recent high school or college graduate. Still, a 25% response was received, and many of the replies were most helpful as clues to an understanding of the state of English teaching and learning as seen through the eyes of these professions.

The various groups chosen for this survey were selected for two basic reasons: (1) the dependence of the groups upon effective communication, and (2) the validity of the opinions of the members of the groups. These criteria are especially applicable to the legislative and law groups represented in this section. Dean Roscoe L. Barrow of the University of Cincinnati College of Law wrote very aptly on this point:

> As you appreciate, competence in comprehension and expression in words is a most important objective of pre-legal education because the power of communication is so important in the work of a lawyer.

This same idea is echoed in a leaflet on the subject of pre-legal education prepared by Dean Erwin N. Griswold of the Law School of Harvard University:

> We stress particularly the importance of acquiring an ability to use the English language. Over and over again we find that many of our students are unable to think accurately because they cannot

express themselves accurately. In giving up classical education our colleges have sacrificed some of the discipline that made for precision in the choice of words and in resulting precision in the choice of ideas. Some work in college to meet those ends is most desirable.

These two statements about the *importance* of the ability to use the English language effectively remind us that there were several replies which expressed an appreciation of the *difficulty* of teaching effective communication under current circumstances. Judge Arthur F. Lederle noted that he "taught law at Wayne University for 17 years, but I am perfectly willing to admit that English teachers perform a greater service for the legal profession than any law teacher can possibly perform." Professor Wilber G. Katz expressed a somewhat similar sympathy when he wrote, "Our own efforts to teach 'legal writing' only show us how hard it is to accomplish very much within a short period."

SUMMARY OF ANSWERS TO QUESTION 1— COMPETENCE IN ENGLISH OF RECENT GRADUATES

The replies to this question might best be presented through the following chart containing the actual comments:

Favorable	Mixed	Unfavorable	No Answer
Legislators			
Replies—14			
"real improvement . . . generally speaking" (1)	"more competent (than before) . . . but still not up to desired" "Fair" (2)	"shockingly low" "growing worse" "poor" "deterioration" "not satisfactory" "not well founded or trained in English" "Not as good as in my generation" (7)	(4)

Favorable	Mixed	Unfavorable	No Answer
Attorneys			
Replies—6			
(0)	"as competent as in a prior generation" "Some young people do very well, others incredibly bad" (2)	Speaking of college graduates: "their speech is pedestrian, imprecise, and solecistic . . . dull" "extremely poor" "Not as high as could be expected" (3)	(1)
Judges			
Replies—6			
"staff used English quite effectively" (1)	"varies greatly even among men of similar ability" (1)	"poor" (1)	(3)
Deans			
Replies—10			
"favorably inclined toward competence" "reasonably competent" "in general, reasonably proficient" (3)	"no significant increase in competency" "between average and poor" (2)	"very low level . . . getting worse" "in general, poor" "Poor" "unsatisfactory on the average" "deplorably bad" (5)	(0)

Note: Each comment represents one reply.

While the state of English teaching in the United States was not in direct scrutiny in these replies, the state of English learning has apparently received a definitive evaluation in these opinions.

SUMMARY OF ANSWERS TO QUESTION 2— AREAS OF IMPROVEMENT NOTED

As expected, most respondents noted that no improvements or no appreciable improvements are apparent in the English language competence of high school and college students. The few who saw improvements mentioned the following areas:

1. improved teaching techniques
2. spelling
3. grammar, especially in oral expression
4. "every area"

SUMMARY OF ANSWERS TO QUESTION 3— AREAS OF DEFICIENCY NOTED

The areas of deficiency are presented in order of frequency mentioned:

1. spelling (13)
2. grammar—grammatical structure (9)
3. written communication—organization—"felicity of expression" (7)
4. vocabulary—use of words (6)
5. punctuation (4)
6. usage (3)
7. oral communication (3)
8. sentence structure (3)
9. enunciation (2)
10. reading (1)

SUMMARY OF ANSWERS TO QUESTION 4— AWARENESS OF THE NCTE PROGRAMS

Only five respondents could write that they were at least "a little" aware of the NCTE programs in curriculum revision, instructional materials, and teacher preparation. Most others gave the indirect impression that they had perhaps never heard of the NCTE.

SUMMARY OF ANSWERS TO QUESTION 5—
RECOMMENDATIONS TO THE NCTE

No clear trend is discernible in the replies; suggestions differ *within* each group and they do *between* groups. The following recommendations for NCTE action, however, were mentioned by at least two respondents in each instance:

1. Wake up to the danger that the sciences may be emphasized "to the detriment of the humanities in the schools."

2. "It seems to me that the solution lies just in harder work and greater self-discipline." We must "recognize the tremendous educational advantages of perspiration."

3. "I do feel . . . that professional school teachers . . . should strongly support you in your efforts to raise standards by safe-guarding your freedom to fail students who do not measure up." Several respondents called for stricter grading and for grading of essay examination papers for expression as well as content. One dean noted that he "would refuse to graduate any student from high school or college, who could not spell, use words and write properly."

4. Two replies stated that qualifications for teaching English should be "stepped up."

5. Many deans called for more composition writing on the high school level and more composition courses on the college level.

6. Of course, a large number of replies called for a return to drilling in the structure of the English language, including pars-ing, diagramming of sentences, identifying parts of speech, etc.

7. A frequent exhortation was in the area of reading. Great literature as well as grammar is the province of English.

8. Mandated courses in Latin and other foreign languages were encouraged.

By far the most frequent recommendation called for a greater publicity effort on the part of the NCTE. The publicity should be directed in two areas: (1) public support for the programs of the NCTE, and (2) public awareness of the difficulties faced by the English teacher in accomplishing the aims of her profession.

CONTRIBUTORS

Congress of the United States

Lister Hill, United States Senate, Alabama

E. L. Bartlett, House of Representatives, Delegate from Alaska

John J. Rhodes, House of Representatives, 1st District, Arizona

Fred Schwengel, House of Representatives, 1st District, Iowa

Wm. H. Avery, House of Representatives, 1st District, Kansas

F. Edward Hebert, House of Representatives, 1st District, Louisiana

Robert Hale, House of Representatives, 1st District, Maine

Lee Metcalf, House of Representatives, 1st District, Montana

Phil Weaver, House of Representatives, 1st District, Nebraska

Charles A. Wolverton, House of Representatives, 1st District, New Jersey

Stuyvesant Wainwright, House of Representatives, 1st District, New York

George McGovern, House of Representatives, 1st District, South Dakota

Henry Aldous Dixon, House of Representatives, 1st District, Utah

	Don Magnuson, House of Representatives, Washington at Large
U.S. District Court Judges	J. Joseph Smith, District of Connecticut
	Melvin J. Marques, Administrative Assistant to the Chief Judge, District of Columbia
	Edward T. Gignoux, District of Maine
	Arthur F. Lederle, Chief Judge, Eastern District of Michigan
	Sidney C. Mize, Chief Judge, District of Mississippi
	Sam M. Driver, District of Washington
U.S. Attorneys	James W. Dorsey, District of Georgia
	Phil M. McNagny, Jr., United States Attorney, Northern District of Indiana
	Charles R. LeMaster, Assistant United States Attorney, Northern District of Indiana
	M. Hepburn Many, Eastern District of Louisiana
	Thomas R. Ethridge, Northern District of Mississippi
	Mrs. Theodore F. Bowes for Attorney Theodore F. Bowes, Northern District of New York

Law School Deans

University of Buffalo, School of Law	Jacob D. Hyman, Dean
University of California, School of Law	William L. Prosser, Dean
University of Chicago, The Law School	Edward H. Levi, Dean
	Wilber G. Katz, Professor of Law

University of Cincinnati, College of Law — Roscoe L. Barrow, Dean

De Paul University, College of Law — Daniel P. Ward, Dean

University of Detroit, School of Law — David C. Bayne, S.J., Dean

Drake University, The Law School — Martin Tollefson, Dean

Fordham University, School of Law — William Hughes Mulligan, Dean

Harvard University, Law School — Erwin N. Griswold, Dean

Indiana University, School of Law — Leon H. Wallace, Dean

10

Opinions of Public Librarians

NATURE OF THE SURVEY

Letters were dispatched to the directors (or persons holding similar positions) of city libraries and of state library commissions. The survey letter asked the following questions about the development of taste in good literature during the past two or three decades:

Where can I get the facts? Have you, for example, any comparative figures on books taken from libraries today and years ago, that would prove anything about reading tastes one way or the other? Are our students borrowing more or less of the classics; more or less of the good moderns; more or less good nonfiction?

Distribution of Replies Received	Letters Sent	Replies Received
Librarians in cities of over 100,000 population	106	47
Libraries in cities of over 50,00 population and less than 100,000	122	40
State commissions		3
Totals	228	90

The following institutions responded to the initial survey letter:

100,000 or more:

Akron Public Library	Akron, Ohio
Albany Public Library	Albany, New York
Allentown Free Library	Allentown, Pennsylvania
Atlanta Public Library	Atlanta, Georgia

Enoch Pratt Free Library	Baltimore, Maryland
East Baton Rouge Parish Library	Baton Rouge, Louisiana
Berkeley Public Library	Berkeley, California
Boston Public Library	Boston, Massachusetts
Buffalo and Erie County Public Library	Buffalo, New York
Public Library of Charlotte	Charlotte, North Carolina
Chicago Public Library	Chicago, Illinois
The Public Library of Cincinnati and Hamilton County	Cincinnati, Ohio
Cleveland Public Library	Cleveland, Ohio
Dallas County Public Library	Dallas, Texas
The Dayton and Montgomery County Public Library	Dayton, Ohio
The City and County of Denver Public Library	Denver, Colorado
Public Library of Washington, D. C.	Washington, D. C.
Duluth Public Library	Duluth, Minnesota
Evansville, Indiana, Public Library	Evansville, Indiana
Fort Worth Public Library	Fort Worth, Texas
Indianapolis Public Library	Indianapolis, Indiana
Kansas City Public Library	Kansas City, Kansas
City of Long Beach Public Library	Long Beach, California
Los Angeles Public Library	Los Angeles, California
Memphis Public Library	Memphis, Tennessee
Milwaukee Public Library	Milwaukee, Wisconsin
Minneapolis Public Library	Minneapolis, Minnesota
New Orleans Public Library	New Orleans, Louisiana
The New York Public Library	New York City, New York
New Bedford Free Public Library	New Bedford, Massachusetts
The Public Library of Newark	Newark, New Jersey
Pasadena Public Library	Pasadena, California
Peoria Public Library	Peoria, Illinois
The Free Library of Philadelphia	Philadelphia, Pennsylvania
Carnegie Library of Pittsburgh	Pittsburgh, Pennsylvania
Library Association of Portland	Portland, Oregon
Reading Public Library	Reading, Pennsylvania
Sacramento City Library	Sacramento, California
St. Louis Public Library	St. Louis, Missouri
The St. Paul Public Library	St. Paul, Minnesota
Salt Lake City Free Public Library	Salt Lake City, Utah

Savannah Public Library	Savannah, Georgia
Tacoma Public Library	Tacoma, Washington
The Toledo Public Library	Toledo, Ohio
Tulsa Public Library	Tulsa, Oklahoma
Utica Public Library	Utica, New York
Wichita City Library	Wichita, Kansas

50,000 to 99,999:

Alameda Public Library	Alameda, California
Mary E. Bivins Memorial Library	Amarillo, Texas
Pack Memorial Library	Asheville, North Carolina
Atlantic City Public Library	Atlantic City, New Jersey
Aurora Public Library	Aurora, Illinois
Binghamton Public Library	Binghamton, New York
Kanawha County Public Library	Charleston, West Virginia
J. Lewis Crozer Library	Chester, Pennsylvania
Clifton Public Library	Clifton, New Jersey
W. C. Bradley Memorial Library	Columbus, Georgia
The Public Library of Concord	Concord, New Hampshire
Davenport Public Library	Davenport, Iowa
Dearborn Public Library	Dearborn, Michigan
East Chicago Public Library	East Chicago, Indiana
Free Public Library of East Orange	East Orange, New Jersey
Fresno County Free Library	Fresno, California
Lane Public Library	Hamilton, Iowa
Hammond Public Library	Hammond, Indiana
Huntington Public Library	Huntington, West Virginia
Free Public Library	Hoboken, New Jersey
Irvington Free Public Library	Irvington, New Jersey
Jackson Public Library	Jackson, Michigan
Joliet Public Library	Joliet, Illinois
Kalamazoo Public Library	Kalamazoo, Michigan
Lancaster Free Public Library	Lancaster, Pennsylvania
Lawrence Public Library	Lawrence, Massachusetts
Lima Public Library	Lima, Ohio
Lincoln City Library	Lincoln, Nebraska
Lorain Public Library	Lorain, Ohio
The City Library	Lowell, Massachusetts
The City Library	Manchester, New Hampshire
Carnegie Free Library	McKeesport, Pennsylvania
Oak Park Public Library	Oak Park, Illinois

Carnegie Free Library	Ogden, Utah
Racine Public Library	Racine, Wisconsin
Roanoke Public Library	Roanoke, Virginia
San Jose Public Library	San Jose, California
Schenectady County Public Library	Schenectady, New York
The Public Library	St. Petersburg, Florida
Topeka Public Library	Topeka, Kansas

State Commissions

Territorial Department of Library Service	Juneau, Alaska
South Carolina State Library Boards	Columbia, South Carolina
State of Vermont Free Public Library Commission	Montpelier, Vermont

ARE OUR HIGH SCHOOL AND COLLEGE STUDENTS READING MORE GOOD BOOKS THAN BEFORE?

Careful interpretation of the letters from libraries of *cities of 100,000 or more* population results in the following breakdown of answers to this question:

Yes (largely unqualified)	32 replies
Yes (qualified)	7 replies
No	2 replies
(No answer)	(6 replies)
Total	47 replies

COMPARATIVE STATISTICS

Very few libraries were able to furnish statistics which would conclusively support a positive or negative answer to the general question posed. Not a single answering library had circulation figures which distinguished between young people (high school and college students or age) and adults for a significant period of time. Most libraries, because of the nature of the recording system, could not determine numbers of the various types of books borrowed. (Writer's suggestion: Libraries might require the answering of certain questions by each borrower during a representative month each year. Questions on a separate slip of paper might deal with number of books borrowed, whether assigned or free reading, fiction or nonfiction, current or classic, etc. Thus a body of comparative figures would be established that would measure the effectiveness of our schools, our libraries, and our culture generally in instilling a love of good books in our young people.)

The following figures are taken from the *affirmative* letters. Statistics from the one negative answer will be given last.

Cincinnati

Our interest in "young people's reading" (high school age) began some 29 years ago with a modest collection of some 700 volumes. Today we have 4000 in our main library collection. Until the past 5 years we had kept no separate figures for this collection. In 1955 the monthly loans averaged 2400; in 1959, the average has been 6250 . . . In our branches where we maintain young people's collections, we have separated statistics for only a year. These collections circulated 11,315 in August 1958 and 12,242 in July 1959.

Dayton

You will be interested to know that in this library system the book circulation increased from less than one million volumes a year in the early 1950's, to about 2,600,000 in 1959. A good portion of this increase has come in children's and young adults' reading.

Evansville

REITZ HIGH SCHOOL LIBRARY
EVANSVILLE, INDIANA
CIRCULATION RECORD

Year	Enrollment	Fiction Circ.	Nonfiction Circ.	Total Circ.
1932–33	923	669	4,949	5,618
1933–34	1,140	1,427	4,293	5,720
1934–35	1,163	2,325	5,545	7,870
1956–57	1,485	17,463	11,635	29,098
1957–58	1,471	15,340	10,350	25,690
1958–59	1,520	14,554	12,963	27,517

Kansas City

I have compared circulation figures for 6 classifications every four years since 1922. The figures indicate more books were used during the 1930's; the fiction figure is especially high. The percentage for useful arts, social sciences, biography and history increased from 1950 on.

Milwaukee

I could offer as additional evidence the increase in nonfiction at the Central Library—from 33% in 1905 to 64% in 1955, although I think you will agree that this does only in part indicate a turning away from light reading. I know that you will feel with me that these figures have to be qualified. Certainly Meredith's *The Egoist* makes far greater demands on the reader than *Please Don't Eat the Daisies*. The 1958 adult figures are as follows:

Year	1958
Central Library Adult Nonfiction	428,885
Central Library Adult Fiction	118,955
Central Library Adult Total	547,840
Neighborhood Library Adult Nonfiction	423,871
Neighborhood Library Adult Fiction	423,253
Neighborhood Library Adult Total	856,124
Adult Grand Total	1,403,964

With juvenile books included, the system circulates over three million a year.

New Bedford

The following is a résumé of adult circulation statistics for 1928 and 1958 for this library. Quantitatively they show an increase in circulation of nonfiction that is significant. Qualitatively one can infer that library users have a more serious intent in using a library than they did 30 years ago.

NEW BEDFORD FREE PUBLIC LIBRARY
COMPARATIVE CIRCULATION OF ADULT BOOKS

	1928	1958
Philosophy	1,711	3,278
Religion & Psychology	1,495	3,428
Social & Economics	3,199	8,690
Language	888	1,169
Science	2,096	3,640
Business & Useful Arts	4,944	12,778
Literature	7,501	9,965
Biography	4,804	9,451
History	3,031	9,535
Travel	4,234	7,425
Periodicals—Misc.	8,663	12,560
	54,305	88,761
Fiction	156,800	131,332
Foreign Language Fiction	5,524	2,654
	216,629	222,747
Population	125,000	109,000

Adult includes high school age (9th grade) and older.

New Orleans

(Figures were supplied for every year from 1939 to 1958; the following figures at four-year intervals should present an adequate picture.)

Years	Adult Nonfiction	Fiction	Juvenile Nonfiction	Fiction	Total
1939	148,791	360,039	197,387		706,217
1942	130,252	389,204	232,062		751,518
1946	120,503	315,322	244,873		680,698
1950	155,010	322,495	306,670	180,720	964,895
1954	193,693	325,365	416,442	216,166	1,241,065
1958	254,737	364,444	434,534	210,360	1,264,075

New York

I can tell you, as a fact for which we have the actual statistics, that the group 13 through 18 years of age accounts for from ¼ to ½ of all books circulated from the adult departments of our branch libraries and that the number of books circulated to this group is steadily rising.

Philadelphia

Here in The Free Library we have noted a marked and steadily growing increase in the use of our nonfiction collections, as the following adult circulation figures indicate:

	1940	%	1950	%	1958	%
Adult Fiction	1,347,700	64	1,360,392	59	1,585,836	49
Adult Nonfiction	763,034	36	942,637	41	1,618,686	51
	2,110,734		2,303,029		3,204,522	

We realize that nonfiction reading per se does not necessarily indicate better quality of reading than does fiction reading. We do hazard a guess that a greater percentage of nonfiction titles is of a higher quality type than is the percentage of quality fiction titles. We have no way of recording the quality of books borrowed whether fiction or nonfiction. A jump from 36% circulation of nonfiction to 51% in 18 years is, however, significant.

Reading

In 1938, 68.9% of the circulation of this library was fiction. In 1958 it was 52%. In volumes circulated, the table below may be useful:

Subject	1938	1958
Religion	2,757	5,415
Sociology	10,851	11,751
Philology	624	2,236
Science	4,270	7,093
Applied Science	11,364	16,108
Fine Arts	7,725	10,063
History	4,890	8,682

Adult nonfiction in 1938 circulated 82,963 and adult fiction 218,849. In 1958 adult nonfiction was 97,040 and fiction 127,571.

In 1938 juveniles borrowed 48,879 nonfiction and in 1958 it had jumped to 92,091. In 1938 juvenile fiction was 68,526 and in 1958 it was 91,253.

Savannah

I can, of course, comment on general reading trends among adults. In the early 1900's when our library was in its first few years of service more than 90% of the books borrowed by adults were fiction. Last year about 45% of the adult loans from the Main Library were nonfiction . . .

Utica

Record of fiction and nonfiction circulated to young people from 1927 to and including 1943:

Year	Fiction	Nonfiction
1927	1,049	2,078
1928	1,241	2,557
1929	1,470	2,479
1930	1,641	2,469
1931	1,333	2,035
1932	1,188	3,036
1933	1,497	4,046
1934	1,769	5,621
1935	1,488	6,933
1936	1,665	6,232
1937	1,109	5,961
1938	1,021	8,385
1939	1,070	6,070
1940	1,053	5,959
1941	746	4,563
1942	684	3,872
1943	359	1,438

Total circulation for 1922 was 27,242 with fiction representing 20,334 of the total and nonfiction 6,908. The nonfiction represented only 25% of the total.

In 1958 the total circulation was 399,820 with fiction representing 211,450 of the total and nonfiction 188,370. The nonfiction has risen from 25% to 47% of the total.

Baltimore (negative answer)

It may be of interest to you to consider the reading, per capita, of adults from 1939 to 1950 as it is analyzed in the *American Library Annual and Book Trade Almanac,* 1959, published by R. R. Bowker Company. On page 6 of this volume the library services branch of the U.S. Office of Education offers figures on reading, per capita, from public libraries. As you will see, in 1939 the reading, per capita, was 5.26; in 1945 it was 3.61; in 1950 it was 3.37 . . .

CONCLUSIONS FROM A STUDY OF THE ABOVE STATISTICS

1. In general, the ratio of total circulation to population is more favorable now than in 1938 or 1928. Per capita figures from public libraries neglect the large circulation of books in school and college libraries, which have grown greatly in recent years and where many students are obtaining their books for free and assigned reading. Per capita figures from public libraries also fail to take account of the increased buying power of the public and the increased availability of inexpensive editions (through paperbacks). People, adolescents as well as adults, are *buying* books where previously they might have borrowed these same books (in fewer numbers) from the public library.

2. The percentage of nonfiction books borrowed has grown in recent years to a point where, in many cases, more nonfiction books are circulated than fiction books. Figures show great nonfiction reading during certain depression years; economic conditions, perhaps, will be found to be the cause.

3. Young people are taking an ever-increasing share of total circulation in our libraries (see above the figures for New York City).

These statistics, admittedly limited and incomplete, are indicative of a change in the qualitative and quantitative reading habits of the American people. And the conclusions indicate that this movement is only the beginning, that libraries can expect a spiraling circulation of books, especially of nonfiction volumes. In addition, the overwhelming opinion of the nation's librarians is that young people are reading more and better books now than ever before.

LARGELY UNQUALIFIED AFFIRMATIVE OPINION

The preponderance of affirmative reaction to the question "Are our high school and college students reading more good books than before?" is shown on page 153 of this chapter. Even the few librarians who qualified their "yes" answers were convinced that "more teenagers are reading more than ever before; that teenagers read about two years ahead of their counterparts 25 years ago; that teenagers *are* reading good nonfiction." Thus Margaret C. Scoggin, Co-ordinator of Young Adult Services, New York Public Library, sums up her general opinion, with the added qualification that these facts may be due to the main fact that there are more teenagers than ever before, and more books available than ever before.

Affirmative reaction centered around these four questions:

1. Are students, on the whole, reading more good books?
2. Are students borrowing more or less of the classics?
3. Are students borrowing more or less of the good moderns?
4. Are students borrowing more or less of the good nonfiction?

ARE STUDENTS, ON THE WHOLE, READING MORE GOOD BOOKS? (Question 1)

Even though many of the librarians noted that it would be impossible to *prove* an affirmative answer to this question, the great majority, on the basis of many years of observation and experience, combined with knowledge and intuition, suggested, with James E. Bryan, Director of the Public Library of Newark, that:

All in all, it is my feeling that our young people are much more intellectually aware and are reading many more worth-while books, particularly those young people with better than average native mental equipment.

Mr. Bryan's opinion could be duplicated almost twoscore times with the opinions of other library directors and workers. The optimism of many of the librarians may derive from any number of the following observations made:

We can say *generally* that the demand for good literature . . . is as strong as ever . . . We find that we must continually replace copies of standard literary classics, and the over-all circulation continues to rise. So we are encouraged. (Elizabeth H. Brand, Head, Popular Library, Toledo P. L.)

I definitely feel that our young people are reading more good books than they did 20 or 25 years ago. One reason is that we have so many more really well written books which they are exposed to in public and school libraries. (Mrs. Helen Kessler, Head, Young People and Children's Department, Peoria P. L.)

Our requests in the Reference Department are mostly for classics and historical novels in the fiction field. (Mrs. Elizabeth Hilderbrand, Head, Reference Department, Peoria P. L.)

Many students are building personal libraries of superior paperbacks. The spur to collecting often comes from a teacher's or librarian's suggestion. (Luana H. Stahkecker, Adult Service Division, Akron P. L.)

Recently, from our observation, children are reading more easily without the fetters imposed by a lack of reading technique. (Mary Louise Rheary, Head, Children's Department, Atlanta P. L.)

Another indication of reading interest is the rapidity with which we have to rebind and replace "standard" titles . . . The logical conclusion is that these are worn out from use by young people, even though we could not prove this statistically. (Harold J. Sander, Director, Indianapolis P. L.)

The evidence from the statistics cited above and these enthusiastic endorsements bear out the thesis that, as Mary Louise Rheary of the Atlanta Public Library expresses it, "The quality of reading by students seems to be definitely on the upswing." Laurence G. Hill, Librarian of the New Bedford Free Public Library, puts it in another form when he writes:

Generally, from my own experience and the reported experience of other public librarians, the trend is toward increased educational and cultural use of the library and away from light recreational reading.

An eminently appropriate conclusion to this section is the following passage from the annual report to the Superintendent of Pittsburgh Public Schools, prepared by Agnes Krarup, Head, Schools Department, Carnegie Library of Pittsburgh:

The high school librarians testify that there is on the whole among young people today a more favorable attitude toward reading, particularly toward reading the classics, than there has been for many years. To be well read has suddenly become the "thing that is done." This is true whether students are preparing for college boards or not. One Pittsburgh school librarian writes concerning the Speed Reading Course begun in September at her school, with a substantial book to be read every week by each student, "Testing and statistical analyses of results by the teacher in charge suggested a remarkable correlation between volume of reading and rates of speed, comprehension, etc. Not indicated by these statistics, but a very evident end-result was the development of taste and discrimination and an unbelievable widening of interests in all directions." Another librarian reports, "During the past year there has been a steady increase in the number of pupils who use the library for serious reference work on individual projects. More of these pupils also read books which are suggested by authorities for college reading, and even the average pupil has begun to read more advanced adult books." . . . "There is evidence that the serious student shows a personal responsibility toward advancing his own learning by reading and searching for knowledge in books." Reports from other schools also mention that more and more stimulation to read outstanding literary works is coming from English classes.

ARE STUDENTS BORROWING MORE OR LESS OF THE CLASSICS; MORE OR LESS OF GOOD MODERN; MORE OR LESS OF GOOD NONFICTION? (Questions 2, 3, 4)

Most librarians would agree with J. S. Ibbotson's observation:

The number of copies of classics, of good moderns, and of good nonfiction which are available in our library and its branches has multiplied many times, and to an extent out of proportion to the population increase. (J. S. Ibbotson, Librarian, Tacoma P. L.)

Ford A. Rockwell, Librarian of the Wichita City Library; Mrs. Varelia H. Farmer, Assistant to the Director, Cleveland Public Library; Esther Norman, Librarian of the Kansas City Public Library; F. Hunter Miracle, Head, Circulation Department, Tulsa Public Library; John T. Eastlick, Librarian of the Denver Public Library; Emerson Greenaway, Director, The Free Library of Philadelphia; and Geraldine Le May, Director, Savannah Public Library, among many others, expressed the belief that there is more reading of good classics, good modern, and good nonfiction now than ever before.

Only two respondents noted the circulation of classics was no greater in 1958 than it was in 1928. Considering the preponderant opinion to the contrary from other librarians, it may be concluded that a lack of interest in the classics can be attributed to a local failure to stimulate interest in these great books. On the other hand, an "interest" in the classics may reflect little more than subtle or overt teacher pressure. Mrs. Max Schenker, Librarian of the East Baton Rouge Parish Library, after noting that "the trend is toward more mature nonfiction," writes:

> We find that the classics are still regarded as school assignments and read as such. Paperbacks make them more available, but do they make them more popular with our youth? Our observations have not led us to think that there has been any increase in voluntary classic reading.

Qualified Affirmative Opinion

Even after qualifying her enthusiastic expression of the opinion that young people are reading more good books today than ever before (see page 160), Margaret C. Scoggin, Co-ordinator of Young Adult Services, New York Public Library, ends her letter with this remark:

> . . . I can assure you that from day to day experience, all of us agree . . . that teenagers read more good books than ever before.

One of Miss Scoggin's sources for this belief is to be found in the pages of *Fifty Years of Best Sellers, 1905–1955* and in the work of the Teen Age Book Club, in which the "rising common denominator of taste and also of the increasing interest in nonfiction" is apparent.

The seven replies which noted a qualified, however enthusiastic, "yes" based their caution on any one or several of the following factors:

1. Increase in overall population (New York Public Library, Public Library of Charlotte, Dallas County Public Library)
2. Increase in school population and subsequent increase in the circulation of books (Dayton Public Library, Minneapolis Public Library, Buffalo and Erie County Public Library)

3. Increase in emphasis upon "research," supplementary reading, free reading of the classics, without indications that the
   practice will be carried into adult life (Dayton Public Library, East Baton Rouge Parish Library, Buffalo and Erie
   County Public Library)
4. Increased availability of books (New York Public Library,
   Buffalo and Erie County Public Library)

Perhaps two quotations will best illustrate the nature of these
cautious "yes" answers:

> It is difficult to form judgment on the quality of literature being
> read by the statistics that are normally gathered on library book
> use, so that judgment on this matter becomes quite subjective.
> Miss Bond (co-ordinator of adult services) notes that there seems
> to be a trend for greater use of good reading by young people, in
> part ascribable to there being more young people finishing their
> high school work each year, and that as the good students in high
> school always did read good material so when the number increases,
> we have many good high school students reading good literature.
> (Raymond E. Williams, Librarian, Minneapolis P. L.)

> It is our belief that reading circumstances in 1959 are so different
> from those 20 years ago that it is almost impossible to compare
> the situations on the same terms . . . It is the opinion of my staff
> members that paperbacks have not had a noticeable effect on the
> level of reading done by young people. More important, perhaps,
> are the extremely attractive, well-illustrated, hard-covered books on
> a wide range of subjects. (Joseph R. Rounds, Director, Buffalo and
> Erie County P. L.)

Negative Opinion

The two respondents who felt that young people apparently
are not reading more good books than ever before based opinions
on one or more of the following factors:

1. Increase in population.
2. ". . . change in school curricula from the 'textbook' approach to the 'research' approach."
3. ". . . there is little time left for reading for pleasure" because of the many other activities with which our students are engaged.
4. "When we consider how low is the reading, per capita, from public libraries in cities where books are easily available, can we be too optimistic over the fine job any of us are doing in teaching people to love reading and the best books? . . . Until high school graduates read from the public library on an average of more than two or three books a year that are not purely informational, I cannot believe that great progress in imparting the love of reading is being made by either teachers or public and school librarians . . . Despite our efforts the large masses of people are not 'fired' for literature . . ."

ARE OUR HIGH SCHOOL AND COLLEGE STUDENTS READING MORE GOOD BOOKS THAN BEFORE?

Letters from libraries in cities of 50,000 to 100,000 population reveal the following distribution of answers:

Yes (largely unqualified)	19 replies
Yes (qualified)	12 replies
No	1 reply
Uncertain	1 reply
No data	7 replies
Total	40 replies

Note: Since replies from the smaller library systems are for the most part similar to the replies from the larger libraries already reported in this chapter, this final section will be greatly abbreviated. All statistics, however, will be reproduced.

Comparative Statistics

With the exception of the last remark, the following statistics are taken from the affirmative letters:

Aurora

Our statistics show more books being read which could be due to an increase in population. Our experience indicates that except for school assignments young people read books chiefly of a frivolous nature.

Kalamazoo

Central High School circulation for the past three years:

	1956–1957	1957–1958	1958–1959
Fiction	31,714	36,704	30,973
Nonfiction	48,547	41,923	40,284
Total	80,261	78,625	71,257

Lancaster

The only figures I can give you are flat circulation statistics which may or may not tell the story . . . nonfiction has increased greatly in recent years. . . .

	1954	1955	1956	1957	1958
Adult Fiction	17,759	36,861	46,467	49,830	54,860
Adult Nonfiction	16,531	36,260	50,804	50,168	56,665
Young People's Fiction	915	10,169	10,731	9,731	9,325
Young People's Nonfiction	779	2,757	3,414	3,954	4,609

Lawrence

We do not keep records of the reading habits of the high school students.

Our students use the adult division when they leave the grammar school. From the adult circulation statistics, I can safely assume that their reading habits are excellent. Our circulation of nonfiction exceeds that of fiction . . .

Lincoln

The only suggestion I might make in regard to comparative statements is that, in the last 10 years, the circulation of books and library materials in Lincoln, Nebraska, has doubled. The population has increased about 30%. The proportion of high school students as users of public libraries is slightly higher than it was 10 years ago.

Conclusions from the above statistics and reports of statistics would be similar to those found on page 158.

Largely Unqualified Affirmative Opinion

A selection of representative comments will serve as an adequate supplement for the corresponding section appearing earlier in this paper.

> All of our staff feels that the circulation of nonfiction has grown considerably in recent years . . . We feel that our local students are studying more seriously and reading more classics and good nonfiction than heretofore . . . (John R. Banister, Director of Libraries, Columbus, Georgia)

> In 1956 nearly 220,000,000 books were circulated to children throughout the United States. The total adult circulation of books for the same period was about 215,000,000. These figures may be an indication of the wide use of public libraries through city, town and county library systems . . . The students read a good deal from public libraries. They read good modern novels a great deal, good nonfiction and quite a few classics but how these would be distributed I do not think I can tell you. (Siri M. Andrews, City Librarian, The Public Library of Concord)

We know that in our own service, it is necessary for us to keep abreast of the better titles available in fiction and nonfiction. (Harold Goldstein, Librarian, Davenport Public Library)

From our observation the difference between students' reading 20 to 30 years ago and today is the reader of good literature has multiplied many times over those of years ago. Outstanding books which over the years have had meager usage—today are receiving steady usage (circulation). (Mrs. Gladys S. Sepin, Director, Lane Public Library)

. . . It is obvious from the interest shown that young adults are learning to be more discriminating in their reading habits and are reading a great deal in the field of nonfiction especially. (Robert K. Pohl, Chief Librarian, Joliet Public Library)

My own feeling is that, thanks to the thousands of *public libraries,* our high school students are reading more good books than ever before in American history. (Charles E. Dalrymple, Director, Lincoln City Libraries)

. . . Our school librarians, who have been serving our local high school students here in our public library over a period of 15 to 30 years, feel that our students are borrowing more of the classical, more good modern and more of the good nonfiction than ever before . . . Our students today are reading better literature than ever before. (Marion M. King, Head Librarian, Lorain Public Library)

Qualified Affirmative Opinion

Qualifications mentioned: Increased availability of books, increased population, shift in emphasis in the high school and college curricula, limited or forced reading of the classics, quantity without quality, reading of nonfiction for specific answers rather than for an overall reading experience.

All respondents, except one, agreed, however, that the reading of good nonfiction and good modern books has increased in recent years.

Negative Opinion

Only one letter from a library in a city of 50,000 to 100,000 population expressed a negative reaction to the question of reading tastes of young people. The comment, *in toto,* is as follows:

> Our statistics show more books being read, which could be due to an increase in population. Our experience indicates that except for school assignments young people read books chiefly of a frivolous nature. It is difficult to persuade high school students to read the classics. Sorry we cannot strengthen your case for worthwhile reading by young people. (Eleanor Plain, Librarian, Aurora Public Library)

Replies from State Commissions

The improvement both in quality and quantity of reading may be indicated by the circulation statistics from all public libraries in South Carolina for the past year which give the figure of 2,986,380 as the total of books read by children and young people up through age 14. Since the selection of books for all public libraries in this state is based upon the very highest standards, I think we can assume that this figure reflects the reading of worth while books. (Estellene P. Walker, Director, South Carolina Library Board)

Our reply is based upon our own circulation of books to the small schools throughout the State and upon general statistics of the local public library as regards high school students.

Students primarily read adult fiction of average quality and better. Classics are read when they have been assigned for a particular school course, or where recommended by parents through our extension service.

Nonfiction in American history and biography is quite popular but science books are the widest read in this classification. (Helen

Dirtadian, Acting Director, Territorial Department of Library Service, Juneau, Alaska)

FACTORS WHICH MAY ACCOUNT FOR THE PRESENT FAVORABLE ATTITUDE ON THE PART OF YOUNG PEOPLE TOWARD INTELLECTUAL DISCIPLINE

The following list is taken from Agnes Krarup's reply:

1. Increasing difficulty in getting into college.
2. National emphasis on the importance of trained minds, following the shock of Sputnik I.
3. Educators' attention to better ways of providing for gifted children, with many challenges to lower grade children such as languages in elementary schools.
4. Advanced College Programs . . .
5. Experiments to improve articulation between elementary schools and high schools; between high schools and college . . .
6. Improved methods of teaching reading in elementary schools during the past decade . . . "extension reading" idea which promotes wide reading.
7. The excellent children's books which stimulate interest and appreciation . . .
8. The realization by school administrators that the rich resources of school libraries, both elementary and high school, challenge the student to read well. English teachers have simultaneously developed more and more skillful techniques for using libraries to promote reading in depth as well as breadth.
9. National Library Week with its nation-wide attention to reading mentioned in articles in almost every magazine.

(Agnes Krarup, Director, School Library Service, Carnegie Library of Pittsburgh)

Other factors, taken from various other letters, follow:

1. Lists of recommended books issued by high schools and by libraries.
2. Displays in school and public libraries.
3. Influence of the Great Books Program; Junior Great Books groups; other reading and discussion groups.
4. Wide availability of paperback editions, leading to home libraries.
5. The result of viewing film and/or TV presentations of the stories.
6. Book clubs such as the Teen Age Book Club.
7. Greater number of "book contacts" each day.
8. Shift in many schools from the single text approach.
9. Inspiring English teaching and teachers.
10. The development of the Work with Young Adults departments in many libraries.
11. Library book talks.
12. Interest in self-improvement.
13. Books designed to catch and hold interest.

STATISTICS IN VARIOUS PUBLICATIONS CITED BY LIBRARIANS

"A nation-wide survey just completed finds two out of three American Teenagers 'currently reading a book' other than a schoolbook. Compared with recent figures on adult reading, this indicates that teenagers out-read the adult population nearly four to one." (*Library Journal,* May 15, 1959) (Cited by H. N. Peterson, District of Columbia Public Library)

If you do not know the article "Teens and Books" in *Scholastic Teacher,* volume 74, no. 11, April 17, 1959, p. 1, you will want to look at it. It shows that two-thirds of the students polled got their books from school or public libraries and that 26% reported buying a book during the preceding thirty days. (Edwin Castagna, City Librarian, Long Beach Public Library)

The *Saturday Review,* in the spring of 1958, referring to the success of the television show called "Sunrise Semester" answers its own question as to the reasons for the popularity in these words: "The answer lies in the fact that a veritable book reading revolution is now going on in America." Classics traditionally deemed too "highbrow" for the general run of citizens are now selling in numbers that astound even the most optimistic book publishers.

The rise in paperbacks is both cause and effect. The connotation, as you so well know, no longer is that of trash. Some interesting figures on the circulation of quality books are given in an article in the *Library Quarterly* of July, 1954, pages 211–235. In 1958, the higher priced paperbacks were expanding even though they were still a small percentage. Recent figures in *Publishers Weekly* and in our local newspapers reveal that, for the Anchor Books, *The Organization Man* was in the No. 1 position . . . (Richard E. Krug, City Librarian, Milwaukee Public Library)

A recent Eugene Gilbert survey reported in the *Cleveland Plain Dealer* for January 18, 1959, states that 40% of the 604 young people polled stated that reading a good book is their favorite entertainment, ranking higher than television and movies. To quote from this survey:

About one in four of the youngsters say they read two books a month—books other than those assigned in school. About the same number, however, say they read for pleasure only when they have time between assignments. The favorite reading matter is adventure stories, although biographies rank almost as high. Also popular are historical novels, romance fiction, mysteries and science stories. Undoubtedly as a result of the recent developments in space technology, science fiction is gaining new popularity . . . (Mrs. Varelia H. Farmer, Assistant to the Director, Cleveland Public Library)

❧ 11 ❧

Opinions of Publishers

NATURE OF THE SURVEY

Letters were sent to a number of major American publishers. In addition to the questions asked in the letter to library directors, the following were posed:

> Do you as a publisher believe that their reading tastes have improved? On what objective evidence do you base your opinion, one way or the other?

DISTRIBUTION OF REPLIES RECEIVED

Number of letters sent: 122   Number of replies received: 43

The following publishers responded to the survey letter:

Abingdon Press	New York
Allyn and Bacon	Boston
American Book Company	New York
The Atlantic Monthly	Boston
Avon Book Division, Hearst Corporation	New York
Ballantine Books	New York
Bantam Books	New York
Columbia University Press	New York
The John Day Company	New York
Dodd, Mead & Company	New York
Duell, Sloan & Pearce	New York
Farrar, Straus & Cudahy	New York
Follett Publishing Company	Chicago
Ginn and Company	Boston

Harcourt, Brace and Company	New York
Harper & Brothers	New York
D. C. Heath and Company	Boston
Hill and Wang, Inc.	New York
Houghton Mifflin Company	Boston
International Universities Press	New York
Little, Brown & Company	Boston
Longmans, Green & Company	New York
McDowell, Obolensky, Inc.	New York
The Macmillan Company	New York
Macrae-Smith Company	Philadelphia
William Morrow & Company	New York
National Association of College Stores	Oberlin, Ohio
Thomas Nelson & Sons	New York
New Directions	Norfolk, Connecticut
The Odyssey Press	New York
F. A. Owen Publishing Company	Dansville, New York
Oxford University Press	New York
Random House	New York
Row, Peterson & Company	Evanston, Illinois
Scott, Foresman and Company	Chicago
Silver Burdett Company	Morristown, New Jersey
Simon and Schuster, Inc.	New York
South-Western Publishing Company	Cincinnati
Teachers College, Columbia University	New York
The Viking Press	New York
John Wiley & Sons	New York
The John C. Winston Company	Philadelphia
A. A. Wynn, Inc.	New York

ARE OUR HIGH SCHOOL AND COLLEGE STUDENTS READING MORE GOOD BOOKS THAN BEFORE?

Yes (with comment or supporting evidence)	16 replies
Yes (without comment)	6 replies
"Apparent" No (in a somewhat related magazine article)	1 reply
No answer	20 replies
Total	43 replies

Comparative Statistics

No publisher could furnish comparative figures on books purchased by secondary and college students today and years ago. A few figures, however, were cited to illustrate a trend in book publishing and sales.

Affirmative Opinion

Of the 22 replies, 16 contained comments or supporting evidence, so that the affirmative opinions were, to a large extent, substantiated by observation and study. Several of these comments and observations will be reproduced here.

Donald A. Eliasson of the Avon Book Division Editorial Department notes that:

> While we have no comparative statistics for you, may I say that the field and metropolitan New York high school and collegiate reader response to paperbacks is constantly growing.

Ian Ballantine of Ballantine Books writes:

> You have, I am sure, come across the Annual Statistics of the American Book Publishers Council. These bulk figures show a constant increase which certainly makes the pessimist that thought television would bring an end to reading look silly . . . There are not any figures to support what every publisher knows, that students are buying a very large number of books . . . Certainly it seems to me that the quality of public taste in book reading is rising by the simple process of comparing the titles published in the last 12 months with the titles published, let us say, in 1945. We could not hope to publish our New Poems, our New Short Novels, or our new September title *Great Cases in Psychoanalysis,* were it not for our substantial sale in college communities.

Roger W. Straus, Jr., President of Farrar, Straus & Cudahy, states:

In general . . . as a trade book publisher, our own figures would indicate an upswing in the reading habits of high school students both in terms of the classics and the semiclassics.

Lawrence Hill of Hill and Wang, Inc., publishers, indicates that

In general terms . . . it would be safe to say that the tremendous growth of quality or higher priced paperback publishing is a definite indication that students and perhaps others are reading more serious literature. It is also interesting to note that there is an increasing number of serious literary works being reprinted by the mass market paperback publishers such as Pocket Books, New American Library, and others.

Arthur H. Thornhill, Jr., Executive Vice President of Little, Brown and Company writes:

Certainly many thousands of young people are now reading books and although they are not always able to purchase books through the regular outlets, they are developing habits by subscribing to clubs and, of course, reading the great variety of paperback titles which are available . . . Whether or not many of the classics are being read, I don't know, although it seems reasonable to assume that this is the case as many fine books have been reprinted in recent years . . . In addition, I have found that in the past 5 or 10 years it has been possible to support the publication of more nonfiction titles and books of extremely high quality than ever before.

Edward E. Mills, President of Longmans, Green and Company, reports:

Certainly, my feeling about the reading tastes of our high school and college students today agrees with yours . . . As for the substance of your questions, while I have no quantitative support, I would say that the observable success of the quality paperback books in campus stores and also the tremendous upsurge of sales of general books, both classics and good moderns, in hand-bound form in the college bookstores over the last 5 years, lend support to your basic contention.

Lee G. Deighton, Vice President of the Macmillan Company, also comments about paperback sales:

I do know that the sales of pocket books to high schools through Scholastic Magazines has now gone into the millions of copies per year . . . From my own family experience, I can tell you that youngsters in suburban Westchester high schools are reading an extraordinary variety of good adult books.

W. R. McCulley, President of Thomas Nelson and Sons, reports:

From the junior high to the high school level, we have found an increase in sale of good nonfiction books . . . The sale of classics with us has had quite an upsurge in the last 5 years—a good many came through school channels, but it would appear that a good number of teachers are turning again to the classics.

William D. Conklin of F. A. Owen Publishing Company suggests that

. . . currently there are many books published specifically for young people . . .

James W. Sarbock, Manager, Educational Division, Oxford University Press, states that

It is our belief that your feeling is correct that high school and college students are reading more good books than ever before. The one development that might well indicate that more students are reading good books is the growth of the paperback editions of high quality in English literature . . . I seriously doubt that such a development would have been possible say 20 years ago.

Jess Stein, Editor, Random House, offers this comment:

We do know that the book industry is publishing more individual titles every year, and we do know that the total number of copies printed is increasing every year . . . We have observed a significant rise in the use of Modern Library in high schools and colleges . . . We have also observed that a very considerable part of the sale of highbrow paperbacks . . . is through college bookstores . . . It is our general impression that secondary and college students today read better books and more books than their parents did; they are reading more modern books than their parents did because they can more easily find low-priced editions; and they are probably reading more nonfiction than their parents did because some of their desire for fictional experience is being satisfied by movies and television. Time dims and distorts our memories, and every generation complains that the current crop of youngsters studies less, reads less, knows less, and talks back more than the preceding generation. We don't agree—at least with regard to learning, reading, and knowing. In short, we believe that secondary and college students will continue to read more and better books as long as we keep finding ways of publishing such books at prices they can afford and as long as we keep increasing the easy availability of books through more stores and other outlets.

Malcolm E. Mellott, Vice President of The John C. Winston Company, states that

My opinion is that our present students are reading just a little more effectively than a generation ago. I can base this on wide contests and observations across the country.

Negative Opinion

Actually the following quotation from "The Quality Fiction Question" need not be regarded as a negative response to the general question proposed, since the article is written for writers and appears in the August, 1959, issue of the *Writer's Digest*. It was sent as a rather general answer to the survey letter, and does not specifically deal with the development of taste in good literature among *present* college and high school students.

The inescapable conclusion is that we are not a nation of book buyers or even book readers. It is humiliating to compare with our own ratios of book sales to population in countries such as England, France, Sweden, Norway, Denmark and Germany. I have read, for example, that there are more bookstores in Paris alone than there are in the United States.

Opinions of
College Bookstore Managers

QUESTION 1

Reasons given for the fact that college students are buying more books than they did 10 or 20 years ago:

1. "There are more books from which to choose and the student is in a better position to buy than he was in the past." (Baylor)

2. "Ten years ago our non-required book sales were in the neighborhood of $10,000. During the past year, they exceeded $100,000, and I'm projecting $150,000 for the current academic year (1959–1960)." (State University of Iowa)

3. "I feel it is because of a larger selection they have to choose from. The previous manager carried about 300 titles and I stock around 3,000 titles." (Kansas State College of Pittsburg)

4. "Ten years or more ago there was no store available from which students could readily buy books." (Knox College)

5. "Their interests are wider, and new books on almost any topic are attractive, available and cheap—none of which was true 10 years ago." (Portland State College)

6. "More good books are available in cheaper form, and more reading is recommended by professors than before, since the financial outlay is no longer exorbitant." (University of Rochester)

7. "I don't think that all of this is due to more interest on the

part of the student, but rather to a change of attitude of newer and younger instructors who have come on the scene and who suggest more supplementary reading for the courses." (Wayne State University)

QUESTION 2

Evidence given that college students are buying more of quality nonfiction:

1. "The type of reading varies and many of the students are eager for self-improvement and will buy many of these books." (Berea College)
2. "Today we are selling in fair volume, books that we couldn't give away 10 years ago." (State University of Iowa)
3. "Our students are buying more quality nonfiction books than before mainly because they have just recently been made available." (Long Beach State College)
4. "Probably one reason for this increase is the enlargement of the trade book section of our store and the addition of many different titles." (Millsaps College)
5. "The greater part of our trade department is made up of nonfiction titles, and sales increase every year at a rate exceeding the increase in registration." (Portland State College)
6. "Yes, because more outside required reading is required." (Providence College)
7. "Since we went on a complete self-service a year ago where we were able to display nonfiction books where the student could examine them, our sale of this particular type of book has more than doubled." (Texas Technological College)

QUESTION 3

Evidence given that the availability of paperbacks has made an impact on buying habits:

1. "Paperbacks have allowed the student to buy more books for the same amount of money. Also many professors are requiring reading outside of texts. These readings can be purchased in paperback. This trend is growing in English, History, and Philosophy. In many courses several paperbacks are required instead of one cloth book. The amount spent on books is no greater and the student has more to read." (Baylor University)

2. "The availability of paperbacks has increased buying of all types of books." (Berea College)

3. "We find at the University of Buffalo that the advent of the paperback, and I mean the good quality book, has done much to make the student want to read. It has also made it easier on the pocketbook so he could afford to read." (University of Buffalo)

4. "The ready availability of more and more quality paperback books has been a boon to the serious reading student, just as the availability of these books was a blessing to the smaller college store which was cautiously entering the nontext field for the first time." (Denison University)

5. "Yes, indeed, the paperback has put good books in the price range of all students." (Florida State University)

6. "Definitely—it brings a wide range of reading matter within the college student's budget." (Houghton College)

7. "Last spring our honorary women's organization on campus published a 15-page list of suggested summer reading books, and the Bookstore sold out of most every good paperback

we had in stock at the time." (University of New Hampshire)

8. ". . . many students are buying quality paperbacks instead of magazines and that many are building their own library." (Parsons College)

9. ". . . a student can buy more books for the same money in quality titles." (Pomona College)

10. "If the paperback titles suddenly reverted to their hardback form and price, sales would drop to an all-time low." (Portland State College)

11. "Yes, increased their scope and assuredly helped to offset normal attitudes toward college store." (St. Louis University)

12. "The availability of the quality paperback is very likely the principal reason why the students of today are buying more nonrequired books." (Utah State University)

QUESTION 4

Why college students today have better reading tastes.

1. "The students in our school read serious books and not light fiction. This I believe is a growing trend." (Baylor)

2. "It depends on the type of influence which will, without any doubt in my mind, guide the student's taste. The instructors and the college store manager play the most important roles in this influence." (Catholic University of America)

3. "I would say that the tastes of our students have always been more serious, sophisticated, of a high degree of intellectual cultivation, and over the 10 years that I have known the campus, these tastes have not declined one whit." (University of Chicago)

4. "College students today, because of the many means of advertising, are reading more today, but they have not neces-

sarily developed better tastes in their reading. They feel that they must read the book that has the most controversial aspects of the day." (Long Beach State College)

5. "Our work in the college store is not only one of selling books, but with instructor co-operation we are in effect guiding the reading tastes of the students, and I feel we have succeeded in this slow process." (University of Rochester)

6. "Their variety in selection is greater." (College of San Mateo)

7. "I do think that many students have a more varied taste in reading than before. That is, they read outside their sphere of study." (Syracuse University)

QUESTION 5

Why college students are developing lifetime habits of reading good books for their pleasure, their self-improvement, their search for better things in life.

1. "I find it hard to believe a student who reads nonrequired serious reading in college will cease such reading when he graduates." (Baylor University)

2. "Yes, I feel that their school years form a great deal of their desires for future life." (Fresno State College)

3. "I do believe college students today are developing lifelong habits of reading good books. Whatever they become accustomed to reading in college, I believe, will be the kind of books they will read throughout life." (Millsaps College)

4. "In observing the thousands of adults registered in our night classes (some of whom buy $20 worth of paperbacks at a time) we are inclined to believe that more and more people are becoming sated with evenings devoted solely to TV and are turning increasingly to reading for entertainment and information." (Portland State College)

5. "Yes—because more is made available." (College of San Mateo)

Negative Replies

1. ". . . I'm afraid that most college students will quit reading just as their predecessors have as soon as they are out of college." (Brigham Young University)
2. "I think that because of the nation-wide advertising based on sensationalism, poor reading habits have developed into a situation which detracts from a student's progress—intellectually and socially." (Catholic University of America)
3. "Unfortunately, I feel only a small percentage are establishing firm habits. Books as items of possession do not rate very highly on most student value scales. Locally, at least, there is no longer any social stigma placed on owning and valuing books." (Knox College)
4. "People spend too much time running around in cars, watching television, and other forms of what we call recreation to have any time left for developing good reading habits." (Utah State University)

QUESTION 6

Reasons for *not* agreeing with criticisms in the public press.

1. "I do not agree with the criticism that students cannot read or have poor reading habits. I believe their reading habits are slowly improving. We shall always have those who are poor readers and who read only what is required. Some people never do any more than is required of them." (Baylor University)
2. "I think the reading habits are improving steadily." (Erskine College)

3. "We definitely believe the reading habits of college students are on the upward grade, and will continue." (Evansville College)

4. "The criticism should be directed at the minority not the majority." (Florida State University)

5. "Definitely not! Because (a) no survey of magazine publication could do justice to the subject as a whole, (b) college students are readily influenced in certain ways and any generalizations about reading habits must take into account the influencing factors as well as the resultant reading habits, (c) civilization does not progress necessarily according to statistics of habits or values of a group within a society." (Knox College)

6. "No. We are a book-minded store and so the faculty encourages using our stores. Students are therefore being *bent* into good reading habits." (University of Massachusetts)

7. "With few exceptions, I do not agree. Our sales records show a marked increase each year in books above the increased number of students, above the increased number of textbooks required, and above the general increased price of textbooks." (University of Rochester)

8. "No. Negative reports impress more people than positive reports." (College of San Mateo)

9. "Not in most cases. Of course, there will always be some who have poor reading habits, but I do *not* think their number is increasing." (Syracuse University)

10. "Many students today, I believe, are more aware of their poor reading habits, and are taking steps to improve them." (Teachers College, Columbia University)

Reasons why college store managers *do* agree with the criticisms in the public press.

1. "I feel that many persons now have poor reading habits, due to our increased speed of living, availability of theaters, and legitimate stage shows, and, of course, television." (Fresno State College)

2. "I believe there is room for great improvement." (Gallaudet College)

3. "Yes, I do agree with the current criticism of the poor reading habits of college students, but I do not feel that I can say they are any worse than they were 10 years ago." (Mt. San Antonio College)

4. "There is still a basis for such criticism, but in the 10 years of my bookstore experience I can report progress in improvement." (Occidental College)

5. "Much of the criticism is justified and the required reading of dry classics may have tended to discourage or fails to awaken an interest in reading." (University of Pittsburgh)

6. "Yes. This may be because they are trained to read poorly with the so-called modern methods as opposed to the alphabet-phonetic method." (San Jose City College)

7. "80% have not improved; other 20% have improved much." (St. Olaf College)

8. "In the main, I do agree with the criticism of the poor reading habits. I do not agree to the extent that these articles tend to disregard the fact that there are still some people that have and are developing good reading habits. The masses, however, are in line for criticism." (Utah State University)

❧ 13 ❦

Opinions of
Commercial Bookstore
Managers

In a talk before a class in New York University, William C. Lengel, editor-in-chief of the Fawcett World Library, stated that the sale of paperbacks in 1960 was expected to reach 300,000,000 copies.[1] That buying habits of America's readers were being affected by the "paperback revolution" has been known for some time. In the preceding chapter it was indicated that 97.16% of the 106 managers of college bookstores believed that the availability of quality paperbacks had made an important impact upon the buying habits of our college students. But what do the managers of the commercial (or noncollege-affiliated) bookstores believe about the buying habits of today's college students in general, and their taste in reading? To secure their opinions, the writer sent a questionnaire to the 1750 members of the American Booksellers Association.[2] There were 160 replies, many of them accompanied by interesting and valuable comments, based on their experience. The statistical summaries of the six questions follow:

---

[1] Reported in *Variety*, May 18, 1960, p. 77.
[2] Our thanks are expressed to Joseph A. Duffy, Executive Director of the American Booksellers Association, Inc., who assisted in the survey.

QUESTION 1

Are college students buying more or fewer books, other than their required textbooks, than their predecessors of 10, 20, or 30 years ago, depending upon your associations with college students?

Yes	*No*	*Uncertain*	*Total*
99 (61.87%)	12 (7.5%)	49 (30%)	160

QUESTION 2

Are they buying more of the quality nonfiction books than before?

Yes	*No*	*Uncertain*	*Total*
103 (64.37%)	19 (11.08%)	38 (18.75%)	160

QUESTION 3

Has the availability of the quality paperbacks made any impact upon their buying habits?

Yes	*No*	*Uncertain*	*Total*
126 (78.75%)	4 (2.5%)	30 (18.75%)	160

QUESTION 4

On the basis of your experience, would you say that college students today have better tastes in reading than before?

Yes	*No*	*Uncertain*	*Total*
79 (49.37%)	33 (20.62%)	48 (30%)	160

QUESTION 5

Do you believe that college students today are developing lifetime habits of reading good books for their pleasure, their self-improvement, their search for the better things in life?

Yes	*No*	*Uncertain*	*Total*
86 (53.75%)	33 (20.62%)	41 (25.62%)	160

QUESTION 6

Do you agree with the current criticism of poor reading habits of college students we so often read in the popular magazines?

Yes	No	Uncertain	Total
45 (28.12%)	75 (46.8%)	40 (25%)	160

CONCLUSIONS

Even though 160 replies represent less than 10% of all the commercial bookstores, they are probably as good a sampling as one can obtain under the circumstances; and they speak for booksellers in 38 states, the District of Columbia, and Canada. What are some valid conclusions?

1. The majority of our commercial booksellers (61.87%) believe that present-day college students are buying *more* books than their predecessors of 10, 20, or 30 years ago.
2. The majority of our commercial booksellers (64.37%) believe that they are buying *more* quality nonfiction than their predecessors.
3. Three quarters of the commercial booksellers believe that the availability of quality paperbacks has made an impact on the buying habits of our college students.
4. Almost half of the commercial booksellers believe that college students have better tastes in reading than before. Only 20.62% believe that their taste is worse.
5. More than half of the commercial booksellers believe that college students are developing lifetime habits of reading good books.
6. Only 28.12% of the commercial booksellers agree with the criticism of poor reading habits in the public press.

It is significant that except for changes in percentages, the managers of commercial bookstores and the managers of college bookstores are in agreement on all 6 questions. Admittedly over 1,000 commercial booksellers did not reply to the questionnaire, and it is possible that had all of them replied, the figures might have been quite different. Nevertheless, it is encouraging to learn from 160 of America's booksellers that our college students (at least in the areas represented) are making a good showing as compared with their predecessors.

Many of the respondents added informative comments, to justify or to amplify their answers. These represent perhaps the most complete set of comments of commercial booksellers on the reading habits of America's college students and merit our consideration.

SURVEY REPLIES FROM BOOKSELLERS

Question 1

Tally McKee
Book-Bargains-By-Mail
516 Sherman Ave.
Pittsburgh 12, Pa.

"Can't say—not in business long enough."

Marvel W. Drought
The Book Bay
2628 N. Downer Ave.
Milwaukee 11, Wis.

"A little more than 10 years ago; we were not in business 20 years ago, so we cannot judge further back."

The Book Home
Colorado Springs, Col.

"Possibly fewer, but not sure."

The Bookshop, Inc.
Meridian and Church Sts.
New London, Conn.

"More—paperbacks and Modern Library for collateral reading."

Carolyn Wellman
The Book Nook
9 Stark St.
Manchester, N. H.

"I have no statistics but I do know that college students are buying many worth while books for pleasure."

Viola Davies Graves
The Book Nook
46 S. Central
Clayton 5, Mo.

"Yes, especially since paperbacks have been available."

Carl J. Miller
The Book Shop
115 W. Monroe St.
Sandusky, Ohio

"I do not believe that they are purchasing more books than their predecessors."

Samuel Oxman
Boonton Stationery & Gift Shop
712 Main Street
Boonton, N. J.

"They do not buy a book simply because they would like to read it, but simply because the particular course they are taking requires it."

E. Gail Loughner
The Book Center of Wilkinsburg
P.O. Box 8675
Pittsburgh 21, Pa.

"Less than 10%, based upon my own experience, buy more, the

others less. Technical students tend to ignore subjects other than supplementary to their own studies."

Mrs. Margaret R. Campbell
 Campbell's Book Shop
 123 S. 7th St.
 Terre Haute, Ind.

"College students are buying more books now than did their predecessors. There are, of course, more students now and they have more money . . ."

D. E. Burgderfer
 The Book Corral
 510 Main St.
 Montrose, Col.

". . . It is, however, my overall feeling that there are too many other things now competing for the time of the average student. . . ."

Jane P. Brown
 William G. Brown Company
 186 Main St.
 Gloucester, Mass.

"There are so many more college students today that naturally they buy more books."

Capitol Stationers, Inc.
 65 Main St.
 Montpelier, Vt.

The owner of this store has this to say of each of the three colleges in his vicinity: "Goddard students (a free thinking school) buy the most books from us. These are books in the order of selling: (1) Better class of pocket books, Mentor, Harper, etc., (2) Modern Library. Vermont College students buy about one book per 25 students from us. Norwich University students almost never buy a book from us."

Jason G. Austin, Mgr.
  Carleton Book Store
  Carleton College
  Northfield, Minn.

". . . However, I can estimate that where our total book sales was in excess of $41,000.00 in 1950, compared to our $85,000.00 in 1959, the difference of $44,000.00 was due to several factors: (1) Increase in price of books, $8,000.00, (2) Increase in enrollment, $13,000.00, Total, $21,000.00. Of the balance about $6,000.00 can be charged off to a greater number of textbooks required and general inaccuracies. That leaves approximately $15,000.00 representing more books sold than ten years ago."

Robert A. Thornton, Jr., Mgr.
  Cokesbury
  Retail Division of the Methodist Publishing House
  150 Fifth Ave.
  New York 11, N. Y.

"I believe college students are buying fewer books other than their required textbooks at the time they are students. However, I believe that the love of books instilled in them by their professors carries over to the point where, if financial means are available, they buy more books than the noncollege people."

David B. Hunt
  David Hunt's Book Shop
  187 Market St.
  Lexington, Ky.

"They are buying more if they can get them in paperback."

Herman B. Fox
  Fox and Sutherland
  15 S. Moger Ave.
  Mt. Kisco, N. Y.

"The college students whom we meet between semesters and summer vacations do read more books other than required according to the influence of their instructors and the sustained interest of the student. When we note this interest we endeavor to stimulate and enlarge this scope."

John Joseph Hagedorn, Book Buyer
Gimbel's
Philadelphia, Pa.

"College students are buying more books from us than they did during the previous 30 years, in number of books sold; I'm not sure in the dollar and cents comparison, as such a heavy percentage is now in paperbacks, costing perhaps ¼ the cost of equivalent hard back texts; paperbacks were a negligible factor even 10 years ago and were infinitesimal before 1940."

Carlton L. Apollonio
The Intimate Bookshop
Paul Smith, Bookseller
Chapel Hill, N. C.

"First, there is little doubt in my mind that students are buying more books now than they did even as recently as 6 or 7 years ago, but the reasons for this are hardly as inspiring as might appear at first glance. The paperback revolution has made it possible for faculty members to require (especially in English courses) to buy as many as 10 to 12 books per semester, each book costing little more than a dollar or so. . . ."

Jane Amann-Jones
Jane's Library Service
3328 17th St. N.W.
Washington 10, D. C.

"College students are using libraries in this area rather than buying books."

Mildred L. Tingley
Little Acorn Book Shop
4 High St.
Pawtucket, R. I.

"College students seem to be buying more of the classics required in outside reading for lit. and other courses . . . now that the books are available in paper."

Helen S. Lowitt
    The Magic Circle Book Shop
    10 Grace Ave.
    Greak Neck, New York

"College students are buying more books in desperation, since the libraries are inadequate."

Harlow Ross
    Ross & Haines, Inc.
    413 S. 4th St.
    Minneapolis 15, Minn.

". . . and it does seem to me that students read more than they did, but this is opinion, not based upon statistics . . ."

James W. Tenney
    Savile Book Shop
    3236 P St. N.W.
    Washington 7, D. C.

"The availability of books for the student has certainly been improved during the past 30 years but in general I would say that 90% of college students are reading less . . . only 10% of the students take an active interest in peripheral reading; the rest are content to stay within the requirements."

George E. Renison, Managing Director
    W. H. Smith & Son (Canada) Ltd.
    224 Yonge St.
    Toronto, Canada

"The total purchases of books other than text books in college book stores has increased enormously but of course the college enrollment has also increased enormously. My own impression is that the students are not buying as many books as their predecessors."

Question 2

The Box of Books
   Alfred, New York

"Not in 'hard back' editions."

Tally McKee
   Book-Bargains-By-Mail
   516 Sherman Ave.
   Pittsburgh 12, Pa.

"There is more interest (it seems to me) in *The Ready-Made Answers*. Many college students want foreign-language translations instead of translating themselves, interlinear Latin and Greek, Answer Books in many subjects, How to Read books, Word Finders (usually the streamlined cheap thesauruses, not the good ones)."

Viola Davies Graves
   The Book Nook
   46 S. Central
   Clayton 5, Mo.

"Yes—result of wider reading."

E. Gail Loughner
   The Book Center of Wilkinsburg
   P.O. Box 8675
   Pittsburgh 21, Pa.

"They who buy and read do so in quantity and variety with classical and near-classical predominating."

Mary Ellen Bailey
   The Book Shop
   11 W. McBee Ave.
   Greenville, S. C.

"College students are buying many non-fiction books . . ."

Capitol Stationers, Inc.
65 Main St.
Montpelier, Vt.

"Almost always the sale of a book by us to a college student is of the better quality of nonfiction book."

Jason G. Austin, Mgr.
Carleton Book Store
Carleton College
Northfield, Minn.

". . . Certainly this wider and now available scope of reading possibilities has awakened latent desires in students to increase their knowledge, if purely from an academic and theoretical viewpoint . . ."

Robert A. Thornton, Jr., Mgr.
Retail Division of the Methodist Publishing House
150 Fifth Ave.
New York 11, N. Y.

"I believe that the quality nonfiction books have higher reading audience among the college graduates than the fiction."

Mrs. Fred Cole
Cole's Book & Card Shop
725 Leopard St.
Corpus Christi, Tex.

"However, for what it is worth, our store sells much more non-fiction than it does fiction."

The Country Bookshop
Southern Pines, N. C.

". . . Those I do see . . . take a keen interest in 'highbrow paperbacks' and the Modern Library."

The Exchange Book Shop
73 Exchange Pl.
New York 4, N. Y.

"Yes—availability of paperbacks is determinate factor."

The Frigate Book Shop
16 E. Highland Ave.
Philadelphia 18, Pa.

"Not quality except paper reprints of good books."

John Joseph Hagedorn, Book Buyer
Gimbels
Philadelphia, Pa.

"They always bought more nonfiction than fiction; I would think *that* percentage hasn't changed much in the past few decades."

Good Office Supply Co.
Tiffin, Ohio

"I believe they are buying more of the worthwhile books for cultural use."

The House of Books, Inc.
9231 Stella Link Rd.
Houston 25, Tex.

"Not as a whole. A small group is accounting for most of the sales."

Carl L. Apollonio
The Intimate Bookshop
Paul Smith, Bookseller
Chapel Hill, N. C.

". . . Obviously, if the student buys a dozen books, picked by the professor, he will be buying 'more of the quality nonfiction books than before'; . . . these purchases are under duress, so to speak.

There is no doubt that more students are being exposed to quality literature by having to enter a bookshop in order to get what the professor has required."

G. G. Brown
Jame & Law Company
217 W. Main St.
Clarksburg, W. Va.

"They are buying more quality nonfiction than ever before."

Jane Amann-Jones
Jane's Library Service
3328 17th St. N.W.
Washington 10, D. C.

"When they do buy, it is more often quality nonfiction."

Gordon W. Bryant, Pres.
Lauriat's
65 Franklin St.
Boston 10, Mass.

". . . and certainly their purchases are a growing proportion of quality nonfiction books, including a great many paperbacks."

Mildred L. Tingley
Little Acorn Book Shop
4 High St.
Pawtucket, R. I.

"In paperbacks only, and only what is assigned. I find that most students have (or take) time only for required work."

The MacMillan Book Shop
248 E. State St.
Salem, Ohio

". . . We have been selling nonfiction so much more than fiction recently that we wonder."

Old Town Books
2040 S. Plaza N.W.
Albuquerque, New Mex.

"Those who do buy form a growing elite, and they are reading more: those who do buy tend to buy good titles—they like the quality paperbounds and they buy real classics, etc."

James W. Tenney
Savile Book Shop
3236 P St. N.W.
Washington 7, D. C.

"If they buy more of the quality nonfiction (who defines quality?) it is on an impulse basis. . . . The more esoteric the better they like it. On the other hand, if you could categorize such authors as Parrington, Hofstadter, etc., in the quality field the answer is, No, they don't buy unless they have to."

Three Arts Shop
6501 Delmar Blvd.
St. Louis 30, Mo.

"We are a college store here, close to the University and sell more nonfiction than fiction."

Robert Dike Blair
The Vermont Book Shop
Middlebury, Vt.

"I think it probable that the students today are buying more worthwhile books simply because so many are available in attractive paperbacks, and the kids do not have too much money to spend voluntarily on books."

Question 3

Anderson's Book & Card Shop
119 So. Jefferson Ave.
Saginaw, Mich.

"The high price of good hardbacks is too much for the average student. He buys more of quality paperbacks because they are cheaper and in greater quantity than 20 years ago. However, they read many 'trash' titles because they are found everywhere."

Frances Pendley
   Angelus Book Shop
   Balcony-Hemphill-Wells
   San Angelo, Tex.

"The paperback books make an appeal to college students. Reading them, *I don't know.*"

Frances Darling
   The Bay Colony Bookshop
   35 Newbury St.
   Boston, Mass.

"We do not have a real student trade—we do not carry textbooks and we are on what one might term a 'Luxury Street' of women's shops etc., but we do have young people coming in and feel that they are intelligent and selective in their purchases. 'Paper books' are a great help."

Catholic Bookshop of New York
   138 W. 32 St.
   New York City, N. Y.

"I would say paperbacks are developing more readers and of a better quality. The low price sells more books of an intellectual level—even in our field."

Educational Center Book Shop
   153 State St.
   Windsor, Vt.

"Quality paperbacks have met the 'buying power' of the student's finances."

Harlow Ross
  Ross & Haines, Inc.
  413 S. 4 St.
  Minneapolis 14, Minn.

"On the whole, I would say that the trend to the buying of paperbacks merely indicates that the student is not fully aware of low-
priced editions already available; Modern Library, Everyman, Oxford World Classics and so on . . . series publications that have
been ready for his use for a number of years, and titles that are
being duplicated to a considerable extent in the paperbacks. Possibly the better and wider distribution of paperbacks is the answer
to some extent."

Robert Dike Blair
  The Vermont Book Shop
  Middlebury, Vt.

"There is no question that the availability of good books in the
paper editions is stimulating the buying and reading of serious
books."

Margaret R. Campbell
  Campbell's Book Shop
  123 S. 7 St.
  Terre Haute, Ind.

"We think the availability of the quality paperbacks is the one
most important factor in the increase in book-buying by students.
Paper-back editions are being recommended as supplementary texts
with increasing frequency by teachers in the college classes. This
has fostered the habit among students of buying books rather than
relying on the library for their outside reading, and the modest
price of the paperbacks puts them within reach of most students."

D. E. Burgderfer
  The Book Corral
  510 Main St.
  Montrose, Col.

"Several revolutions are being recognized in the book business.

For one, the paper-backed book, once held in disrepute because of the usual low forms of literature treated in such editions, is now becoming an important teaching tool in many high schools. Many schools, in fact, even sell them to the students on the premises, usually through the school library. Much higher class literature is now finding its way into these volumes, and I strongly suspect that many students who otherwise might not be reading anything of much worth may now be doing so."

Gordon W. Bryant, Pres.
Lauriat's
65 Franklin St.
Boston 10, Mass.

"There is no doubt that the entry of paperbacks in the picture in America has been a tremendous stimulus to the sale of good books to young people."

J. F. Albright
Cokesbury
1910 Main St.
Dallas 1, Tex.

"Some, but most prefer the permanent hard books to keep for permanent reference."

Helen S. Lowitt
The Magic Circle Book Shop
10 Grace Ave.
Great Neck, N. Y.

"The paperbacks are a great boon and students buy enthusiastically."

Kingsport Office Supply
200–202 Market & Commerce Sts.
Kingsport, Tenn.

"I do notice that since better books are in paperbacks they buy them rather than going to the libraries for them."

Richard D. Marting, V. Pres.
The Marting Bros. Co.
Portsmouth, Ohio

"Paperback books have definitely made an impact upon the buying habits of college students. The lower price of paperbacks has permitted the student to buy more books with the same amount of money, yet the student is not taking this money saved to buy more of the better books but is probably using the money to buy more 'trash,' with the result that the better and more thought-provoking books are not being purchased."

Sheridan Square Chemists
10 Sheridan Sq.
New York 14, N. Y.

"Having a bookshop in the heart of Greenwich Village gives us a point of view rather different from others. We firmly believe that there is a hard core of readers who are quite happy about 'paperbacks' because of price, etc. This hard core is most usually college educated."

Capitol Stationers, Inc.
65 Main St.
Montpelier, Vt.

"We experience a great problem in buying paperback books due to the use of magazine distributors as the paperback distributors . . . they do not let us select our own choice of titles and give us about 98% junk. We could do much better by the student if we could select titles. The student has without question bought more paperbacks and this type of book is a great help to the college student."

Theodore Wilentz, Sec'y.
The Eighth Street Bookshop, Inc.
32 W. 8th St.
New York 11, N. Y.

"Tremendous. Students of today grow up as book buyers. . . ."

Herman B. Fox
Fox & Sutherland
15 S. Moger Ave.
Mt. Kisco, N. Y.

"University press and major publishers' paper books are the greatest blessing for the students and do attract the students of both high school and college."

Jane P. Brown
Wm. A. Brown Co.
Gloucester, Mass.

"Yes, it's made it possible for them to own books they would otherwise have read only in libraries."

John Joseph Hagedorn, Book Buyer
Gimbels
Philadelphia, Pa.

"The paperback books have *completely changed* the buying habits of book lovers and book buyers in *all* age groups, students and non-students. We stock here about 3500 different paperback titles, perhaps 7500 hardback titles. . . ."

Question 4

The Bookmark, Inc.
97 Central Sq.
Pittsburgh 28, Pa.

"Our bookstore is less than a year old, so we're no experts. However, we've been greatly impressed by the caliber of reading done by young people—as opposed to their parents!"

Viola Davies Graves
The Book Nook
46 S. Central
Clayton 5, Mo.

"Yes, they receive more ideas through reading and can compare and contrast the books read."

Samuel Oxman
Boonton Stationery & Gift Shop
712 Main St.
Boonton, N. J.

"I believe that college students have better tastes in reading than before because the high schools are giving better English courses today and require so much outside reading of good books."

The Bookstore
203 A N. Blvd.
De Land, Fla.

"Our guess is: Inflation has curtailed frivolous purchases; result is improved buying trend in percentages of total sold."

Jason G. Austin, Mgr.
Carleton Book Store
Carleton College
Northfield, Minn.

"I feel that the present-day educated youth is more interested in good reading, as a whole, but still temper their intellectual pursuits with occasional bursts of reading of the voluminous trash that is available."

The Edward Madison Co.
427–429 Bloomfield Ave.
Montclair, N. J.

"Maybe not better taste, but a greater variety of subjects."

Carlton L. Apollonio
The Intimate Bookshop
Paul Smith, Bookseller
Chapel Hill, N. C.

". . . I am afraid that students today do not 'have better tastes in reading than before.' . . . More and more students get to college without having learned the rudiments of the English language . . ."

James W. Tenney
Savile Book Shop
3236 P St. N.W.
Washington 7, D. C.

"More esoteric, not better. They lack the foundations."

Mrs. Margaret R. Campbell
Campbell's Book Shop
123 S. 7th St.
Terre Haute, Ind.

"The availability of quality paperbacks has certainly given students an opportunity to develop better tastes in reading, but our acquaintance among students is not wide enough for us to have formed an opinion about their tastes."

Gordon W. Bryant, Pres.
Lauriat's
65 Franklin St.
Boston 10, Mass.

"We do feel that college students have better tastes in reading than in years past. It seems to improve constantly; perhaps because more young people are going further in school today than heretofore."

J. F. Albright
Cokesbury
1910 Main St.
Dallas 1, Tex.

"Yes, schools are doing a better job, starting at the elementary level."

Helen S. Lowitt
The Magic Circle Book Shop
10 Grace Ave.
Great Neck, N. Y.

"College students *don't have as good taste* as formerly. They buy what is required and have no further interest or curiosity."

Tally McKee
Book-Bargains-By-Mail
516 Sherman Ave.
Pittsburgh 12, Pa.

"More esoteric, perhaps—searching for they know not what."

Mildred L. Tingley
Little Acorn Book Shop
4 High St.
Pawtucket, R. I.

"No. Their tastes are only forming in college. They have done less reading before than their predecessors."

George E. Renison, Managing Director
W. H. Smith & Son (Canada) Ltd.
224 Yonge St.
Toronto, Canada

"The answer to Question 4 is very difficult. I feel that the selection offered to the students is a vastly wider and vastly better one than it has ever been in the past. On this basis, I think that the students are reading more and have better taste in their reading. Whether this comes from opportunity or as a result of better education, I am not able to say."

Agatha E. R. Delaney
Taga Book Shop
53 Fourth St.
Troy, N. Y.

"I would *not* say they have better *tastes* in reading than before, but better *opportunity* due to inexpensive paperbacks."

Marvel W. Drought
The Book Bay
2628 N. Downer Ave.
Milwaukee 11, Wis.

"They are more serious-minded anyway, especially in the fields of science. The proportion with good reading tastes in literature is still small and perhaps decreasing."

Question 5

Barber's Book Store
215 W. 8th St.
Fort Worth 2, Tex.

"I might qualify the term 'good books' but they are reading more nonfiction for purposes listed."

The Box of Books
Alfred, N. Y.

"I question the 'lifetime.' I do not know. From observation of alumni, I wonder whether the habit continues after the impetus of college is over."

John Q. Burch
4206 Halldale Ave.
Los Angeles 62, Calif.

"It seems to me that the average serious scholar of today is disposed to be so immersed in his specialty that he pays a price for it by being very poorly informed on other matters."

E. Gail Loughner
The Book Center of Wilkinsburg
P.O. Box 8675
Pittsburgh 21, Pa.

"They are much more confused than youth has a right to be. The reading of books, like alcoholic consumption is habit-forming. I don't know what the better things in life are."

Mary Ellen Bailey
The Book Shop
11 W. McBee Ave.
Greenville, S. C.

"Generally speaking we do believe that college students are developing good reading habits and are seeking a higher plane of living."

Mary Schornherst
  Everyman's Bookshop
  113 W. College Ave.
  Tallahassee, Fla.

"When I was in college I did not have money to purchase the books I wanted. Many students seem to have money to buy books with, but in my shop they buy them for others, not for themselves. This may indicate more interest. People so often buy for others what they *want* themselves."

Highland Park News Co.
  13527 Woodward Ave.
  Highland Park 3, Mich.

"The causes for *lack* of continued reading after graduation (if any) should be examined in the light of the poor instruction in the schools. Less *analysis* and more extensive 'reading for reading's sake' might be the answer."

G. G. Brown
  The James & Law Co.
  217 W. Main St.
  Clarksburg, W. Va.

"I believe that college students today develop the habit of reading good books largely for self-improvement and secondly for pleasure."

Kingsport Office Supply
  200–202 Market & Commerce Sts.
  Kingsport, Tenn.

"My personal opinion is that beginning in the grades and continuing through high school there is too little required reading of the great books. Therefore, children do not develop a taste for these, they read too many condensations—enough to get by. I am speaking of the majority."

Richard D. Marting
   The Marting Bros. Co.
   Portsmouth, Ohio.

"The answer is definitely NO. Apparently the prevailing idea is to do the smallest amount of reading required—and not only the least amount but the easiest type of reading. Any book requiring concentrated reading is avoided."

Sheridan Square Chemists
   10 Sheridan Sq.
   New York 14, N. Y.

"We also believe that the emergence of T.V. these past 10 years has ruined the reading habits of the present student generation."

Capitol Stationers, Inc.
   65 Main St.
   Montpelier, Vt.

"The *real* college student is developing as you say but I believe they only represent a small percentage of the total student body. Many college students are in college but do not realize what for until long after graduation. These students are not book buyers."

Theodore Wilentz, Secy.
   The Eighth Street Bookshop, Inc.
   32 W. 8th St.
   New York 11, N. Y.

"Yes, with qualifications. If our culture emphasizes the material things in life as the 'better things in life,' the pressures of making a 'proper' living could destroy good habits that are being built up."

Herman B. Fox
   Fox & Sutherland
   15 S. Moger Ave.
   Mt. Kisco, N. Y.

"Reading, like any habit must find attraction, and as long as writers and teachers create a universal outlook, reading will continue.

Limited and circumscribed thoughts do not awaken further thought."

J. F. Albright
    Cokesbury
    1910 Main St.
    Dallas 1, Tex.

"Yes, they have been taught the value of books and reading."

Helen S. Lowitt
    The Magic Circle Book Shop
    10 Grace Ave.
    Great Neck, N. Y.

"Furthermore, *few* read for enjoyment and many find reading difficult. And they have no criteria for judgment as far as I can see, because they have read so little and have no vocabularies."

Tally McKee
    Book-Bargains-By-Mail
    516 Sherman Ave.
    Pittsburgh 12, Pa.

"Not really—compared to 50 or 100 years ago. Far too many sensate distractions."

Mildred L. Tingley
    Little Acorn Bookshop
    4 High St.
    Pawtucket, R. I.

"The colleges certainly seem to be trying to develop reading habits and I think *all* Americans are going to read more and better things in the future than they have in the past . . . that there is going to be a revulsion from materialism in this country . . . that it has already begun."

George E. Renison, Managing Director
W. H. Smith & Son (Canada) Ltd.
224 Yonge St.
Toronto, Canada

". . . I do not think most colleges at the present time truly encourage students to read for pleasure. Most colleges seem to have settled for the practice of putting a maximum amount of prescribed knowledge into the student's memory during his period at the university rather than presenting him with the maximum number of interesting problems which will take the rest of his life to answer."

Carl J. Miller
The Book Shop
115 W. Monroe St.
Sandusky, Ohio

"From my experience I must honestly state that college students may have better tastes in reading now than in the past . . . and yet . . . in literature and the humanities, no."

Robert A. Thornton, Jr., Mgr.
Cokesbury
150 Fifth Ave.
New York 11, N. Y.

"This question poses a very stringent problem, but my opinion would be that in the years immediately following college, reading habits slack off (probably for various reasons) for a number of years and then pick up again to the development of reading an average of 5 books a year."

W. R. Rockhill
Old Fort Books
811 S. Calhoun St.
Ft. Wayne, Ind.

"College students today are perhaps developing habits of reading good books, but the demands of earning a living will limit their reading time so much that these habits may drop by the wayside."

Marsh & Anne Cross
   Their Book Shop
   1410 S. Tejon St.
   Colorado Springs, Col.

"Not the majority—but the minority is as fervent as ever."

Question 6

E. Lichenstein
   Barnes & Noble, Inc.
   105 Fifth Ave.
   New York 3, N. Y.

"I find often that college students are a serious, thoughtful lot, and I think we will have a solid citizenry to anticipate."

Barr-Hurst Book Shop
   14–16 W. Orange St.
   Lancaster, Pa.

"We have no doubt that many college graduates of today don't read, but the percentage of those who do is rising, we feel. Many students of our local college buy books in our store, and certainly many local college graduates."

Good Office Supply Co.
   Tiffin, Ohio

"I believe people like to condemn the whole when it applies only to a few."

Hartman's Books, Inc.
   1513 Fifth Ave.
   Seattle 1, Wash.

"*NO,* as usual, the many who read are not sensationalists, so they don't get the publicity."

Jane Amann-Jones
Jane's Library Service
3328 17th St. N.W.
Washington 10, D. C.

"I believe the current 'bad reading habits' stem from the days of elementary school when the alphabet was thrown out."

Presbyterian Book Store
118 W. 5 St.
Charlotte 2, N. C.

"I believe their reading habits are poor and they are struggling to overcome them."

Fred S. Shields
Shields Books & Stationery
516 W. Lewis St.
P.O. Box 490
Pasco, Wash.

". . . that the reading requirements are more stringent in the smaller schools and the students are developing better reading habits. In the larger universities where mass classes are the rule there is more truth to the criticism. The top students and those who are genuinely interested in securing a good education are reading the better books and developing the good reading habits."

Smith & Butterfield
305–307 Main St.
Evansville 2, Ind.

"I think this is like the teen-age problem—the bad ones are publicized—the good ones aren't!"

Jane P. Brown
Wm. A. Brown Co.
Gloucester, Mass.

"I don't read of poor reading habits of *college students*. They are all working so hard to stay in the college of their choice, that they must spend most of their time with required reading."

John Joseph Hagedorn, Book Buyer
  Gimbels
  Philadelphia, Pa.

"Only in the field of their *magazine* habits; far too many still buy such trash as *Mad, Down Beat,* and even—alas—*Comics.* Far *too few* buy the quality magazines such as *Reporter, Progressive, Atlantic Monthly, Harper's Bazaar, Saturday Review, New Yorker."*

Herman B. Fox
  Fox & Sutherland
  15 S. Moger Ave.
  Mt. Kisco, N. Y.

"Current criticism of college students is based on the past habits of home and, to a great extent, on school environment. Books neatly arranged on shelves do not arouse the fascination for the contents. Quotation of the contents do attract attention and, with proper guidance, we find that both young and adults become aware of their own creative ability and comprehension."

Marvel W. Drought
  The Book Bay
  2628 N. Downer Ave.
  Milwaukee 11, Wis.

"Yes; my personal belief is that it stems from poor reading instruction with the 'new' methods used in the last 20 years."

Agatha E. R. Delaney
  Taga Book Shop
  53 Fourth St.
  Troy, N. Y.

"I don't think enough of our college students' reading is channeled in the right direction. More emphasis should be stressed in the selection of the correct type of reading. Lack of this tends to develop poor reading habits for which our college students are greatly criticized."

Mildred L. Tingley
Little Acorn Book Shop
4 High St.
Pawtucket, R. I.

"Yes, and some of the blame for it lies in the elementary schools where they were guinea pigs for the 'word recognition' system of learning to read before they knew the alphabet. We do a tremendous business in this town on books for remedial reading for all ages up through high school."

W. R. Rockhill
Old Fort Books
811 S. Calhoun St.
Ft. Wayne, Ind.

"We feel that the criticism of poor reading in college students may be valid in that many students enter college with poor reading and studying habits, but they are soon dropped. I have a personal notion that our elementary reading curriculum needs much revision to accommodate children with visual deficiencies that keep them from responding to the modern techniques of sight reading."

Carl J. Miller
The Book Shop
115 W. Monroe St.
Sandusky, Ohio

"I think that there is truth in the criticism of college students about poor reading habits . . . but, I believe, the criticism should be directed against family and secondary training."

⇘ 14 ⇙

Opinions of
College Librarians

Addressing the conference on "The Undergraduate and Lifetime Reading Interest," held at the University of Michigan on February 21–22, 1958, Dean Lester Asheim of the Graduate School of Library Science of the University of Chicago, spoke pessimistically of the findings of research:

"Reporting the findings of research on reading is always a thankless task. The findings are invariably discouraging to those who are interested in promoting the use of the book . . ."[1]

The numerous articles listed at the end of Dean Asheim's study represent perhaps the most significant studies of the reading of American college students in recent decades. Yet these studies, intensive as they are with respect to a single institution or a group of institutions, are limited in scope. Actually no one can speak for the reading tastes and habits of the millions of college students in our 2011 institutions of higher learning. At best, we can speak for only a portion of them.

The two preceding chapters have presented the opinions about book-buying and reading habits of our college students held by managers of college bookstores and owners or managers of commercial bookstores. Although only about one tenth of the bookstore managers expressed their opinions, there was a higher percentage of replies from the college librarians.

[1] Quoted from Dean Asheim's paper on "A Survey of Recent Research" in *Reading for Life,* edited by Jacob M. Price, Ann Arbor, University of Michigan Press, 1959, p. 3.

All institutions of higher education (2011) listed in Part 3 of the *Education Directory* of the U.S. Office of Education for 1959–1960 were addressed. Each librarian was asked a series of 6 questions about the reading habits and tastes of today's college students. They were invited to comment freely, and hundreds of frank and perceptive comments were made. A total of 467 librarians replied or 23.22% of all our college librarians. It is probable that their views represent the largest collection of its kind ever made, and as such they deserve careful consideration. The questions and the replies follow. A special section of opinions will follow the statistics and the generalizations that can be made.

QUESTION 1

Are college students reading more or fewer books, other than their required textbooks, than their predecessors of 10, 20, or 30 years ago, depending upon your own association with college students?

Yes (More)	No	Uncertain
230 (64.06%)	75 (20.08%)	38 (10.57%)

Related	Total	No Data*
16 (4.45%)	359	108

QUESTION 2

Are they reading more of the quality nonfiction books than before (i.e., 10, 20, or 30 years ago)?

Yes	No	Uncertain
241 (69.45%)	57 (16.42%)	43 (12.39%)

Related	Total	No Data
6 (1.72%)	347	120

* In calculating the percentages, only the replies with definite answers were included. Over 100 replies were received from librarians who either had no data, did not wish to venture an opinion, or had not been appointed long enough to make comparative judgments. By "related" we mean that replies were made but that they referred only tangentially to the questions.

QUESTION 3

Has the availability of the quality paperbacks made any impact upon their reading habits?

Yes	*No*	*Uncertain*	*Related*	*Total*	*No Data*
275 (77.46%)	44 (12.39%)	32 (9.01%)	4 (1.12%)	355	112

QUESTION 4

On the basis of your experience would you say that college students today have better tastes in reading than before?

Yes	*No*	*Uncertain*	*About the Same*
133 (39.46%)	107 (31.69%)	40 (11.86%)	26 (7.71%)

	Related	*Total*	*No Data*
	31 (9.11%)	337	130

QUESTION 5

Do you believe that college students are developing lifetime habits of reading good books for their pleasure, their self-improvement, their search for the better things in life?

Yes	*No*	*Uncertain*	*Related*	*Total*	*No Data*
199 (57.69%)	102 (29.56%)	31 (8.98%)	13 (3.76%)	345	122

QUESTION 6

Do you agree with the current criticism of the poor reading habits of college students we so often read in the popular magazines?

Yes	*No*	*Uncertain*	*Related*	*Total*	*No Data*
173 (51.03%)	114 (33.64%)	11 (3.24%)	41 (12.09%)	339	126

In the appendix all the libraries which responded are listed.

CONCLUSIONS

Although less than one fourth of the colleges and universities in the country responded to the inquiries, 41 states were represented, plus Washington, D. C., the Canal Zone, and Puerto Rico. Large universities as well as colleges with a few hundred students; state universities as well as private sectarian colleges; old as well as new colleges were represented. In short, what we have is as complete a sampling of opinion of librarians as is available anywhere. The following conclusions have been based on this sampling.

1. Almost two thirds of the college librarians believe that present-day college students are reading *more* nonrequired books than their predecessors of 10, 20 or 30 years ago. This is almost the exact percentage of commercial booksellers who believe that they are buying more books.

2. More than two thirds of the college librarians (69.45%) believe that present-day college students are reading more quality nonfiction than their predecessors.

3. More than three quarters of the college librarians believe that the availability of quality paperbacks has made an impact upon the reading habits of present-day college students.

4. Almost 40% of the librarians believe that today's college students have better tastes in reading. Thirty-one percent believe that their taste is worse.

5. The majority of the college librarians believe that present-day students are developing lifetime habits of reading good books.

6. The majority of the college librarians agree with the criticism of poor reading habits, although the reasons vary. More than a third do not agree.

It is of some interest to compare the replies to Questions 3 to 6 as given by the managers of college bookstores, managers of commercial bookstores, and college librarians.

Question 3—Paperbacks

Yes

College bookstore managers	97%
Commercial bookstore managers	78%
College librarians	77.46%

Question 4—Better Tastes in Reading

Yes

College bookstore managers	56.6%
Commercial bookstore managers	49.37%
College librarians	39.46%

Question 5—Lifetime Habits of Reading

Yes

College bookstore managers	63.20%
Commercial bookstore managers	53.75%
College librarians	57.69%

Question 6—Criticism of Reading

Yes

College bookstore managers	33.01%
Commercial bookstore managers	28.12%
College librarians	51.03%

Some interesting contradictions seem to exist in these replies. Although the majority of the librarians believe that our present-day students read more books, read more quality nonfiction, and are developing lifetime reading habits, yet 51% still agree with the criticism in the public press. All three groups of respondents agree on the impact of the quality paperbacks.

Many of the librarians explained their answers in considerable detail, and extracts from these replies now follow. They indicate the tremendous interest that our college librarians have in the reading habits of our students and their efforts in stimulating permanent reading interests. These replies indicate also some of the beliefs our librarians hold concerning the relationship between methods of instruction and withdrawal of books from the college library; the effect of the personality of the instructor and his own love for reading, upon the reading of his students; the relationship between the borrowing system of the library and the reading habits of the borrowers; the effect of movies and television upon reading (interesting differences of view are expressed); and the presence of plenty of good books.

Incomplete as these replies are from the standpoint of all the colleges in the land, they are probably as complete a representation of points of view to be found in any source at present.

TOTAL LIBRARIANS AND STATES REPRESENTED

1. Alabama	5	26. New Mexico	4
2. Arizona	3	27. New York	42
3. Arkansas	6	28. North Carolina	12
4. California	45	29. North Dakota	6
5. Colorado	5	30. Ohio	21
6. Connecticut	6	31. Oklahoma	8
7. Delaware	1	32. Oregon	8
8. District of Columbia	6	33. Pennsylvania	27
9. Georgia	17	34. Puerto Rico	1
10. Illinois	28	35. Rhode Island	2
11. Indiana	12	36. South Carolina	6
12. Iowa (State U.)	6	37. South Dakota	1
13. Kansas	11	38. Tennessee	7
14. Kentucky	6	39. Texas	11
15. Louisiana	5	40. Utah	3
16. Maine	6	41. Vermont	2
17. Maryland	12	42. Virginia	7
18. Massachusetts	21	43. Washington	8
19. Michigan	16	44. West Virginia	7
20. Minnesota	15	45. Wisconsin	10
21. Mississippi	5	46. Wyoming	1
22. Missouri	12	47. Canal Zone	1
23. Nebraska	6	Total	464
24. New Hampshire	3	Anonymous	3
25. New Jersey	11	Total	467

COLLEGES REPRESENTED IN THE SURVEY
(BY STATE)

Alabama

Alabama College	Montevallo, Alabama
Athens College	Athens, Alabama
Birmingham-Southern College	Birmingham, Alabama
Miles College	Birmingham, Alabama
St. Bernard College	St. Bernard, Alabama

Arizona

Arizona State College	Flagstaff, Arizona
Grand Canyon College	Phoenix, Arizona
Phoenix College	Phoenix, Arizona

Arkansas

Hardin College	Searcy, Arkansas
Henderson State Teachers College	Arkadelphia, Arkansas
Hendrix College	Conway, Arkansas
Shorter College	North Little Rock, Arkansas
Little Rock University	Little Rock, Arkansas
University of Arkansas	Fayetteville, Arkansas

California

Army Language School	Presidio of Monterey, California
California Institute of Technology	Pasadena, California
College of Marin	Kentfield, California
College of the Holy Names	Oakland, California
College of the Siskiyous	Weed, California
Compton College	Compton, California
Foothill College District	Mountain View, California
Fresno City College	Fresno, California
Fuller Theological Seminary	Pasadena, California
Glendale College	Glendale, California
Immaculate Heart College Library	Los Angeles, California
Los Angeles Conservatory of Music	Hollywood, California
Los Angeles Trade Technical Junior College	Los Angeles, California
Marymount College	Los Angeles, California
Menlo School and College	Menlo Park, California
Occidental College	Los Angeles, California

Palomar College	San Marco, California
Palo Verde College	Blythe, California
Pasadena City College	Pasadena, California
Sacramento City College	Sacramento, California
Sacramento State College	Sacramento, California
San Diego State College	San Diego, California
San Fernando Valley State College	Northridge, California
San Jose City College	San Jose, California
Santa Monica City College	Santa Monica, California
Santa Rosa Junior College	Santa Rosa, California
St. Mary College	St. Mary, California
Scipps College	Claremont, California
Sierra College	Auburn, California
Southern California School of Theology	Claremont, California
University of California	Davis, California
University of California	La Jolla, California
University of California	Riverside, California
University of San Diego	San Diego, California
University of San Francisco	San Francisco, California
University of Santa Clara	Santa Clara, California
	Chico, California
Los Angeles County Art Institute	Los Angeles, California
Bakersfield College	Bakersfield, California
University of California	Berkeley, California
University of California	Los Angeles, California
Fresno State College	Fresno, California
Stanford University	Stanford, California
San Bernardino Valley College	San Bernardino, California
San Jose State College	San Jose, California

Colorado

Colorado College	Colorado Springs, Colorado
Colorado School of Mines	Golden, Colorado
Colorado State College	Greeley, Colorado
University of Colorado	Boulder, Colorado

Connecticut

Berkeley Divinity School	New Haven, Connecticut
Connecticut College	New London, Connecticut
Danbury State College	Danbury, Connecticut
University of Connecticut	Storrs, Connecticut

| Wesleyan University | Middletown, Connecticut |
| Yale University | New Haven, Connecticut |

Delaware

| Goldey Beacon School of Business | Wilmington, Delaware |

Washington, D. C.

District of Columbia Teachers
   College
Gallaudet College
Majorie Webster Junior College
Oblate College
Trinity College
Washington Missionary College

Florida

Barry College	Miami, Florida
Embry Riddle Aeronautical	
Institute	Miami, Florida
Florida Christian College	Tampa, Florida
Florida State University	Tallahassee, Florida
Orlando Junior College	Orlando, Florida
Gulf Coast Junior College	Panama City, Florida
St. Petersburg Junior College	St. Petersburg, Florida
Stetson University	DeLand, Florida
University of Miami	Coral Gables, Florida

Georgia

Armstrong College	Savannah, Georgia
Atlanta University	Atlanta, Georgia
Emmanuel College	Franklin Springs, Georgia
Georgia Institute of Technology	Atlanta, Georgia
Georgia Military College	Milledgeville, Georgia
Georgia Southwestern College	Americus, Georgia
Interdenominational Theological	
Center	Atlanta, Georgia
North Georgia College	Dahlonega, Georgia
Norman College	Norman Park, Georgia
Piedmont College	Demorest, Georgia
Savannah State College	Savannah, Georgia
Southern State College of Pharmacy	Atlanta, Georgia
Paine College	Augusta, Georgia

Wesleyan College	Macon, Georgia
University of Georgia	Athens, Georgia
Georgia State College	Atlanta, Georgia
Mercer University	Macon, Georgia

Idaho

Idaho State College	Pocatello, Idaho
North Idaho Junior College	Coeur D'Alene, Idaho

Illinois

Amundsen Junior College	Chicago, Illinois
Art Institute of Chicago	Chicago, Illinois
Belleville Junior College	Belleville, Illinois
Bradley University	Peoria, Illinois
Carthage College	Carthage, Illinois
Chicago City Junior College	Chicago, Illinois
Chicago-Kent College of Law	Chicago, Illinois
Chicago Theological Seminary	Chicago, Illinois
Chicago Medical College	Chicago, Illinois
Felician College	Chicago, Illinois
Greenville College	Greenville, Illinois
Illinois College	Jacksonville, Illinois
Illinois State Normal University	Normal, Illinois
Kendall College	Evanston, Illinois
Lincoln College	Lincoln, Illinois
Lyons Township High School and Junior College	La Grange, Illinois
Moody Bible Institute	Chicago, Illinois
Northern Illinois State College	DeKalb, Illinois
Principia College of Liberal Arts	Elsah, Illinois
Rosary College	River Forest, Illinois
Saint Xavier College	Chicago, Illinois
Springfield Junior College	Springfield, Illinois
Southern Illinois University	Carbondale, Illinois
University of Chicago	Chicago, Illinois
University of Illinois	Urbana, Illinois
Northwestern University	Evanston, Illinois
Wheaton College	Wheaton, Illinois
	Moline, Illinois

Indiana

Anderson College	Anderson, Indiana
Butler University	Indianapolis, Indiana

Concordia Senior College	Fort Wayne, Indiana
DePauw University	Greencastle, Indiana
Indiana State Teachers College	Terre Haute, Indiana
Lain Technical Institute	Indianapolis, Indiana
Marion College	Marion, Indiana
Oakland City College	Oakland City, Indiana
St. Benedict College	Ferdinand, Indiana
Valparaiso University	Valparaiso, Indiana
West Baden College	West Baden Springs, Indiana
University of Notre Dame	Notre Dame, Indiana

Iowa

Marycrest College	Davenport, Iowa
Mason City Junior College	Mason City, Iowa
Webster City Junior College	Webster City, Iowa
William Penn College	Oskaloosa, Iowa
Iowa State University of Science and Technology	Ames, Iowa
University of Dubuque	Dubuque, Iowa

Kansas

Baker University	Baldwin, Kansas
Bethany College	Lindsborg, Kansas
Coffeyville College	Coffeyville, Kansas
Friends University	Wichita, Kansas
Junior College and Senior High School	Fort Scott, Kansas
Kansas State University of Agriculture and Applied Science	Manhattan, Kansas
Sterling College	Sterling, Kansas
Tabar College	Hillsboro, Kansas
University of Kansas	Lawrence, Kansas
University of Kansas City	Kansas City, Kansas

Kentucky

Georgetown College	Georgetown, Kentucky
Nazareth College	Louisville, Kentucky
Paducah Junior College	Paducah, Kentucky
St. Mary's College	St. Mary, Kentucky
University of Kentucky	Lexington, Kentucky
Western Kentucky State College	Bowling Green, Kentucky

Louisiana

Centenary College of Louisiana	Shreveport, Louisiana
Dillard University	New Orleans, Louisiana
Tulane University	New Orleans, Louisiana
Southern University	Baton Rouge, Louisiana
Louisiana State University	Baton Rouge, Louisiana

Maine

Bates University	Lewiston, Maine
Bowdoin College	Brunswick, Maine
Colby College	Waterville, Maine
Nasson College	Springvale, Maine
Westbrook Junior College	Portland, Maine
Washington State Teachers College	Machias, Maine

Maryland

U.S. Naval Academy	Annapolis, Maryland
Eastern College of Commerce and Law	Baltimore, Maryland
Frederick Community College	Frederick, Maryland
Goucher College	Towson, Baltimore, Maryland
Hood College	Frederick, Maryland
Montgomery Junior College	Takoma Park, Maryland
St. Charles College	Catonsville, Maryland
St. Joseph College	Emmitsburg, Maryland
St. Mary's Seminary Junior College	St. Mary's City, Maryland
State Teachers College	Salisbury, Maryland
University of Maryland	College Park, Maryland
Woodstock College	Woodstock, Maryland

Massachusetts

Amherst College	Amherst, Massachusetts
Babson Institute	Babson Park, Massachusetts
Boston College	Chestnut Hill, Massachusetts
Boston University	Boston, Massachusetts
Harvard College	Cambridge, Massachusetts
Lasell Junior College	Auburndale, Massachusetts
Massachusetts Institute of Technology	Cambridge, Massachusetts
Massachusetts School of Art	Boston, Massachusetts
Mount Holyoke College	South Hadley, Massachusetts

New Bedford Institute of Technology	New Bedford, Massachusetts
New England College of Pharmacy	Boston, Massachusetts
Newton Junior College	Newtonville, Massachusetts
Nichols College	Budley, Massachusetts
Northampton Commercial College	Northampton, Massachusetts
State Teachers College	Boston, Massachusetts
State Teachers College	Bridgewater, Massachusetts
University of Massachusetts	Amherst, Massachusetts
Woods Hole Oceanographic Institution	Woods Hole, Massachusetts
Worcester Polytechnic Institute	Worcester, Massachusetts

Michigan

Adrian College	Adrian, Michigan
Calvin College and Seminary	Grand Rapids, Michigan
Central Michigan University	Mount Pleasant, Michigan
Community College Library	Muskegon, Michigan
Emmanuel Missionary College	Berrien Springs, Michigan
General Motors Institute	Flint, Michigan
Henry Ford Community College	Dearborn, Michigan
Hillsdale College	Hillsdale, Michigan
Eastern Michigan University	Ypsilanti, Michigan
Western Michigan University	Kalamazoo, Michigan
Michigan State University	East Lansing, Michigan
Northern Michigan College	Marquette, Michigan
Suomi College	Hancock, Michigan
University of Michigan	Ann Arbor, Michigan
Wayne State University	Detroit, Michigan
Western Theological	Holland, Michigan

Minnesota

University of Minnesota	Minneapolis, Minnesota
Northwestern College	Minneapolis, Minnesota
College of Saint Teresa	Winona, Minnesota
Augsburg College	Minneapolis, Minnesota
Bemidji State College	Bemidji, Minnesota
Brainerd Junior College	Brainerd, Minnesota
College of Saint Benedict	Saint Joseph, Minnesota
The College of Saint Catherine	Saint Joseph, Minnesota
Minnesota Bible College	Minneapolis, Minnesota
North Central Bible College	Minneapolis, Minnesota

St. Cloud State College	St. Cloud, Minnesota
St. John's University	Collegeville, Minnesota
Macalester College	Saint Paul, Minnesota
Rochester Junior College	Rochester, Minnesota
Moorhead State College	Moorhead, Minnesota

Mississippi

Blue Mountain College	Blue Mountain, Mississippi
Mary Holmes Junior College	West Point, Mississippi
Mississippi State College for Women	Columbus, Mississippi
Mississippi State University	State College, Mississippi
Tougaloo Southern Christian College	Tougaloo, Mississippi

Missouri

Central College	Fayette, Missouri
College of St. Theresa	Kansas City, Missouri
Culver-Stockton College	Canton, Missouri
Harris Teachers College	St. Louis, Missouri
Kansas City Art Institute	Kansas City, Missouri
Kemper School	Boonville, Missouri
Maryville College of the Sacred Heart in St. Louis	St. Louis, Missouri
Southwest Baptist College	Bolivar, Missouri
Southwest Missouri State College	Springfield, Missouri
St. Louis University	St. Louis, Missouri
University of Missouri	Columbia, Missouri
Washington University	St. Louis, Missouri

Nebraska

Union College	Lincoln, Nebraska
Dana College	Blair, Nebraska
McCook College	McCook, Nebraska
Midland College	Fremont, Nebraska
Nebraska State Teachers College	Peru, Nebraska
Nebraska State Teachers College	Wayne, Nebraska

New Hampshire

St. Anselm's College	Manchester, New Hampshire
Keene Teacher's College	Keene, New Hampshire
Dartmouth College	Hanover, New Hampshire

New Jersey

Drew University	Madison, New Jersey
Glassboro State College	Glassboro, New Jersey
Newark College of Engineering	Newark, New Jersey
Newark State Teachers College	Union, New Jersey
Paterson State College	Paterson, New Jersey
Rutgers University	Camden, New Jersey
Saint Peter's College	Jersey City, New Jersey
Stevens Institute of Technology	Hoboken, New Jersey
Theological Seminary	New Brunswick, New Jersey
Rutgers State University	New Brunswick, New Jersey
Westminster Choir College	Princeton, New Jersey

New Mexico

College of St. Joseph	Albuquerque, New Mexico
New Mexico Institute of Mining and Technology	Socorro, New Mexico
New Mexico College	University Park, New Mexico
New Mexico Western College	Silver City, New Mexico

New York

Niagara University	Niagara University, New York
Nazareth College of Rochester	Rochester, New York
Concordia Collegiate Institute	Bronxville, New York
Long Island University	Brooklyn, New York
Bard College	Annandale-on-Hudson, New York
Brooklyn Law School	Brooklyn, New York
Cazenovia Junior College	Cazenovia, New York
Hartwick College	Oneonta, New York
The College of Saint Rose	Albany, New York
Dominican College of Blauvelt	Blauvelt, New York
Elmira College	Elmira, New York
General Theological Seminary	New York, New York
Molloy Catholic College for Women	Rockville Centre, New York
Alfred University	Alfred, New York
Dutchess Community College	Poughkeepsie, New York
Bank Street College of Education	New York, New York
Keuka College	Keuka Park, New York
Ladycliffe College	Highland Falls, New York
La Salette Seminary	Altamount, New York
Maryknoll Sisters Motherhouse	Maryknoll, New York

New York Law School	New York, New York
Pratt Institute	Brooklyn, New York
Rensselaer Polytechnic Institute	Troy, New York
Roberts Wesleyan College	North Chili, New York
Rosary Hill College	Buffalo, New York
Russell Sage College	Troy, New York
St. Bernard's Seminary	Rochester, New York
Saint Joseph's Seminary	Dunwoodie, Yonkers, New York
State University of New York Agricultural and Technical Institute	Morrisville, New York
State University of New York Agricultural and Technical Institute	Cobleskill, New York
State University College on Long Island	Oyster Bay, New York
Mohawk Valley Technical Institute	Utica, New York
Orange County Community College	Middletown, New York
State University of New York College of Education	Oswego, New York
University of Rochester	Rochester, New York
City College	New York, New York
Columbia University	New York, New York
Cornell University	Ithaca, New York
New York University	New York, New York
State University of New York	Plattsburg, New York
University of Buffalo	Buffalo, New York
Syracuse University	Syracuse, New York

North Carolina

Atlantic Christian College	Wilson, North Carolina
Asheville-Biltmore College	Asheville, North Carolina
Bennett College	Greensboro, North Carolina
Duke University	Durham, North Carolina
Mars Hill College	Mars Hill, North Carolina
North Carolina State College	Raleigh, North Carolina
Pembroke	Pembroke, North Carolina
Pfeiffer College	Misenheimer, North Carolina
Pineland College	Salemburg, North Carolina
Warren Wilson College	Swannanoa, North Carolina
University of North Carolina	Chapel Hill, North Carolina

North Dakota

North Dakota School of Forestry	Bottineau, North Dakota
North Dakota State School of Science	Wahpeton, North Dakota
State Normal and Industrial College	Ellendale, North Dakota
State Teachers College	Dickinson, North Dakota
State Teachers College	Minot, North Dakota
State Teachers College	Valley City, North Dakota

Ohio

Hiram College	Hiram, Ohio
Baldwin-Wallace College	Berea, Ohio
Ashland College	Ashland, Ohio
Antioch College	Yellow Springs, Ohio
Bluffton College	Bluffton, Ohio
Case Institute of Technology	Cleveland, Ohio
Cincinnati Bible Seminary	Cincinnati, Ohio
Denison University	Granville, Ohio
Heidelberg College	Tiffin, Ohio
John Carrol University	Cleveland, Ohio
Mt. St. Mary's Seminary	Norwood, Ohio
Franklin University	Columbus, Ohio
Ohio College of Applied Science	Cincinnati, Ohio
University of Toledo	Toledo, Ohio
Wittenberg University	Springfield, Ohio
University of Cincinnati	Cincinnati, Ohio
University of Dayton	Dayton, Ohio
Kent State University	Kent, Ohio
Miami University	Oxford, Ohio
Ohio University	Athens, Ohio
Western Reserve University	Cleveland, Ohio

Oklahoma

University of Oklahoma	Norman, Oklahoma
Oklahoma State University	Stillwater, Oklahoma
Cameron State College	Lawton, Oklahoma
Connors State Agricultural College	Warner, Oklahoma
Eastern Oklahoma A & M College	Wilburton, Oklahoma
Oklahoma Christian College	Oklahoma City, Oklahoma

St. Gregory's College	Shawnee, Oklahoma
University of Tulsa	Tulsa, Oklahoma

Oregon

Lewis & Clark College	Portland, Oregon
George Fox College	Newberg, Oregon
Mt. Angel College	Mt. Angel, Oregon
Multnomah College	Portland, Oregon
Multnomah School of the Bible	Portland, Oregon
Northwest Christian College	Eugene, Oregon
Oregon State System of Higher Education	Corvallis, Oregon
University of Oregon	Eugene, Oregon

Pennsylvania

University of Pittsburgh	Pittsburgh, Pennsylvania
Elizabethtown College	Elizabethtown, Pennsylvania
Bryn Mawr College	Bryn Mawr, Pennsylvania
Allegheny College	Meadville, Pennsylvania
State Teachers College	Millersville, Pennsylvania
Alliance College	Cambridge Springs, Pennsylvania
Albright College	Reading, Pennsylvania
Beaver College	Jenkintown, Pennsylvania
Bucknell University	Lewisburg, Pennsylvania
Gettysburg College	Gettysburg, Pennsylvania
Juniata College	Huntingdon, Pennsylvania
Keystone Junior College	La Plume, Pennsylvania
Kings College	Wilkes Barre, Pennsylvania
Lebanon College	Annville, Pennsylvania
Jefferson Medical College	Philadelphia, Pennsylvania
Moore Institute of Art	Philadelphia, Pennsylvania
Muhlenberg College	Allentown, Pennsylvania
Philadelphia Museum School of Art	Philadelphia, Pennsylvania
Rosemont College	Rosemont, Pennsylvania
Seton Hill College	Greensberg, Pennsylvania
Susquehanna University	Selinsgrove, Pennsylvania
Thiel College	Greenville, Pennsylvania
York Junior College	York, Pennsylvania
University of Pennsylvania	Philadelphia, Pennsylvania
Pennsylvania State University	University Park, Pennsylvania
Temple University	Philadelphia, Pennsylvania
Carnegie Institute of Technology	Shenley Park, Pittsburgh, Pennsylvania

Puerto Rico

University of Puerto Rico   Rio Piedras, Puerto Rico

Rhode Island

Providence College   Providence, Rhode Island
Barrington College   Providence, Rhode Island

South Carolina

Newberry College   Newberry, South Carolina
Anderson College   Anderson, South Carolina
Furman University   Greenville, South Carolina
Lander College   Greenwood, South Carolina
Wofford College   Spartanburg, South Carolina
Medical College of South Carolina Charleston, South Carolina

South Dakota

Yankton College   Yankton, South Dakota

Tennessee

Tennessee Wesleyan College   Athens, Tennessee
Union University   Jackson, Tennessee
University of Tennessee   Knoxville, Tennessee
Bethel College   McKenzie, Tennessee
Meharry Medical College   Nashville, Tennessee
Milligan College   Milligan, Tennessee
Maryville College   Maryville, Tennessee

Texas

Alvin Junior College   Alvin, Texas
East Texas Baptist College   Marshall, Texas
LeTourneau Technical Institute
   of Texas   Lubbock, Texas
Navarro Junior College   Corsicana, Texas
Paris Junior College   Paris, Texas
Texas Lutheran College   Seguin, Texas
University of Dallas   Dallas, Texas
University of St. Thomas   Houston, Texas
Sam Houston State Teachers
   College   Huntsville, Texas
Baylor University   Waco, Texas

Utah

Brigham Young University	Provo, Utah
Westminster College	Salt Lake City, Utah
Weber College	Ogden, Utah

Vermont

Goddard College	Plainfield, Vermont
University of Vermont	Burlington, Vermont

Virginia

Radford College	Radford, Virginia
Eastern Mennonite College	Harrisonburg, Virginia
Mary Baldwin College	Staunton, Virginia
Sweet Briar College	Sweet Briar, Virginia
University of Virginia	Charlottesville, Virginia
Virginia Polytechnic Institute	Blacksburg, Virginia
Sullins College	Bristol, Virginia

Washington

Central Washington College of Education	Ellensburg, Washington
Eastern Washington College of Education	Cheney, Washington
Olympic College	Bremerton, Washington
St. Edwards Seminary	Kenmore, Washington
Seattle Pacific College	Seattle, Washington
Western Washington College of Education	Bellingham, Washington
University of Washington	Seattle, Washington
Grays Harbor College	Aberdeen, Washington

West Virginia

Davis and Elkins College	Elkins, West Virginia
Glenville State College	Glenville, West Virginia
Greenbrier College	Lewisburg, West Virginia
Shepherd College	Shepherdstown, West Virginia
West Liberty State College	West Liberty, West Virginia
West Virginia Wesleyan College	Buckhannon, West Virginia
Wheeling College	Wheeling, West Virginia

Wisconsin

Holy Family College	Manitowoc, Wisconsin
Marian College	Fond Du Lac, Wisconsin
County Teachers College	Richland Center, Wisconsin
Waushara County Teachers College	Wautoma, Wisconsin
Wisconsin State College and Institute of Technology	Platteville, Wisconsin
Wisconsin State College	Whitewater, Wisconsin
Wisconsin State College	La Crosse, Wisconsin
Wisconsin State College	River Falls, Wisconsin
Wisconsin State College	Oshkosh, Wisconsin
Viterbo College	La Crosse, Wisconsin

Wyoming

Northern Wyoming Community College	Sheridan, Wyoming

Canal Zone

Balboa High School and Canal
  Zone Junior College

SURVEY REPLIES FROM COLLEGE LIBRARIANS

Question 1

Wilma Heisser
  Phoenix College
  1202 W. Thomas Rd.
  Phoenix, Ariz.

"Yes. 58–59 we averaged 1,000 per month additional circulation over 57–58 and are running about 900 per month above last year (58–59)."

Thomas J. Toohey
  Glendale College
  1500 N. Verdugo Rd.
  Glendale 8, Calif.

"I would say that there has been a definite increase in the amount and the quality of the reading done by our students, but I'm afraid that most of it has been required by instructors."

Alec Ross
  Menlo School and College
  Menlo Park, Calif.

"Students are reading fewer books than did their predecessors of 10 years ago. They are also doing less reading in their required text books."

Norah E. Jones
  University of California
  The University Library
  Los Angeles 24, Calif.

"While college students are probably reading fewer books, other than their required textbooks, on their independent initiative, they are required to read more than before from faculty-suggested lists of collateral works which supplement their texts and lectures."

Wallace B. Hoffman
  Regis College
  W. 50th & Lowell Blvd.
  Denver 21, Colo.

"It is my impression that students are reading more books, other than their required textbooks, than their predecessors of 20 or 30 years ago. They are reading the same number of books as their predecessors of 10 years ago. There seems to be more reading done in the preparation of class work, term papers, etc., than was formerly the case."

Hazel A. Johnson
  Connecticut College Library
  New London, Conn.

"We believe that college students are reading more books, other than their required textbooks, than their predecessors of 10, 20 or

30 years ago. I believe however, that superior students have always read fairly widely."

James E. Skipper
  The University of Connecticut
  Storrs, Conn.

"With the improvement of library facilities and admission standards, it has been my observation that during the past 10 years students are reading more and better books. This general statement does not apply in institutions with an inadequate number of books, or where the faculty does not encourage reading. I don't believe that individual motivation to read has increased, but this factor can be influenced by proper encouragement."

H. Eugene Craig
  Interdenominational Theological Center
  Atlanta 15, Ga.

"Definitely, college students are reading more books. Their reading ability is far advanced over the student of 20 or 30 years ago which makes for faster and more reading. The economic condition enables them to be able to purchase more books of their own, and though the television takes up more of their time there is some stimulus to reading gained therefrom."

Annette Buurstra
  Calvin College and Seminary Library
  1345 Franklin St., S.E.
  Grand Rapids 6, Mich.

"They are reading more than 10 years ago. At least they are borrowing more books. Our student enrollment has increased 44% since 1950 but I found that in a comparative two week period the average number of books borrowed each day had increased nearly 200%. Of course, most of this is because of increased assignments of outside reading."

Willard O. Mishoff
Mississippi State College for Women
Columbus, Miss.

"On this campus, there is evidence that students do more reading than in past years primarily because more books and periodicals are available than formerly, on a greater variety of subjects. Reading requirements for many courses, moreover, are more extensive than in years past, due in a considerable degree to the widening range of knowledge in so many fields."

Arthur E. Jones, Jr.
Drew University
Madison, N. J.

"The average college student is required to do more reading today than at any time in the past. I suspect that the amount of non-required reading he does is about the same. The percentage of students of college age who attend college, however, has changed more radically than the reading habits of the average students."

Donald F. Cameron
Rutgers, The State University
New Brunswick, N. J.

"We at Rutgers are sure that undergraduates read more from the University Library than they did 25 years ago. . . ."

Ruth M. Miller
Hartwick College
Oneonta, N. Y.

"I think the college students are reading more books other than their required textbooks; however, I feel that this reading is forced on them. Textbook teaching has been frowned on for the last 10 years."

Frederick L. Taft
  Case Institute of Technology
  University Circle
  Cleveland 6, Ohio

"Case students read more books than they did 20 years ago because we make them do so, because we have more books in our library from which to select reading, and because engineering students seem to me to be more conscious of the necessity of reading now than then. Also, too, the students coming to engineering schools today are less narrowly interested."

Wanda J. Calhoun
  Heidelberg College
  Tiffin, Ohio

"I can only go back 10 years in my association with college students to the time when I was a college student myself, and I would say that the students today are reading slightly more books than we did when I was in college. Actually I think the amount of additional reading a college student does depends to a large extent upon the enthusiasm and encouragement of the faculty. Some professors naturally inspire students to do additional outside reading while other professors do not."

Ilo Fisher
  Wittenberg University
  Springfield, Ohio

"I believe they are reading more. In the first place, there are more books available than there were 10, 20 or 30 years ago, and they cover a wider variety of subject matter."

Robert D. Gault
  Northwest Christian College
  Eleventh & Alder
  Eugene, Ore.

"Students in our college have such a heavy study load of required material that they have very little opportunity for any additional reading. We have attempted to make available a selected browsing collection of good reading, but the students simply do not have the time to make much use of it. I believe that the students certainly have a vast amount of good reading material available to them today over what their predecessors had—of course much poorer literature, also."

Helen S. West
  Philadelphia Museum School of Art
  Broad & Pine Sts.
  Philadelphia 2, Pa.

"Our students are, I think, reading more books other than their texts than did their predecessors of 10 years ago. This is largely due to the fact that more of our students are taking degree courses today—not, unfortunately, due to increased interest in reading, per se."

Elizabeth C. Welborn
  Lander College
  Greenwood, S. C.

"Statistics which I have will be of little help to you. However, they show that circulation has doubled in the last 5 years. Still this says nothing for our enrollment has also doubled. Another factor enters in. We are doing more screening of those we take in which means that we are getting more intelligent students, and more intelligent students do more reading."

Martha Hackman
  Occidental College
  Los Angeles 41, California

"I would say that during the past three or four years there has been a noticeable increase in the amount of unassigned reading. This may be due in part to the increasingly superior type of student which we have been receiving. It may also reflect a change in teaching methods here, particularly in the Department of English, which seems to be stressing more and more the works of modern writers."

Mrs. James C. Bonner
  Georgia Military College
  Milledgeville, Georgia

"Fewer—but I believe they relate reading to television, to movies, to world events, making a depth of interest stimulated by all mediums of communications."

Mrs. Dorothy A. Bradley
  The Principia College of Liberal Arts
  Elsah, Illinois

"We believe the students are reading more now than in the past. However, we do not have any statistics for previous years to prove this. Our observation is that our students are doing very little reading for pleasure. A great deal of reading is required by our faculty."

Sister Margaret Mary
  Saint Joseph College
  Emmitsburg, Maryland

"I believe that college students are definitely reading more books, other than their required textbooks, than their predecessors of 10, 20 or 30 years ago. As far as the last 10 years are concerned, in our own library the annual circulation has risen from 4,173 to 20,704. This, I believe is due to an entirely different type of teaching and the addition of seminars and discussion groups to the curriculum."

Norma Hovden
  University of Minnesota
  Minneapolis 14, Minnesota

"Probably more but more superficially. Quantity versus quality."

B. H. D. Director of Libraries
Niagara University
Niagara University, New York

"My observation is that the same small group of college students spend their spare time in the library, and withdraw general reading books. Most of the others consult or withdraw books pertaining to their studies, or for aid in preparing term papers or other assignments."

Thelma R. Bumbaugh
Hiram College
Hiram, Ohio

"According to the figures available the students read 38.2 books per student in 1947–48 and 46.3 books per student in 1958–59."

Agnes E. Painter
Allegheny College
Meadville, Pennsylvania

"According to statistics that have been kept here since 1930, the average number of books used per student has not changed to any great extent over the years. The teaching methods have changed. There are fewer books on reserve which must be read in the Library. This means that there are more books taken on stack circulation. The general average remains the same."

R. C. Janeway
Texas Technological College
Lubbock, Texas

"College students are reading more. Ten years ago the average student borrowed 7 books for use outside the library. For 1958/59 that figure is 14. So far this year our circulation is running more than 25% over this time last year."

Clifford P. Wolfsehr
Central Washington College of Education
Ellensburg, Washington

"In my opinion (and judging from published reports of reading surveys) I believe that, *on the average,* college students are reading fewer books today than 10, 20 or 30 years ago, in spite of better collections and freer access to books. The evidence for this statement seems to me obvious and convincing."

Evelyn Crouch
West Virginia Wesleyan College
Buckhannon, West Virginia

"In my short experience with college students, I find them about the same as in former years. Most of the books used have to do directly with their school assignments. Many say they wish they had time to read other books, but they have too much else to do. However, there are a few who find the time and do read the outstanding books. There may be more than I realize."

Marian College
390 E. Division Street
Fond du Lac, Wis.

"Only because of multiplications of activities and the need for so many college students to work to meet financial needs."

Question 2

Abi Russell
Alabama College
Montevallo, Ala.

"More quality nonfiction books appear to be circulating in recent years. Since our college has been coeducational only four years, this may be due to the addition of men who are particularly interested in science and world affairs."

Alec Ross
Menlo School and College
Menlo Park, Calif.

"The reading of quality nonfiction is at an all time low in my experience."

Marvin W. Cragun
Sacramento City College
Sacramento 18, Calif.

"In some fields of nonfiction there has been a fairly lively interest. Biography has become more popular and the type of nonfiction which interprets some phase of historical period has also been in favor. Nonfiction as a whole does not fare so well as in the twenties."

Norah E. Jones
University of California
The University Library
Los Angeles 24, Calif.

"As simple pleasure-reading has declined, partly due to pressures of other time-consuming commitments, nonfiction has come to constitute the major part of the college students' reading. The authoritativeness and practical applicability of the nonfiction are qualities which are more likely to be valued than literary style."

Wallace B. Hoffman
Regis College
W. 50th & Lowell Blvd.
Denver 21, Colo.

"They are definitely reading more of the quality nonfiction books than before, but I feel that there are more quality nonfiction books to read than there were before. Specifically, I think you will agree that the works of Churchill are more interesting and readable than were the biographies of Pershing."

Sister Marita, CHM
Marycrest College
Davenport, Iowa

"Our collection is made up of nonfiction books and most of them circulate within the year. We have a small fiction section and what fiction they usually read is in connection with literature classes. The Public Library is used for nonfiction books as well."

Mother M. V. Coleman
Newton College of the Sacred Heart
885 Centre St.
Newton 59, Mass.

"I am aware that the students are reading much more nonfiction than they did before. They read around their subjects in history, political science, etc., and save fiction to read after heavy tests or a hard day. As an incentive, we have subject rooms with the newest and best books. . . ."

Willard C. Mishoff
Mississippi State College for Women
Columbus, Miss.

"The consensus here is that students are reading more quality non-fiction books than heretofore, because their interests are becoming broader, due possibly to such influences as television documentaries and travel experiences, to say nothing of newspapers and newsreels. Again, more attractive and popular nonfiction is available than formerly as is evident from the files of the *Publishers' Weekly.*"

John A. Sperry, Jr.
Culver-Stockton College
Canton, Mo.

"The quality of non-fiction books read by the small minority is good but here again I must emphasize that the vast majority of college students avoid reading like the plague."

Marie Winka
    Maryville College of the Sacred Heart in St. Louis
    St. Louis, Mo.

"Yes, they are reading better books—fiction and nonfiction; such as Dostoevski, Mauriac, Chekov, T. S. Eliot, Eugene O'Neill, and Thomas Merton."

Max Langham
    Nebraska State Teachers College
    Peru, Neb.

"Indications are, according to our statistics in circulation, that nonfiction reading surpasses fiction here. I am bothered by this, as other librarians too, in that we feel they are missing much *educational* and aesthetic experience in the process."

Edward A. Chapman
    Rensselaer Polytechnic Institute
    Troy, N. Y.

"Yes. As judged by our inability to keep our rack of better paperbacks attractively full. Believe format and colorfulness of the paperback an important factor in more voluntary student reading of quality nonfiction."

Thomas A. Hunt
    State Normal and Industrial College
    Ellendale, N. D.

"My reaction, personally, to the question concerning quality nonfiction books is a definite yes. This is definitely influenced, however, by the fact that coercion is placed upon individuals by the instructors of the college. Not only for term papers and individual projects, but also from the standpoint of additional reading assignments, the result is obtained."

Ilo Fisher
    Wittenberg University
    Springfield, Ohio

"I believe they are. We do not purchase many fiction books; only those that are representative in some way—author, style, reflections of the times, etc.—are purchased by our library. Practically all unassigned reading from library books is nonfiction."

Martha Hackman
    Occidental College
    Los Angeles 41, California

"A good deal of their reading is nonfiction, but I couldn't really say whether this has increased more in proportion to fiction."

Mrs. James C. Bonner
    Georgia Military College
    Milledgeville, Georgia

"In my opinion, if their teachers read, they read these. I find that the modern youth are perfectly able to make relationships. Many nonfiction books crystallize the conditions of our times, and I find that young men like to recognize the figures of speech suggested by such phrases as "the affluent society," "the organization man." I regard many quality nonfiction books as "building blocks" to acquiring contemporary vocabulary."

Mrs. Dorothy A. Bradley
    The Principia College of Liberal Arts
    Elsah, Illinois

"They are reading more quality nonfiction books for two reasons: first, we have a younger faculty who are reading themselves and discussing and recommending these books; second, more is being demanded of the students in the form of term papers or research writing."

Thelma R. Bumbaugh
Hiram College
Hiram, Ohio

"I do not have figures broken down for the 1947–48 reports so I do not know how much of this was nonfiction books. The percentage of nonfiction read in 1958–59 was 89.7 and I believe that this is a higher percentage than in former years."

Agnes E. Painter
Allegheny College
Meadville, Pennsylvania

"The students have never made any great use of the Library for fiction reading. There is little fiction buying other than that used directly or indirectly in literature courses."

R. C. Janeway
Texas Technological College
Lubbock, Texas

"Yes. While our general circulation has more than doubled, the circulation from our recreation collection has declined. It is my belief that recreational reading is being provided by inexpensive paperbacks."

Question 3

Fr. Frederick Smith, O.S.B.
St. Bernard College
St. Bernard, Ala.

"Paperbacks are tremendous, tho I don't care for them personally for library use, but they have given people books they could not afford before."

Raylene M. Steelman
Hendrix College
Conway, Ark.

"Yes, the resulting ease of acquiring books of their own has led to more reading. Relatively low cost leads more instructors to require purchase of these books for class-connected reading."

Thomas J. Toohey
    Glendale College
    1500 N. Verdugo Rd.
    Glendale 8, Calif.

"I think that the paperbacks have had an effect . . . that the instructors have added these books to their list of textbooks, and that few of the students, in great contrast to students in the colleges and universities in this area, buy any without the stimulus of class requirements."

Alec Ross
    Menlo School and College
    Menlo Park, Calif.

"The only observable impact of ready availability of quality paperbacks has been to lower the respect for books in general. (This has important consequences in terms of care of library books, but I assume that this is beyond the scope of your present investigation.)"

Mrs. Kent M. Dale
    Palo Verde College
    Blythe, Calif.

"From observations I would say that quality paperbacks have definitely made an impact upon the reading habits of students. Perhaps it is a 'back-door' method, but many are reading good literature in spite of themselves."

Marvin W. Cragun
    Sacramento City College
    Sacramento 18, Calif.

"What little interest shown in the nonfiction field is attributable, I believe, to the reprints now available of standard titles in quality paperbacks. It has also helped to reawaken an interest in the better fiction."

Norah E. Jones
University of California
The University Library
Los Angeles 24, Calif.

"The availability of many standard works in paperback format has certainly made it possible for students to buy for themselves a greater variety of good books than ever before. Long friendships with books which live on one's shelves are of course far preferable to brief acquaintances with books on mere visit from library collections, and the building of personal libraries is an important aspect of the development of lifetime reading habits. Faculty members watch paperback publication with great interest, and frequently choose as assigned readings those selections which their students may purchase cheaply. Students themselves naturally find paperbacks both convenient and attractive, and their easy accessibility is surely providing a wholesome stimulus to much worthwhile reading."

Hazel A. Johnson
Connecticut College Library
New London, Conn.

"Students at Connecticut College purchase and read many of the quality paperbacks. Our college book store stocks them rather heavily, and the girls do use them in many of their courses. They also include them in their entries in the Students Personal Libraries contest held each year."

James E. Skipper
The University of Connecticut
Storrs, Conn.

"To a limited extent, yes. Librarians are trying to promote building personal libraries through the purchase of paperbacks and are attempting to get faculty to require their purchase, rather than placing textbooks on assigned reading shelves in libraries."

John W. Pattillo
Georgia Institute of Technology
Atlanta 13, Ga.

"We believe that paperbacks have made a substantial impact on student reading habits. Our college bookstore stocks a wide variety and we are in the process of establishing a paperback collection in the library. The aim of this collection will be to provide additional copies of popular books and the classics, and to provide books which we would not normally buy in hard back editions. We would not be doing this if the interest did not warrant it."

H. Eugene Craig
Interdenominational Theological Center
Atlanta 15, Ga.

"Yes. The vast sales in this area attest to this. Actually many students have discovered the Bible through the paperbacks."

Robert M. Lightfoot, Jr.
Bradley University
Peoria, Ill.

"The availability of quality paperbacks has undoubtedly had some effect—but they have been available too short a time for anything like an accurate measure of this effect to be made yet."

Sister M. Tobias, O.P.
Rosary College
River Forest, Ill.

"I believe paperbacks have definitely affected the reading of our students, but primarily in the curricular areas—required and recommended reading. This is our first year for our paperback book shop, and it is well patronized, with steady sales. There seems to be a great enthusiasm and appreciation of the paperbacks at least among a small group of eager readers."

H. L. Boisen
  Butler University Library
  Indianapolis 7, Ind.

"The availability of paperbacks has made a difference in the buying of books; who can say if it has made an impact upon reading? I know some people who do wishful buying but never get to reading."

Fred W. Hanes
  Indiana State Teachers College
  Terre Haute, Ind.

"Very little. Students with intellectual interests—a small minority of American college students—find the quality paperbacks a means to an inexpensive personal library. The average student's reading habits have not been affected."

Luella C. Benson
  Nasson College
  Springvale, Me.

"The availability of quality paperbacks has made some difference in what the students are reading. Our town does not have a real book store. There is one store which deals entirely in paperbacks, but it does not lean very heavily toward the quality titles. However, it will, and frequently does order any title a student wants. . . ."

Mother M. V. Coleman
  Newton College of the Sacred Heart
  885 Centre St.
  Newton 59, Mass.

". . . Background reading is needed for their essays; so without a doubt paperbacks have made profound increases in their reading habits. They are beginning to love reading."

Mrs. W. H. Greely
  Newton Junior College
  Newtonville 60, Mass.

"Yes, indeed! Students will ignore a hardbound title, quality or nonquality, and borrow or even buy the same title in paperback. The library at N.J.C. sells paperbacks for the convenience of the students and this is proved daily. We try to be selective."

Hugh Montgomery
  University of Massachusetts
  Amherst, Mass.

"The inexpensive paperback has helped the teaching program in providing worthwhile books in quantity and has brought back into print a number of worthwhile, formerly out of print, classics."

Annette Buurstra
  Calvin College and Seminary Library
  1345 Franklin St., S.E.
  Grand Rapids 6, Mich.

"Our bookstore manager reports that the sale of quality paperbacks continues to increase. I think more of the classics and current nonfiction are read because they are more attractive and available in paperback editions."

John A. Sperry, Jr.
  Culver-Stockton College
  Canton, Mo.

"There can be no question that the quality paper books have a great influence upon the reading habits. Unfortunately the distribution of quality paper books is uneven and in our particular region it is extremely difficult to get good paperback books other than by mail."

Marie Winka
Maryville College of the Sacred Heart in St. Louis
St. Louis, Mo.

"Yes, the quality paperbacks have made an effect on their reading habits at least judging by the number they buy. In our library we sell a limited amount of paperbacks. They are very popular with the girls and it is quite consoling how many good things they buy just because they are available in the inexpensive edition."

Arthur E. Jones, Jr.
Drew University
Madison, N. J.

"The availability of paperbacks has meant, so far as I can judge, more ownership of the books the student reads and perhaps less dependence upon the Library for these. It has contributed to the quality of materials read simply by virtue of making so many titles readily available."

Andrew L. Bouwhuis S.J.
Saint Peter's College
2645 Hudson Blvd.
Jersey City 6, N. J.

"Paperbacks have contributed a great deal, the owner can read at his leisure; he can reread; he owns, and ownership is practically essential. The range in quality and quantity will depend on the stimulus given by the instructor."

Ruth M. Miller
Hartwick College
Oneonta, N. Y.

"We have recently added a collection of paperbacks to the resources of the college bookstore. They are being sold to our students in surprising numbers. However, it is quite possible that they deal directly with the courses being taught. One can always hope that availability of this type of book will have a positive impact on students' reading habits."

Elena Horton
Orange County Community College
Middletown, N. Y.

". . . I would say that quality paperbacks have not been available to the students until quite recently in the college community. The college bookstore reports that they sell quite well. This may have affected their reading habits in the library, and probably has to the extent of stimulating increased reading of certain authors."

Thomas A. Hunt
State Normal and Industrial College
Ellendale, N. D.

"Quality paperbacks have had a definite influence upon reading habits—again a personal reaction. This is an agricultural community and the financial resources of the students are not such to warrant expensive books for individual usage. It has been my pleasure to note students purchasing quality paperbacks for individual usage. . . ."

D. W. Ferguson
State Teachers College
Valley City, N. D.

"I cannot see that the paperbacks have changed the situation greatly. My impression is that the average student is averse to spending money on books of any kind—of course, there are exceptions. In general, I think that the largest market for quality paperbacks is among more mature readers."

Frederick L. Taft
Case Institute of Technology
University Circle
Cleveland 6, Ohio

"Yes, an enormous one, for many students seem to buy them even though we have multiple copies available for their humanities courses on reserve."

Lois E. Engleman
  Denison University
  Granville, Ohio

"On this campus, at least, I believe the availability of quality paperbacks has made a decided impact on the reading habits of our students; in addition to increased classroom use of paperbacks, students have bought widely perhaps up to 10,000 copies a year from the broad book stock available in the college book store. . . ."

Ilo Fisher
  Wittenberg University
  Springfield, Ohio

"It certainly has. I think the reading public has obtained much satisfaction from 'quality' paperbacks. Our library is stocking them and we are encouraging students to purchase 'quality' paperbacks. We have had students purchase a hardback for study at home and a paperback of the same title for use in class."

Robert D. Gault
  Northwest Christian College
  Eleventh & Alder
  Eugene, Ore.

"Some of our faculty members actually encourage students to purchase paperback editions of worthy books. Many of the professors have collections of these editions in their own libraries. The availability of 3 such stores within a two-block radius of the campus also encourages this type of thing."

Martha Hackman
  Occidental College
  Los Angeles 41, California

"There seems to be a connection between the availability of quality paperbacks and the increase in reading, although which is cause and which effect I couldn't say. Most students do seem to be aware of the potentialities of the paperback market."

Sister Margaret Mary
    Saint Joseph College
    Emmitsburg, Maryland

"The availability of quality paperbacks has affected to some extent the reading of our students. This is particularly true in the case where novels must be read for a course. Formerly, the Library was supposed to supply these books and since sometimes the copies were not adequate, the books were too often only skimmed or perhaps not read at all."

Norma Hovden
    University of Minnesota
    Minneapolis, Minnesota

"Yes, easier and cheaper access to books allows them to build up an inexpensive library."

Ruth Gibbons
    Union University
    Jackson, Tennessee

"Very definitely the availability of quality paperbacks has influenced reading habits. We sell paperbacks in our library and I am convinced students buy them who would not otherwise buy books. Also, I believe taste in reading is improving among college students."

Sadie A. Hartzler
    Eastern Mennonite College
    Harrisonburg, Virginia

"Decidedly. Cheapness of these items permits those who want to buy books to do so. The attractive covers, the pull of others buying, etc., cause many to buy and read "

John Cook Wyllie
University of Virginia
Charlottesville, Virginia

"Yes. E.g., when a movie like *The Brothers Karamazov* hits town, formerly the first dozen people who wanted to read the book could get it from the library. Paperbacks enable us to stockpile quickly against sudden demands, so that last year in a period of one month, between two and three hundred people read this book. Similarly, when Faulkner was Writer in Residence, the circulation of paperback Faulkners ran into four figures here."

Clifford P. Wolfsehr
Central Washington College of Education
Ellensburg, Washington

"Of course the availability of the quality paperbacks has made an impact upon the reading habits of college students. . . . The point of significance is, are they reading and buying as many quality paperbacks as one should hope or expect? Only on campuses with solid and unusual academic programs (such as Reed College, in Portland, Oregon) does one find vigorous merchandising of quality paperbacks. . . . Again, do we want to be satisfied with a little improvement? An evaluation of the impact of quality paperbacks should be made in terms of the as-yet disproportionate and unfortunate gap between general use and potential value."

Question 4

Abi Russell
Alabama College
Montevallo, Ala.

"As for better tastes in reading, I am often encouraged with what some freshmen have read in high school and are interested in reading while in college; but much too frequently we encounter the opposite type who select their books on the basis of those with the fewest pages. The mature students—many of the men who have had Army, Navy and Air Force training—show discrimination in their selections."

Mrs. Adrian Hughes
  Birmingham-Southern College
  Birmingham 4, Ala.

"Taste is created by having the best available and *publicized!* The library has owned many of the same titles now in paperback which have circulated perhaps once or twice to those who may have responded when the title was on a new book shelf or best seller list or on special display. The fact that the professors have taken a shine to the paperbacks and push them in class has resulted in the tremendous rush to purchase by so many students. The circulation and browsing in a college library should be in the care of a book-oriented, enthusiastic personality. If that were the situation I would have better means for comparison for you."

Alec Ross
  Menlo School and College
  Menlo Park, Calif.

"On the basis of my experience college students have less 'taste' in reading than did their predecessors of 10 years ago. To develop reading taste one must read."

Mrs. Kent M. Dale
  Palo Verde College
  615 E. Hobsonway
  Blythe, Calif.

". . . I find this trend: our superior students read good books and have good habits; our average students would like to read more but because of regular school work and the pressure of outside activities have little time for reading; our poor students seldom read anything they are not compelled to read."

Marvin W. Cragun
    Sacramento City College
    Sacramento 18, Calif.

"I should say that college students today have less good taste than those of a generation ago, poorer judgment, and only a small spoonful of imagination."

Norah E. Jones
    University of California
    The University Library
    Los Angeles 24, Calif.

"In their search for definite and reliable information, college students are anxious to consult reputable and authoritative works, and show an exacting critical sense in selecting these."

Wallace B. Hoffman
    Regis College
    Denver 21, Colo.

"No, but in some cases it definitely depends upon the home background. We also notice that movies will in some cases cause students to read specific classics, such as the current interest in *Ben Hur.*"

John W. Pattillo
    Georgia Institute of Technology
    Atlanta 13, Ga.

"Georgia Tech is a state college. Therefore we have students from widely varying backgrounds. There are those who have developed and are continuing to develop good reading habits. And of course there are those who have not and probably never will. Perhaps some of these will respond to library encouragement. At any rate we hope so and feel that the effort is very much worth while."

Eli M. Oboler
    Idaho State College
    Pocatello, Idaho

"In general, I would say that college students definitely do have better tastes in reading than the group which was attending college during the late '40's and early '50's. Part of this is due to the paperback habit, part of this is due to better college libraries, and part of this is due to more inspiration by college faculty toward good reading."

Robert M. Lightfoot, Jr.
    Bradley University
    Peoria, Ill.

". . . I'd say the older generation was ahead; in other words, the top 25% of a generation ago probably had better tastes than the top 25% today, simply because it was a more selective group then than now."

Fred W. Hanes
    Indiana State Teachers College
    Terre Haute, Ind.

"I am not sure what you mean by 'better tastes.' If you mean more intelligent and discriminating tastes, I would say no. The American student, like his parents, lets high-powered comments of critics, etc., form the basis for his judgments. While he is not so prone as earlier generations to let traditional values influence his tastes, he is more susceptible to predigested views firmly implanted by the mass media of communication."

Valdon L. Johnson
    Webster City Junior College
    Webster City, Iowa

"I sincerely believe that literature is 'feeling the pinch' of our present stress on technology. More and more students are requiring that a book fill a 'practical' purpose. Some students who do read fiction, poetry, and so forth, are devoting themselves to the modern literature of revolt—a sort of mid-century Dadaism. It seems that the literary appetite of a majority of our students today can be satisfied only by the reading of contemporary works."

Sarah White Jackson
    Westbrook Junior College
    Portland 5, Me.

"What is one man's taste is another's torment! I really can't say on this one. I find lively student interest in course readings that are on what is generally conceded to be a high literary level. But I also find that most students have little if any background to this reading."

A. P. Valakis
    New England College of Pharmacy
    70–72 Mt. Vernon St.
    Boston 8, Mass.

"The mass media have so influenced our students that even though they may be reading more, their 'taste' has remained unaltered. T.V., radio, journalism, and Madison Avenue are not interested in improving taste; they are interested in selling products. Tragically enough, they have succeeded in both of these interests."

Mother M. V. Coleman
    Newton College of the Sacred Heart
    885 Centre St.
    Newton 59, Mass.

"On the basis of my experience, I would say that college students today have far better tastes in reading than before, chiefly because of their special guidance on the part of trained teachers and professors, who are more conscious of their duties than before."

Max Langham
    Nebraska State Teachers College
    Peru, Neb.

"Question four intrigues me. Taste in this sense cannot be implied except by observation of what is being read. A close scrutiny of individual discrimination in free selection would seem to show lesser tastes according to the standards of a decade or more ago. However, the new age brings with it more than was encompassed a few short years ago and such transitory seeking would not be conclusive for a period of time yet. I think the student's reading reflects experimentation rather than taste at this point in his life."

Edward A. Chapman
Rensselaer Polytechnic Institute
Troy, N. Y.

"Unable to give a direct reply but more and more students seem to be aware of book review media such as New York *Times Book Review,* etc., requesting items ahead of normal staff selection."

Mildred Larsson
North Dakota State School of Science
Wahpeton, N. D.

"Probably they do. There has probably been a decline in the reading of romanticized material and a corresponding literary increase of material of a sociologic nature."

Thomas A. Hunt
State Normal and Industrial College
Ellendale, N. D.

"The quality of reading taste is improving locally. My experience of the past four years is such that a feeling of optimism is present. A large percentage of the majors of elementary education classes and English classes is presently realizing the deficiency of earlier reading training. Standard fiction is read to improve the background. My thinking is such that those individuals will develop a reading habit which will carry into the teaching field—and add to the effectiveness of the individual as an individual or as a teacher. This is one element which is stressed in literature and library-science-reading courses."

Ilo Fisher
   Wittenberg University
   Springfield, Ohio

"There are less taboos on the selections of reading titles than there were some years back. From that point of view, I think students are doing wider reading and are interested in more subjects. I am a little uncertain as to the interpretation of the word 'tastes.' One young fellow told me that he doesn't like any of the modern poetry because it is so much concerned with content that he feels the style is sacrificed. When he wants to read poetry, he reads the old masters. This is one instance, but it may be indicative."

Helen S. West
   Philadelphia Museum School of Art
   Broad and Pine Sts.
   Philadelphia 2, Pa.

"I feel that students of today have been poorly prepared in their secondary schools in the matter of taste in reading—or indeed reading at all. Some of our students freely admit that until they came to us they had done so little reading that they were appalled at the thought of actually reading a *whole* book. This sounds incredible, but it is true!"

Donald F. Cameron
   Rutgers, The State University
   New Brunswick, N. J.

"My own opinion is that more good books are being read in colleges now than in the past, and that fewer textbooks are being read. This I call a very good sign. I hope you agree with me."

Martha Hackman
   Occidental College
   Los Angeles 41, California

"This, of course, depends upon what you mean by better. I believe they are less repelled by the brutal, the sordid, the pessimistic in their reading. A paperback collection selected for the Browsing Room by a student committee about two years ago gives an idea of the type of reading students choose. Authors included are, among others, D. H. Lawrence, Scott Fitzgerald, Baudelaire, Gide, Rilke, etc., all rebels and outcasts of previous generations. There is also a heavy representation in the fields of philosophy and religion as represented by Sartre, Heidegger, Jaspers, Niebuhr, etc."

Norma Hovden
University of Minnesota
Minneapolis 14, Minnesota

"Probably wider tastes because they are exposed to information about books by communication media but not better."

Agnes E. Painter
Allegheny College
Meadville, Pennsylvania

"I doubt that the reading tastes of the student of today are any better, or any worse, than those of the student of the thirties. Our students read, or say they read, everything from comic books to Proust (they buy the comic books, we furnish Proust) and from Kant to Will Rogers."

R. C. Janeway
Texas Technological College
Lubbock, Texas

"Taste is difficult to measure, but with students borrowing more books from the college library, improved taste is an anticipated concomitant."

John Cook Wyllie
University of Virginia
Charlottesville, Virginia

"No. There are vastly more students who read, but to compare the hundreds who read widely 30 years ago with the thousands who read widely today shows nothing in favor of either group. Students, naturally trying to participate in the spirit and vivacity of their own age, tend to be enamored of the contemporary, and your question therefore boils down to whether contemporary literature is better now than X-number of years ago. I personally think it is neither better nor worse, only more contemporary."

Clifford P. Wolfsehr
   Central Washington College of Education
   Ellensburg, Washington

"My answer to the previous question, of course, forms the basis of a *No* to this question. I fail to see any convincing evidence that 'the average college student' (who is lower than his counterpart of years gone by simply because of the inevitable lowering of standards with the rise of mass education: greatly increased quantity inevitably tends to diminish quality), has better taste than before."

Robert Hertel
   Illinois State Normal University
   Normal, Illinois

"I don't believe there has been any noticeable change in reading tastes than could be explained on any other basis than the fact that writing even in popular magazines has been more seriously oriented since the last war."

Marianna Kahler
   Michigan State University
   East Lansing, Michigan

"In your question about 'better tastes in reading,' we did not feel that we had enough experience from previous years to draw an opinion but were inclined to say that the tastes in reading have remained about the same over the last 10 years."

Question 5

Yvonne Elaine Leonard
Immaculate Heart College Library
2070 E. Live Oak Dr.
Los Angeles 28, Calif.

"Certainly lifetime reading habits for good books to foster pleasure, self-improvement, and the search for the better things of life, are being formed by many students. Of course, one wishes more college persons were developing along these lines, but the outlook could be far worse."

Alec Ross
Menlo School and College
Menlo Park, Calif.

"Pleasure reading among college students today is almost non-existent. Reading for self-improvement is not typical of college students. This comes later, if at all. Reading and what you term 'the better things of life' seem, in my observation of students, to be opposed to one another."

J. R. Blanchard
University of California
Davis, Calif.

"College students today may not be developing lifetime *habits* of reading good books for their pleasure, their self-improvement, their search for the better things in life, but the desire seems to be there. So many hold jobs and are married that they have little time to cultivate the *habit*. You do hear many say, on graduation, 'Now, I hope I'll have time to read!' "

Norah E. Jones
University of California
Los Angeles 24, Calif.

"Since the inculcation of a lifetime interest in good books is a basic aim of all educational endeavor, college students are certainly in a far better way to develop good reading habits than any other segment of the population. That much encouragement and assistance is needed to strengthen this development goes without saying."

Virginia Lee Wicox
Colorado School of Mines
Golden, Colo.

"I do believe that college students today are developing lifetime reading habits judging from the titles and subject matter selected by our students in addition to their required reading for their courses. It is particularly, we believe, pronounced in our institution where the required reading is predominantly technical and scientific in nature. We realize that engineering schools, and we are no exception, are becoming increasingly aware of the need for professional engineers with a balanced educational background, and since much of this cannot be obtained in the technical curriculum, the Library attempts to give opportunity to round out and encourage the nontechnical interests and reading for self-improvement and social development."

Wallace B. Hoffman
Regis College
W. 50th & Lowell Blvd.
Denver 21, Colo.

"No. Today's students have not yet learned that reading can be for recreation. They still depend largely for their entertainment on television, radio, movies and spectator sports."

James E. Skipper
The University of Connecticut
Storrs, Conn.

"I don't believe that their inherent motivation has improved, but environmental and curricular patterns have improved."

Gertrude M. McKenna
Wesleyan University
Middletown, Conn.

"There is a tendency to lean rather heavily on established evaluations; to accept the opinions of others rather than to evaluate on the basis of individual and independent judgment."

Elizabeth Coffee
Piedmont College
Demorest, Ga.

"I fear that 'lifetime habits of reading good books . . .' are developed before the person comes to college or not at all. This is not a judgment. It is probably my seeing that my campaign to get students to read more and better books has no obvious success. I shall continue to try."

Eli M. Oboler
Idaho State College
Pocatello, Idaho

"I believe that college students today are developing good lifetime habits of reading, and that the biggest surprise of the '60's and '70's will be the steadily rising quality of books read by the adults who are now in college."

Sister M. Tobias, O.P.
Rosary College
River Forest, Ill.

"I'm afraid that the answer to this one is an unfortunate negative. With the exception of a small minority, it seems, from the informal comments of many of our alumnae, that reading dwindles to nothing—and frequently is not even missed. There are notable exceptions, of course. The reason often lies in marriage and large families, which leave no leisure time for personal pursuits, even reading."

Fred W. Hanes
  Indiana State Teachers College
  Terre Haute, Ind.

"I am sad to say that I do not. A single answer cannot serve satis-
factorily in this case. Some students are developing the qualities
you mentioned. However, I am sad to say that the great majority
are not. As colleges tend toward more specialized vocational teaching, we are creating a generation of the 'educated' who are cultural
juveniles."

A. P. Valakis
  New England College of Pharmacy
  70–72 Mt. Vernon St.
  Boston 8, Mass.

"We are trying to inculcate these habits, but we are not succeeding.
'Is it required?' or 'Will it help me to increase my yearly gross?'
are still the sole motivating factors."

Andrew L. Bouwhuis, S.J.
  Saint Peter's College
  2645 Hudson Blvd.
  Jersey City 6, N. J.

"Probably 40% (that may be high) of the students are developing
lifetime reading habits. Most college graduates have extremely little
leisure in the 15 years after graduation. Professional training, law,
medicine, engineering, journalism, etc., absorb their energies; making their way in business; marriage, establishing a home militate
against much reading. However, the college bookstores note increase in book sales in May, due to students buying in for summer
reading."

Mrs. Alice B. Griffith
  Mohawk Valley Technical Institute at Utica
  Utica, N. Y.

"I believe a great deal of evidence points to the fact that college students are not developing lifetime habits of reading good books for pleasure."

Lois E. Engleman
Denison University
Granville, Ohio

"While I would like to believe that the college students today are developing 'lifetime habits of reading good books' that seems to me an assumption that can be tested only in the future and I am not optimistic enough to believe that there will be radical change in the pattern of adult reading in the United States despite the efforts of teachers at secondary and college level combined with the equally sincere efforts of the librarians of the country."

John B. Nicholson, Jr.
Kent State University
Kent, Ohio

"The responsibility for the provocation for the student to read, and read intelligently, to read, and to read with appreciation, must lie in the hands of the teacher, and in the light of your particular interest, it should lie in the hands of the teacher of English."

Robert D. Gault
Northwest Christian College
Eleventh & Alder
Eugene, Ore.

"Yes, I have known of many students who have had many new doors to books opened to them as a result of their college work. Few students have the time to devote to this reading at present, but will no doubt delve into it when once out of college."

Helen S. West
Philadelphia Museum School of Art
Broad and Pine Sts.
Philadelphia 2, Pa.

"I wish I could say that our students are developing good lifetime habits of reading for pleasure and profit, but I really cannot. They are so eager to become high-salaried professionals in their fields that most of their time is spent in that preparation. They see little use for any 'fringe' cultural activities, and will, I fear, drop them as soon as they can."

Martha Hackman
   Occidental College
   Los Angeles 41, California

"I feel that much of this reading is motivated not so much by pleasure or self-improvement although these enter in, of course, as by a search for meaning and values."

Mrs. James C. Bonner
   Georgia Military College
   Milledgeville, Georgia

"I definitely believe that college students are developing lifetime habits of reading, even more than formerly. There is wider selection, more imaginative presentation. The art of photography is enhancing book illustration. The more the student has in his college curriculum, the more 'laymen's interest' he seems to have in many fields to pursue in the future."

Robert R. Hertel
   Illinois Normal University
   Normal, Illinois

"Regrettably, I don't think there is too much carry-over to adult life from the rather rigorous reading demands of college life."

Katherine Walker
   Northern Illinois State College
   DeKalb, Illinois

"The few students who have been influenced by college professors or librarians to develop lifetime habits of reading good books is most encouraging. Students who are already readers when they reach college are more apt to develop even better reading habits."

Dorothy A. Bradley
   The Principia College of Liberal Arts
   Elsah, Illinois

"Our students borrow serious books for holiday and vacation reading. Therefore, we hope that they are developing lifetime habits."

Sister Margaret Mary
   Saint Joseph College
   Emmitsburg, Maryland

"I am uncertain about the answer to this question. I honestly think, from surveys that are taken of the type of reading done by rather recent college graduates, that college students apparently are failing to develop lifetime habits of reading good books."

Marianna Kahler
   Michigan State University
   East Lansing, Michigan

"Yes, we firmly believe that college students are developing lifetime habits of good reading. This has been accomplished, we think, through the faculty who have encouraged and helped their students to find good habits."

Floda V. Smith
   Union College
   Lincoln 6, Nebraska

"In regard to reading of college students, I should like to make this comment. I believe that many college students do not have time for the reading of good books for pleasure because of their heavy school program and assignments. We have a number of students who work a considerable part of their way through college. Many of these students use the library a good deal in connection with outside reading, research papers, and general study.

However they do not have time or make time for general leisure reading as we feel they should."

The Library
   Oklahoma State University
   Stillwater, Oklahoma

"Probably not, since according to our critics American adults after graduating from college soon succumb to the pressures of a way of life which, altho not anti-intellectual, is essentially nonintellectual."

Agnes E. Painter
   Allegheny College
   Meadville, Pennsylvania

"I believe that the college students of today have less time to read than they did, say in the thirties. The students today are busy with so many things, but they are finding the answers to many of their problems in the Library. Many of them express the hope that when they finish college they will be near a library where they may get books to read. They do read after college. This I know for our town circulation has more than doubled in the past 20 years. The majority of our town patrons are college graduates of this or some other college."

John Cook Wyllie
   University of Virginia
   Charlottesville, Virginia

"I believe that despite some of the pedagogical devices still used in colleges (e.g., the Reserve Book Reading) a small but growing percentage of students succeed in preserving an interest in reading through four years of college. The number who come to college with the habit is growing; the number who later develop it is growing; the number who are discouraged from it in college is diminishing. The illiteracy of scientists seems to me to be dangerously increasing."

Clifford P. Wolfsehr
  Central Washington College of Education
  Ellensburg, Washington

"A big, fat *No* to this one, with an ironic laugh, spontaneously induced by the tragic gulf separating the reality from the wishful thinking implied by the mellifluous rhetoric of the question."

Robert F. Kidd Library
  Glenville State College
  Glenville, West Virginia

"Yes. I believe that curricular reading fosters reading habits that will last beyond student days."

Question 6

Fr. Frederick Smith, O.S.B.
  St. Bernard College
  St. Bernard, Ala.

"This one I cannot answer in merely a yes or no. Our student body is made up of a wide scale of students from city, well-educated backgrounds to almost the unlettered individual of the backwoods type, where the latter is almost taught how to read over again. As I said before, there is a vast improvement and there is room for ever-increasing improvement. The change is terrific and just a few years of observation can enlighten one's mind to these facts. I believe that one has to experience working with people of these types and not merely read about them to get the full value and see the strides made in the educational field, particularly here in the South."

Wilma Heisser
  Phoenix College
  1202 W. Thomas Rd.
  Phoenix, Ariz.

"No, I do not agree with the current criticism. However, the reading range is from very exceptional, i.e., reading 6 to 8 books in 48 hours, to almost an inability to read adult material. So I would say the criticism is partly justified."

Yvonne Elaine Leonard
Immaculate Heart College
2070 E. Live Oak Dr.
Los Angeles 28, Calif.

"Current criticism is indeed varied. Numerous librarians feel that 'poor reading habits' grow simply because the students are pressed for time to investigate any kind of books other than those assigned via class work. . . ."

Alec Ross
Menlo School and College
Menlo Park, Calif.

"Poor reading habits of college students are undeniable. However, I feel that the popular press has concentrated too much on 'quality' reading, rather than reading in general. In my opinion, the basic problem stems from students' inability to concentrate on what they are reading. My personal experience leads me firmly to the conviction that the problem originates in the actual teaching of reading in the grade schools. The materials from which reading is learned are such that reading becomes a chore. . . ."

Marvin W. Cragun
Sacramento City College
Sacramento 18, Calif.

"I certainly do. They just cannot read—let's face it. They cannot read fast enough to do college level work, so they cheat. They are not thorough enough to assimilate the ideas read, so they are bored. The way has been made too easy and the textbooks piled too high for them to get an education."

Rev. Charles Dollen
University of San Diego
San Diego 10, Calif.

"The reading habits are not poorer in our experience. It is criminal, however, that many, many students are kept from college by lack of preparation in high schools and elementary schools."

H. Eugene Craig
    Interdenominational Theological Center
    Atlanta 15, Ga.

"Yes I do agree with the current criticism of the poor reading habits of college students. This, however, is not that they are poorer readers than the students of a generation ago, but rather that the standards and requirements of today are so much higher. By comparison they are far superior, but by prevailing standards they are way down the ladder."

Eli M. Oboler
    Idaho State College
    Pocatello, Idaho

"I disagree with the current criticisms of the poor reading habits of college students, which I believe are based on limited sampling and a predisposition to pessimism. True, our college students do not do the kind of reading that is done at Oxford or Cambridge, but then there is a much greater percentage of American students attending college than in England, and those who do have surprisingly good taste."

Sister M. Tobias, O.P.
    Rosary College
    River Forest, Ill.

"Undoubtedly some of the current criticism is justified. We still find some remedial reading program necessary for some of our freshmen. Because our admissions policy is quite selective, we probably do not have the poorest readers among our students, however. And there are many and brilliant exceptions."

H. L. Boisen
    Butler University Library
    Indianapolis 7, Ind.

"No, I do not agree with the current criticism of poor reading habits among college students as a generalization. We are getting poor readers who formerly did not go to college, and we must do what we can for them. It makes a good topic for sensational journalism."

Fred W. Hanes
    Indiana State Teachers College
    Terre Haute, Ind.

"I most heartily agree with current criticism of the poor reading habits of college students and I wish that more educators would concern themselves with this problem which is of primary importance in American education."

Lucile Rogers
    Junior College and Senior High School
    Ft. Scott, Kans.

"Many college students do have poor reading habits but the fact that our college students are not the select group they used to be is a factor here. We are trying to educate the masses so we are going to find many among this group of lesser ability. Another point here is that today the trend is to 'pass' every child in every grade instead of requiring him to repeat a grade when he has not done work of a required standard. We often find students being advanced year after year when some intense remedial and/or repeating a grade would give them a much better basis but they do not get the advantage of either."

Cathryn M. Feather
    Eastern College of Commerce and Law
    3 W. Mt. Vernon Pl.
    Baltimore 1, Md.

"I agree that many college students possess poor reading habits but this does not necessarily mean that they make unwise selections. They actually have poor reading habits so far as the skills are concerned. We offer a course in Rapid Reading which has been very beneficial to those who have pursued it."

John A. Sperry, Jr.
Culver-Stockton College
Canton, Mo.

"Yes, I agree very much with the current criticism of the poor reading habits of college students and feel that it reaches the proportion of a national disgrace."

Marie Winka
Maryville College of the Sacred Heart of St. Louis
St. Louis, Mo.

"There is still much to be done and I think many college students could profit by remedial reading courses to increase their speed and comprehension. . . ."

Max Langham
Nebraska State Teachers College
Peru, Neb.

"Question 6 shows the degree of *expertise* in America today. The critics seem to have left their haven of literature and music and invaded all realms of life. I am not an expert but in my humble opinion self-determination has not been shortened or even lengthened over the years. Perhaps it is more that what we expect of today's students is poor in comparison. Aggregate numbers can never justify high academic ability. It's what we are *doing with scholastic aptitude* that rates severe criticism."

Arthur E. Jones, Jr.
Drew University
Madison, N. J.

"I don't find college students of this generation are much better or worse than those of a previous generation. There may be more diversification of reading experience and less commonly shared reading experience among the present group. Maybe the best ones are better and the worst ones worse. At least, I'll agree that there is as much room for improvement as at any time in the past."

Andrew L. Bouwhuis, S.J.
Saint Peter's College
2645 Hudson Blvd.
Jersey City 6, N. J.

"There is ample evidence of poor reading habits—taking habits in the broad and various meanings of that word even in this context—in many students. Broad unfavorable generalizations, however, are not justified."

Ruth M. Miller
Hartwick College
Oneonta, N. Y.

"I thoroughly agree with the criticism of the poor reading habits of the college students. Our students come to us with poor backgrounds in literature. Many of them have not faced the discipline of reading books which are too difficult for them; hence, they have great difficulty in college when this type of reading is forced on them without direct supervision."

Rice Estes
Pratt Institute
Brooklyn 5, N. Y.

"Yes, to a certain extent. I don't think reading habits are necessarily worse. We merely have more students and therefore the habits seem worse. But these have always been bad in America compared to Western Europe."

Kathryn Parke
State University of New York
Agricultural and Technical Institute
Cobleskill, N. Y.

"Far more serious, in my opinion, is the plain fact that far too many of them *cannot* read, even for the purposes required for their assignments. It may be that this technical junior college accepts too many poorly prepared students, but we are more or less committed to take high school graduates, and why should people be graduated from high school, if they cannot comprehend anything more difficult than the sports page of the newspaper? I know that their handicap is real, not just laziness, because I have for years taught a class in literature to some of our supposedly better students, and they are genuinely helpless, it seems—yet with a little individual help they do improve. Why could they not have had this help earlier?"

Alice B. Griffith
Mohawk Valley Technical Institute
Utica, N. Y.

"It is probable that college students have poor reading and study habits. If this is so, it can hardly be expected that these students would choose reading as a pleasurable pastime. If reading is a difficult task, surely it would not be chosen as a leisure-time activity."

Elena Horton
Orange County Community College
Middletown, N. Y.

"To Question 6, I would suggest that a certain percentage of college students read well and copiously. Others read only at the suggestion of instructors, and still others not at all. But it would surprise me if the percentages vary a great deal over previous generations. If they do, I would suspect that more students read well through sheer availability of more reading materials."

Thomas A. Hunt
State Normal and Industrial College
Ellendale, N. D.

"Although this answer to the question concerning the current criticism may seem inconsistent, my reaction is that it is true; however, many individuals are realizing this deficiency and are actually dong something about the realization to begin a program to counteract this difficulty. Remedial work is being done by instructors and by individuals on a voluntary basis."

Frederick L. Taft
  Case Institute of Technology
  University Circle
  Cleveland 5, Ohio

"We have been testing them as freshmen and encouraging them to improve their reading with a reading laboratory, so I should have to say that one thing they do not know is how to read rapidly for the most part. Nor do they, when they arrive, recognize the imperative need to read to stay in college. Many colleagues in mathematics, physics, and chemistry attribute their failure in those courses to their inability to read the texts. You might say they can read, but not at the speed nor the level they must for college. . . ."

Wanda J. Calhoun
  Heidelberg College
  Tiffin, Ohio

"I think much of this criticism is true, but when I was a student we also read some of this same 'trash' which we now criticize the students for reading. I actually think it is just a phase all of us go through, and if you are really interested in continuing your education throughout your lifetime, good reading habits will be formed as you realize the need for them. Of course, television and other mediums make it easy for the lazy person to forget about reading good books."

Elizabeth C. Welborn
  Lander College
  Greenwood, S. C.

"According to one of our English professors, there is much truth in this. He says: 'Students who read more, read more, but more students are not reading.'"

Los Angeles County Art Institute
2401 Wilshire Boulevard
Los Angeles 57, California

"In short, while they frequently display good taste in their choice of reading (assuming they read at all) their skills are so rudimentary, for the most part, that I wonder they can understand anything of what they do read."

Mrs. James C. Bonner
Georgia Military College
Milledgeville, Georgia

"The inability to read is deplorable. Our school is very 'democratic' and many have never developed accuracy or speed in reading. Their own written work is even worse. In most cases, they can but they won't."

Robert R. Hertel
Illinois State Normal University
Normal, Illinois

"I don't believe that these articles are too reliable in a statistical sense. What the authors do not consider is the fact that many students have differing reasons for attending college today than before the war and these reasons many times have little relation to academic pursuits."

Sister Margaret Mary
Saint Joseph College
Emmitsburg, Maryland

"Yes, I do agree with the current criticism in popular magazines. Many students say that they have all they can do to keep up with the course work, term papers, etc., which are assigned to them. They say they would like to read but do not have time. However, an observation of the manner in which they spend their leisure time during the school years and the little reading they do during the summer would seem to prove that they prefer to spend their free time in other pursuits than reading."

Marianna Kahler
    Michigan State University
    East Lansing, Michigan

"On the whole, the current criticism of college students is a trend among journalists, 'the thing to do,' and we feel that the results of surveys taken to indicate this negative attitude have been based on a very small minority."

Norma Hovden
    University of Minnesota
    Minneapolis 14, Minnesota

"Hard for them to be selective. Most students tend to acquire scanning habits and are unoriginal in their opinions. Modern college tends to stress preparation for successful business or professional life."

Thelma R. Bumbaugh
    Hiram College
    Hiram, Ohio

"I am afraid that most of the criticism of poor reading habits is justified. Students with good reading habits are in the minority."

Ruth Gibbons
    Union University
    Jackson, Tennessee

"I have to agree with the current criticism of the poor reading habits of college students because I think the good readers are in such small minority. Even though reading has increased in our college community it still lags behind in the running with other college activities."

R. C. Janeway
Texas Technological College
Lubbock, Texas

"Yes and no. I find that our students often have difficulty with the mechanics of reading, but since academic success and intellectual interest require reading ability, adjustment is made. Those who survive improve their reading ability. Reading habits of college students are largely a matter of atmosphere. If reading (or the admission that one reads) is unpopular on the campus, students will not read (or admit that they read). On the other hand, if student and faculty conversation often contains reference to books and reading, then more and more students will read."

John Cook Wyllie
University of Virginia
Charlottesville, Virginia

"I have not seen the criticisms, perhaps because I don't read the right magazines. I am, however, familiar with the statistical fact that 15% of American college students never check a book out of their college library. I can say that this percentage in this University coincides with the slightly larger percentage of those who fail to complete the academic requirements successfully."

Clifford P. Wolfsehr
Central Washington College of Education
Ellensburg, Washington

"I agree with anyone who says that *the average* college student reads very little in college of anything that is not required reading, except for some low-level recreational reading."

Robert F. Kidd Library
Glenville State College
Glenville, West Virginia

"Yes, to some extent. However, the student who cannot read usually does not stay in college."

Interpretations, Summations, and Conclusions

Attitudes Toward English Teaching represents the contributions of over 1250 educators, business executives, editors, librarians, publishers, legislators, and judges.

The organization and the interpretation of the mass of facts and opinions represented by the communications received is no easy task, particularly because there are so many contradictory statements. Yet even these many replies represent only a sampling of opinion; and any conclusions drawn must be viewed as based on only a part of the evidence. To know what *all* the college presidents believe about the teaching of English, we would have to receive 2011 replies instead of the 79 listed in this study. Likewise, 63 business executives represent only a small fraction of those whose opinions might have been consulted.

Although the opinions expressed represent many aspects of our society, both professional and commercial, the respondents showed a rather unusual unanimity in their interest in the subject of English instruction and their wish to see it strengthened and improved. Time and time again in the pages of this report quotations have been made from successful people in various walks of life, testifying to the paramount importance of our subject. That they came from teachers of English should surprise no one. That these views were also shared by bankers, civil service administrators, judges, etc., is very comforting at a time when other nonhumanistic disciplines have secured so many headlines and such large governmental and foundation funds. On the question "What do successful people in all walks of life think about the importance of English?" we can say unequivocally on the basis of these replies, that English is of central importance. To many respondents, it was *the most important subject in the curriculum.*

A few random samplings will indicate the importance of our area. From leaders in business came the following testimonials to the economic importance of a good English training:

1. Teach the economic importance of a good background in English. (Goodyear Tire and Rubber)
2. I know of no more valuable asset in business life than the ability to express one's thoughts with clarity and precision. (Merck)
3. In the business world, English, in the sense of communication, is the way management gets its job done. There is little risk of oversimplification in saying that good managers are good communicators, poor managers are usually the opposite. (Shell Oil)
4. As we all know, the rapid growth and importance of communication makes a ready command of English for speaking and writing an indispensable asset, not only in business and industry but in everyday living. (U.S. Steel)
5. . . . it is vital that all scholastic levels be impressed with the extreme importance of having a better than average knowledge of English, especially grammar and vocabulary, if they expect to move ahead in the business world. (Equitable Life Assurance)

Not only for economic success but for personal growth and development is English recognized as of great importance.

6. There is no line of endeavor we can follow competently without a good grounding in the language we use and

none in which our proficiency would not be improved with greater fluency. (Continental Can)

7. This is a very important subject as the ability to express oneself well is extremely important in transmitting ideas to others. (Libbey-Owens-Ford Glass)

8. Carry on your efforts to show students why they are limited without proper equipment in English. (Scott Paper)

9. We do wish to emphasize the importance of knowing the proper use of English as a means of communication and expression as well as the cultural identification it provides. (Shell Oil)

10. Teachers of English occupy a more vital position than ever in our educational program. (U.S. Steel)

11. A continual upgrading of the general level of ability to utilize English would serve the best interests of the nation. (Westinghouse)

12. At an early age students should be inculcated with the knowledge that a love of English and a command of English are prerequisites to success as adults. (Yale and Towne)

Pleasant as these encomia are, they are coupled nevertheless with frank criticisms, which merit the serious study of all of us in our profession.

Almost from the time when English became a subject to be taught in the high schools and the colleges, there have been criticisms of the results. In fact, the history of the teaching of English in America might very well be called the history of the criticism of the teaching of English. Much of this criticism was valuable, valid, and necessary, and has contributed to the rich body of methodology and research we possess today. English teachers at all levels are exposed to such criticisms because their subject affects almost everybody. Almost everybody in school or college today takes some kind of English, whether it be in the simple storytelling of the kindergarten or in the specialized research of the graduate seminar. Where there are so many products, it is to be expected that there will be many opinions expressed about the quality of products.

Since the individual chapters indicate the answers to the questions about the preparation in English in detail, it will not be necessary to repeat them here. The answers show, if anything, a wide difference of opinion, and should make one cautious about glib generalizations.

Are our entering college freshmen better or worse in their preparation in English? Spokesmen for 26 out of 79 responding institutions think they are better prepared than those of 5 to 10 years ago. Many colleges are not sure, and have no ways of knowing. Some colleges have statistical evidence over the years and feel that there has been a decline in preparation. Far too many of the respondents were frank in admitting that they had no statistical evidence, but that they could give personal impressions at best. It would seem, perhaps, that more statistical evidence one way or the other would be desirable, if only to put an end to the charges and countercharges that have characterized so much discussion of education in the past few years, especially since Sputnik I was sent into orbit.

Whether statistical evidence or personal opinion is the basis for the comments on certain aspects of our English instruction, it should be of interest to readers of this report to know what has come in for most serious criticism and what our respondents offer by way of suggestions for improvements.

WRITTEN COMPOSITION

Of the 79 replies from college presidents, 24 criticized the written composition of recent (past 5 to 10 years) entrants. Since the details are indicated in the appropriate chapter of this report, we need not repeat them here. This weakness was noted by almost all other groups of respondents. An examination of the number of recommendations to improve written composition will reveal how large a place this aspect of English occupies in the thinking of the respondents. Thus, of a total of 76 different items of suggestion made by college presidents for the NCTE to improve the teaching of English, the largest number of recommendations were for written composition (39). In other words, almost one half of the respondents made recommendations that would, in their opinion, strengthen the writing program. Summarizing the highlights of these 39 recommendations, we come to the following:

1. More writing in high school. (Alabama, Boston, Brown, Case I.T., Harvard, Kansas, Maine, Oberlin, M.I.T., Ohio State, Oregon, Princeton, Rhode Island, Rutgers, Southwestern, Virginia, Wisconsin, Yale)
2. Careful correction by instructor. (Cincinnati, Chicago, Carnegie I.T., Oberlin, M.I.T., Ohio State, Rhode Island, Rutgers, Southwestern)
3. More instruction and experience in writing simple exposition. (Alaska, Carnegie I.T., Texas)
4. Practice in essay and report writing. (Oklahoma)
5. More exercises in analytical writing. (Stanford)
6. Very specific instructions for each assignment. (Cincinnati)
7. Encourage student to take pride in expressing himself. (USAFA)
8. Insist on high quality; training in neatness and accuracy. (Southwestern)
9. More short themes with careful correction. (Colorado, Ohio State)
10. Conditions to be established to permit teachers of English to have time needed for thoughtful criticism of student essays. (Chicago, Brown)

11. Training in writing in the whole curriculum as well as the section of it. (Bowling Green SU)
12. Stress on more effective teaching of the art of writing. (New Hampshire)
13. Developing among public school teachers an awareness of the importance of composition in all phases of education. (Louisiana SU)
14. More uniform and extensive teaching of writing throughout the junior high school and high school years. (Vermont)
15. Insistence upon the importance of fundamental disciplines in written composition. (North Carolina, Brown, Amherst)
16. One theme of 500 words per month—minimum through all three years of high school. (Maine)

It is obvious from these recommendations that more practice in writing and more correction of students' writing would please college teachers of English. Here and there they have indicated the kind of writing they would prefer to a greater degree. Those who have asked for more frequent writing and more careful correction in the secondary schools are well aware of the time required to carry out such a program. Hence it is not surprising that 20 college respondents made recommendations that in their opinion would make it humanly possible for secondary school teachers to mark all the compositions necessary for an adequate program.

RECOMMENDATIONS FOR ENGLISH TEACHERS' LOAD IN SECONDARY SCHOOL

1. Establish reasonable work load requirements for secondary English teachers. (Boston, Brigham Young, Michigan, Ohio State, Tennessee, Texas, Utah)

Specifics

   (a) 60–65 students in classes of 20–22 (Cornell)
   (b) Four classes—maximum of 80 students (U. of Connecticut)
   (c) Four classes of 25 students apiece (Arkansas)
   (d) No more than 100 students (Case I.T.)
   (e) Fewer sections of fewer pupils (U. of Washington)
   (f) Reduce number of students (Cincinnati, Colorado, Florida, Kansas)

2. Persuade authorities to lighten burden of English teachers (Carnegie I.T., Chicago)
3. Relieve English teachers of "fringe" assignments—extracurricular activities, P.T.A., nonacademic functions. (Ohio State College of Engineering)

Criticisms of written expression have been made by representatives of the various groups represented in this survey, and these have been summarized in the various chapters. Their recommendations to English teachers are of considerable interest because they are frank, designed to be helpful, and represent a fairly high level of commercial and professional success. These are highly educated ladies and gentlemen who have frequently risen to the top of their profession and who have more than a passing interest in education.

RECOMMENDATIONS ON WRITTEN COMPOSITION BY BUSINESS EXECUTIVES

The 63 business executives made recommendations to the Council in 56 categories, ranging from "academic standards" to "word construction." On the matter of written composition, 13 executives had recommendations. Since there were also 13 recommendations on spelling and 11 on vocabulary building, it is clear that the written composition of the employees of big business has been of considerable interest to them.

These are the major recommendations made to our teachers with respect to written composition:

1. English composition should be taught in every grade of school as long as the student attends school. (Borden)
2. Only by writing can people learn to write. Practice in writing is more effective than grammar drill, diagramming of sentences, or other forms of grammar study. (Motorola)
3. Wanted: development of a writing style which expresses clearly, accurately, and vividly the intended message by study of the best literature and repeated assignment of written exercises. (Liberty Mutual)
4. In the matter of writing we are interested in accuracy, completeness, understandability and the effect that the written word has on the reader. (Brown Shoe)
5. More assignments in the writing of letters, reports, surveys, compositions, and essays. (U.S. Steel)
6. Improvement could be made by training in expository writing. (Swift)
7. Perhaps curriculum changes to require more time for English subjects would result in more effective expression. (Texas Co.)

RECOMMENDATIONS BY CIVIL SERVICE ADMINISTRATORS

Civil service administrators made recommendations in 25 categories, ranging from "acceleration" to "written composition," which drew the greatest number of recommendations (8). Apparently, college presidents, business executives, and civil service administrators are in agreement on this one point: the importance of skill in written expression and the need to improve it.

Because the demands for writing in civil service are somewhat specialized, it is of interest to know the recommendations which follow:

1. Place more emphasis on brevity (consistent with clarity) in written communications (Director Operations, 3700 Military Training Wing CATC)

2. I think, therefore, that even at the expense of lengthening the number of years required for engineering or scientific training, additional effort should be placed on the training in composition. I do not deprecate the need for those aspects of cultural English which are taught in the normal English course. I feel, however, that for engineers and scientists oral and written expression should be improved. (Deputy Director, Research and Development, U.S.A.)

3. . . . requiring a higher portion of students, no matter what their technical interest, to take courses in expository writing. (Director, Bureau of Programs and Standards, U.S. Civil Service Commission)

4. I hope greater emphasis can be placed on the fundamentals of English and the discipline of writing. (Director of Information, Department of Agriculture)

5. Provide intensive practice in composition (e.g., report-writing or brief-writing) in connection with classwork in all subjects where this is practicable. (Director of Personnel, Department of Commerce)

6. A student should be taught to carefully think through a particular subject and express his ideas precisely, forcefully, and briefly on paper. There is no substitute for plain, old composition drill in my view. In addition, teachers in all subjects should feel a responsibility for their students' writing. That

is, history, science and geography teachers should take it upon themselves not only to teach their own particular subjects but also to help the student express well on paper his ideas on these subjects. Teachers should correct examination papers for both subject matter and writing ability. (Director Information, Publications and Reports, U.S. Department of Labor)

7. It is my feeling and the feelings of my colleagues with whom I have discussed this matter that perhaps we fail to some extent in our English instruction because we still give courses in "rules" throughout the elementary school, secondary school and the first year of college, but we seldom fail students because they cannot write coherent English. One good course in mechanics, possibly in the sophomore year of high school, might be enough, if it were kept a good stiff course which couldn't be passed without a fair degree of mastery. In other years a goodly amount of writing and speaking with high standards of performance expected, could be varied in subject matter to move from immediate experience to thoughtful essays requiring a basis of knowledge which could not be copied from encyclopedias. (Chief of the English Training Branch, Information Center Service, U.S. Information Agency)

In addition to these recommendations from 7 different U.S. civil service agencies, there are several recommendations in the booklet *Observations on Competence in English of Recent College Graduates and Suggestions for Improvement,* prepared by E. H. Morse, Jr., Director, Accounting and Auditing Policy Staff. This 55-page booklet is based upon replies received from 100 different individuals who are employed in the Washington office and the 19 regional offices of the U.S. General Accounting Office.

Since copies of this interesting report may be obtained upon request from Mr. Morse at the U.S. General Accounting Office, Washington 25, it will not be necessary to repeat what has been so well summarized in this booklet.

RECOMMENDATIONS TO IMPROVE WRITTEN COMPOSITIONS MADE BY EDITORS

Three sets of editors were invited to express their opinions about the competence in English of recent graduates from high schools and colleges. Since their concern is primarily with the written word, their comments and recommendations are of considerable interest. The 35 magazine editors who replied to our inquiry made recommendations in 19 different categories ranging from two in "achievement" to 7 in "written composition." These recommendations were equaled by 7 in spelling and 7 in reading. Following are the specific recommendations:

1. Much greater concentration in grade school on solid grounding in . . . English composition. Require students at all levels to do much more written work than is now demanded in most American schools. I would like to see every student required to produce at least one paper of 1,000 words or more every week; these papers to be rigidly graded and criticized by teachers who have both the competence and time for such work. (John Fischer, Editor, *Harper's*)

2. If I were a teacher, I would make my English pupils rewrite and rewrite their compositions. It is by self-editing that clear and emphatic writing is learned, not in just having teacher (or editor) point out errors. (Mabel H. Schubert, for the Editors of *Life*)

3. *All* (not just the work in English classes) written work be marked for errors and graded for competence in English,

and that teachers require that work not competent be re-written with errors corrected. (Betsy Talbot Blackwell, Edi-tor-in-Chief, *Mademoiselle*)

4. . . . the Council should put its major effort into seeing that students are taught to write, and that they are made to write as much as possible in all forms. Benjamin Franklin learned to write by writing and by copying. Can you think of any-one who wrote better prose? He had very little of what used to be called methodology. (Sey Chassler, Executive Editor, *Pageant*)

5. . . . I favor . . . the practice of clear, simple communication rather than encouraging them too soon in flights of what's called creative writing. (Howard Allaway, Editor, *Popular Science*)

6. Insist upon more actual writing of compositions in both high school and college. The only way to learn to write is to write, write, and write—with, of course, proper supervision and correction. (Ben Hibbs, Editor, *Saturday Evening Post*)

RECOMMENDATIONS FROM NEWSPAPER EDITORS TO IMPROVE WRITTEN COMPOSITION

There were 25 newspaper editors who replied to our inquiry. Three of them made specific comments on written compositions in addition to those who discussed such items as "spelling," a "return to basics," and "standards."

1. The Council should concentrate on enlisting the efforts of teachers of other subjects in high school in placing more em-phasis on written composition. Students should be required to get more experience in writing. This might be accom-plished by providing more opportunity for written reports and summaries of research in subjects other than English. Standards for acceptance of these reports should be as rigid

as those required in English classes. (Richard H. Woodbury, Editor, *Portland* (Maine) *Sunday Telegram*)

2. . . . anyone in school or college planning to make his living by writing should be required to have that writing subjected to searchingly detailed, *but* always constructive, criticism. (Richard P. Kleeman, News Editor, *Minneapolis Tribune*)

3. Increase emphasis on . . . the science of writing. (Roderick J. Watts, Managing Editor, *Houston Chronicle*)

RECOMMENDATIONS FROM EDUCATION EDITORS TO IMPROVE WRITTEN COMPOSITION

Of the education editors who responded, 6 made recommendations with respect to written composition, the largest number of recommendations in any one category. Four of the more significant recommendations follow:

1. I think one of the greatest improvements in English teaching, so far as the use of English in writing is concerned, would be to give more emphasis to the more formal aspects of writing. Perhaps we have gone somewhat too far in emphasizing the pleasure that can be had in writing rather than acceptability in form, spelling, and grammatical structure. In other words, we should not take enthusiasm for skill. (E. I. F. Williams, Editor, *The Educational Forum*)

2. . . . the Council can promote more effective teaching of composition through encouraging English teachers to provide more supervised practice in English written composition. Perhaps even more important, the Council should use its influence to get teachers of other subjects to insist on better written English. (R. H. Eckelberry, Editor, *Educational Research Bulletin*)

3. . . . continue to require written and oral presentations of topics, issues, and subjects, with a special emphasis on the

clarity and skill of effective presentations. (Paul E. Elicker, Editor, *Bulletin,* National Association of Secondary School Principals)

4. . . . The Council should encourage efforts to have students do more writing in school, to arrange for teaching loads (or assistance) so that the students can have the benefit of the criticism of their output, and that this criticism reflect to some extent views of modern scholars as to what makes writing good, rather than rigid insistence upon adherence to formal rules of grammar and rhetoric. (Maurice L. Hartung, Chairman, Board of Editors, *School Review*)

RECOMMENDATIONS BY DEANS OF LAW SCHOOLS AND MEMBERS OF THE HOUSE OF REPRESENTATIVES

Characteristic recommendations by both of these groups that resemble in substance some of those cited earlier refer to such oft-repeated items as greater frequency of writing, more careful correction by qualified teachers, insistence upon high standards, and greater self-criticism.

1. Additional emphasis in high school and college on . . . composition . . . would greatly aid the pre-law student in preparing for his professional study. (Roscoe L. Barrow, Dean, U. of Cincinnati Law School)

2. The high schools should be encouraged to reinstitute . . . weekly compositions. (William Hughes Mulligan, Dean, Fordham University Law School)

3. . . . increase the amount of required work in English composition and literature. (Roger Howell, Dean, University of Maryland Law School)

4. I can only suggest that we recognize that high school and the first year of college are the last years we are going to be

able to teach formally these boys and girls English literature and composition. Therefore, in these years we must
redouble our efforts to teach both by precept and example
of the great writers of the past . . . the basic principles of
material. Practice of these principles under the supervision
of the instructor for longer periods than at the present time
should help to give this fundamental training. (Lee Metcalf,
H.R., Montana)

GENERAL CONCLUSIONS

It has been deemed advisable to quote many of the recommendations on the improvement of written composition so that a
fairly representative picture could be obtained, ranging from the
views of college presidents to deans of law schools. Diverse as the
backgrounds of our respondents are, certain recommendations
have appeared with such consistency that they might be considered as representative of their thinking. Among the recommendations are:

1. Greater frequency of writing.
2. More time for correction.
3. Administrative provisions to enable teachers to correct
   papers.
4. Insistence upon high standards both in content and form
   before a paper is accepted.
5. Greater participation by *all* teachers in improving written
   composition, not only those in the English Department.

It could be said with reasonable assurance that the Council has
been making these recommendations for years, in its publications
of the Commission on the Curriculum, its annual resolutions, and
in various publications of one or more of its committees. It is to
be hoped that constant iteration of the need for reducing teacher
load in the secondary school may influence administrators and

budget directors to make the necessary provisions for teacher time. It is gratifying that outstanding men and women in professions other than our own have agreed so consistently with our own points of view and understand the difficulties under which our colleagues must operate. From such understanding, it is hoped improvements will come in working conditions, which will in turn result in increased effectiveness in written composition at all levels.

RECOMMENDATIONS CONCERNING GRAMMAR

In the contemporary discussions concerning the educational needs of our times, one frequently reads the recommendations to "return to the fundamentals," "more grammar," "greater insistence upon correctness," and the like. These recommendations seem to vary with the groups making them in intensity and in frequency. Since all the respondents of this survey were asked to comment on the deficiencies observed in recent high school and college graduates, it is not surprising that "grammar" was mentioned by nearly all groups. A few of the comments from the college presidents are typical:

1. There is a definite lack of understanding of grammar. (Alabama)
2. Their grammar is still not what it should be. (Amherst)
3. Many students still do not know the first essentials of grammar. (Cincinnati)
4. The knowledge of grammar, deplorable. (De Paul)
5. Students know far less grammar than they used to, and this handicaps their work whenever they must decipher a difficult passage of prose or poetry or revise their own writing. (Earlham)
6. Possibly less well prepared in knowledge of formal grammar. (Maine)

7. Smaller competence in such fundamentals as . . . grammar. (South Carolina)

8. They do not know the parts of speech. (U.S. Air Force Academy)

These 8 comments were the only ones specifically directed toward deficiencies in grammar by the respondents from 79 colleges and universities.

COMMENTS ON GRAMMAR FROM BUSINESS

Typical of some of the comments by business leaders were the following:

1. Grammar is a complete mystery to almost all recent graduates. (Borden)

2. We believe that deficiencies exist in grammar. It appears that high school graduates are well drilled in grammar but that they may forget much of their training when they continue with college. (Campbell Soup)

3. There does appear to be a basic weakness in . . . knowledge of some of the common rules of grammar (said of female graduates who must fill typing and stenographic positions). (Chase Manhattan Bank)

4. Reduced reading experience is not only reflected in a lack of background in literature but also in a reduced capacity to understand grammar and to use it properly. (Commercial Investment Trust, Inc.)

5. The deficiencies I have noticed are mainly in the lack of a formal grasp of grammar. (Continental Can)

6. One comment on deficiency in English competence is that too many people, college graduates as well as high school graduates, have to learn some of the basic rules of grammar while on the job. (DuPont)

7. . . . we find a marked lack of knowledge of the basic rules of grammar . . . (Equitable Life Assurance Society)

8. . . . it is our experience that competence is lacking in all areas: namely, spelling, grammar . . . (Equitable Trust)

9. Limited training in the language of the market place—grammar that is simple and direct . . . (General Mills)

10. The deficiencies seem to begin with poor spelling and run through the areas of grammar . . . (International Business Machines Corporation)

11. Their (high school graduates) grammar has also left much to be desired. (John Hancock Mutual Life Insurance)

12. We do find many high school and college graduates whose grammatical usage is not good. (Koppers)

13. The most noticeable deficiencies have been in simple grammar and rhetoric. (Liberty Mutual Insurance Company)

14. . . . failure to follow basic principles of grammatical construction. (Merck)

15. Deficiencies range all the way from the most elementary violations to basic rules of grammar . . . (Motorola, Inc.)

16. Incorrect grammar. (Sears, Roebuck)

17. In other words, a lack of knowledge of grammar. (Sunshine Biscuits)

18. Most glaring deficiencies in the past 5 or 10 years have been in spelling, grammar and punctuation. (U.S. Steel)

It is obvious from these representative criticisms that those who have been in contact with large numbers of employees in business and industry have noticed deficiencies in grammar. Similar statements were made by representatives of the U.S. Civil Service Agencies, editors, and judicial and legislative personnel. These criticisms are not new in the history of the teaching of English in America and some of the recent statements might easily be paralleled by others of 50 and 75 years ago.

Nor have recommendations for improvement been few, both then and now. It may be of interest, however, to study these recommendations of our respondents which may have especial significance to us today as we constantly search for more effective approaches to increase the competence of our students today.

From the colleges, there were six recommendations to improve the teaching of grammar:

1. Cease emphasizing drill in grammar independently of practice in composition or as a substitute for it. (Ogilvy, Head, Department of English, University of Colorado)
2. Knowledge and understanding of grammatical terminology may be the shortest way to correct usage; these are a necessity where the student takes foreign languages. (Hankins, Head, Department of English, Maine)
3. Urge them (high school teachers) to reduce to a minimum the time now spent on formal grammar. (P. Stewart, Texas)
4. In some instances this insufficiency in writing derives from an overinsistence upon grammar unapplied to composition. (Clapp, Head, Department of English, Utah)
5. . . . trying to bring about more uniform and extensive teaching of grammar . . . throughout the junior high school and high school years. (Hughes, Head, Freshman English, Vermont)
6. That formal grammar be emphasized in grade and high schools. (Murphy, President, Villa Madonna)

Even among these 6 respondents, there is evidence of a difference of opinion about the place of grammar instruction in our schools. Perhaps the most marked contrast is between President Murphy's recommendation to emphasize formal grammar and Powell Stewart's urging to reduce to a minimum the time now spent on formal grammar.

Related to instruction in grammar were these two recommendations pertaining to drill:

1. Cut out other aims, such as childish drills. (Mattione, Dean, Regis)
2. This lack of training in itself again leads to a tendency to drill rather than direct writing. (Clapp, Utah)

Although the "fundamentals" were never clearly defined and one cannot always equate them with grammar, at least 5 of the college respondents wished greater emphasis on fundamentals.

1. By stressing the mastery of fundamentals in elementary and high school, plus some regular practice in writing. (Hankins, Maine)
2. . . . time devoted in high school to instruction in English be spent on primary and fundamental matters to the exclusion of much peripheral matter now included. (Horner, North Carolina)
3. All the way along there is need for greater thoroughness for a mastery of the fundamentals one by one. (Kelso, M.I.T.)
4. We suggest a return to the teaching of fundamentals, and we believe that whatever can be done to encourage students to take pride in expressing themselves well in their native English should be done. (McDermott, U.S. Air Force Academy)
5. . . . being a bit old fashioned, by stressing first and last, a return to fundamentals. (Stewart, Vanderbilt)

RECOMMENDATIONS BY BUSINESS EXECUTIVES

Recommendations to the NCTE concerning the teaching of grammar were even more numerous among our friends in the business community. Some recommendations resembled those of the college persons; in general there was the demand for more teaching of grammar.

1. English grammar should be learned in elementary school. Four more years of drilling in high school are essential if the student is to make language an effective tool. (Borden)

2. . . . the greatest good can be accomplished by a college freshman English course which insures the learning of grammar and develops a consciousness of it. (Campbell Soup)

3. . . . better grounding in the fundamentals of grammar. (Chubb and Company)

4. . . . a more intensive program requiring courses in grammar, rhetoric, and composition on the primary and secondary level than is now apparent in the school system. (America Fire Insurance)

5. There is need for greater effort to instill in the minds of our children, from the very beginning of school, the rules of grammar. (DuPont)

6. More emphasis on . . . grammar that is simple and direct (as used in business letters and reports). (General Mills)

7. Continue English grammar . . . on a review basis through high school. (Goodyear Tire and Rubber)

8. . . . secretaries need more thorough training in the basic skills . . . grammar. (Source withheld on request)

9. . . . increased emphasis should be placed on the fundamentals of grammar, including much drill in the diagramming of sentences. (Liberty-Mutual Insurance Company)

10. It may be helpful if your Council can encourage greater attention from grammar school right through college levels to . . . grammatical usage. (Metropolitan Life)

11. . . . place stronger emphasis on the basic fundamentals of English, emphasizing grammar. (Socony Mobil Company)

12. . . . more stress on the mechanics of grammar. (Philco)

13. We have felt the need for improving the grammar . . . of our employees, particularly stenographers, for quite some time. (Standard Oil)

14. . . . greater emphasis placed on grammar, and the technical phases of English. (Sunshine Biscuits)

15. We feel that grammatical correctness is as important in an underwriting report as it is in a critical comment on *Hamlet*. (Travelers Insurance)

16. Further stress on teaching grammar so that it will be understood. (U.S. Steel)

These 16 recommendations pertaining to greater stress on grammar constitute the largest number in any single category made by 63 business executives. That grammar is important in the opinion of our colleagues in business is obvious. Only 8 of the college respondents made similar recommendations.

Closely allied to greater stress on grammar was the return to "the fundamentals" requested by business executives. Six of them referred to this:

1. . . . high schools . . . should stress the fundamentals more. (Carrier Corp.)

2. . . . better grounding in the fundamentals of grammar, syntax, punctuation, spelling, and handwriting. (Chubb and Company)

3. . . . more concentration and practice on those fundamentals of English which spell the difference between good and bad writing and speaking. (John Hancock)

4. . . . place stronger emphasis on the basic fundamentals of English, emphasizing grammar, spelling, syntax, diction, and reading skills. (Socony Mobil Oil)

5. Increase drills on fundamentals in spelling, syntax, and the essentials of speech. (Pfizer)

6. . . . more time should be spent in high school on fundamental English skills, particularly spelling. (Sears, Roebuck)

RECOMMENDATIONS FROM CIVIL SERVICE ADMINISTRATORS

Altogether the 29 civil service administrators made recommendations in 25 categories, ranging from "acceleration" to "written composition." Concerning grammar, these three recommendations were made:

1. Emphasize grammatical principles in the speaking medium. (Director of Operations, 3700 Military Training Wing, ATC)
2. Provide intensive review of English grammar in high school and in freshman years of college. (Director of Personnel, Department of Commerce)
3. . . . grammar . . . needs more attention in our schools. (Deputy Assistant Postmaster General)

The two statements concerning "fundamentals" were:

1. I hope greater emphasis can be placed on the fundamentals of English and the discipline of writing. (Director of Information, Department of Agriculture)
2. . . . but I would recommend constant drilling in the fundamentals of English as a possible source of improvement. (Director of Personnel, Interstate Commerce Commission)

As was stated earlier in this chapter, E. H. Morse, Jr., Director, Accounting and Auditing Policy Staff of the U.S. General Accounting Office, elicited comments from 100 employees, supervisors of recent college graduates and regional office managers. Their references to grammar merits particular attention since they came from the largest single group of any U.S. agency in this survey.

RECOMMENDATIONS FROM THE U.S. GENERAL ACCOUNTING OFFICE

1. I feel that raising the standards for completion of existing English courses and placing more emphasis on basic grammar . . . would help to correct the deficiencies.

2. To require a full four years of English courses in high school with no substitutions permitted. These courses should be concentrated in the study of the rules of grammar, sentence and paragraph structure, composition, and literature.

3. Basic composition and grammar both written and oral should be made a part of each course in the college curriculum rather than being a separate and distinct area. Most students have completed their formal English work by the time they are juniors and their application of basic composition and grammar principles depends upon the subject matter and the teacher in courses other than English.

4. I recommend that more emphasis be placed on the fundamentals of grammar on the high school level.

5. More adequate indoctrination in grammar, sentence structure, and correct word usage at both the high school and college levels.

6. English classes should emphasize application of grammar.

7. All staff members stated that more emphasis should be placed on English in colleges, particularly with respect to grammar, spelling, and composition.

8. . . . more emphasis be placed on grammatical construction in English courses.

9. A writer should have a good knowledge of grammar and grammatical terms. He should know the parts of speech and their uses.

10. It may be that disregard for grammar is part of today's

apparent rebellion against circumscription and discipline. Students should be made to understand that discipline still has a place and that they cannot hope to write correctly and clearly without making use of the basic tools of writing, which are the rules of grammar. Students should be shown that these rules were not established arbitrarily and not taught merely for their own sake; it can easily be demonstrated that abiding by the rules contributes to both the clarity and the logic of the writing.

11. It would be well to return to the teaching of parsing or diagramming so that students will acquire the habit of examining their sentences to see that everything fits together properly and that nothing is left over.

12. First, don't let them escape without a good foundation in the basic building blocks of spelling and grammar because deficiencies here will retard them to a degree disproportionate to their over-all capabilities.

13. Our experience has shown that, if one is equipped with a good basis in spelling and grammar, improvement in construction and composition has come with practice.

14. Extend teaching of grammar and English composition all through grammar school, high school, and college.

15. I recommend that additional emphasis be placed on writing and the basic principles of grammar and punctuation.

16. I believe the Council could be of help in producing students better equipped in all phases of English by pursuing forcibly a program designed to sell college faculties and the students on the need for additional training in the practicable application of the basic rules to both oral and written composition.

17. The elementary rules of good grammar should be continually emphasized . . .

18. The present unsatisfactory conditions would seem to call for greater emphasis on and better teaching of, the fundamental basic rules of grammar.
19. More required courses in English, particularly composition and grammar, be included in curricula at all school levels.
20. More intensive courses of study in the use of the language in high school with particular emphasis upon spelling and grammar.
21. Some college graduates appear to know the rules of grammar but are unable to apply them in composition.
22. Diagramming of sentences is very useful in learning the parts of speech and their use in sentences.

It is rather significant that these recommendations for greater emphasis on grammar were made by supervisors of employees trained in accounting and allied disciplines. In their honest opinion, such training would have enabled their employees to express themselves more effectively in oral and written forms.

RECOMMENDATIONS BY EDITORS

Our editorial respondents likewise had recommendations for greater emphasis on grammar. Thus, Sumner Blossom of Crowell-Collier thought ". . . that the grade schools should offer more intensive training in the fundamentals of grammar." John Fischer, editor of *Harper's*, wished "much greater concentration in grade school on solid grounding in . . . grammar." The editor of *Popular Science* declared, "I favor drilling the young in grammar." More specifically, Marjorie L. Burns, Copy Editor of *Cosmopolitan*, would "make students learn to conjugate verbs . . . and decline nouns and adjectives." Kay Thomas, Managing Editor of *Charm*, had an interesting observation on diagramming: "In teaching construction, I am a great believer in diagramming of sentences. I found my own children learned the parts of speech and the relations of phrases to main clauses much more readily after I had taught them how to diagram."

Returning to "fundamentals" was asked by Charles A. Fell, editor of the *Birmingham News,* C. B. Lindeman, Publisher of the *Seattle Post-Intelligencer,* and Robert Bottorff, Executive Editor of the *Wall Street Journal.* Emphasis on grammar was deemed desirable by Dave Peugeot, of the *Buffalo Evening News,* and D. F. Caswell, Education Editor of the *Los Angeles Examiner.* A. Ranger Tyler, Associate Editor, *New York State Education,* would like greater drill on the structure of the language.

RECOMMENDATIONS FROM JUDICIAL AND LEGISLATIVE PERSONNEL

Grammar and the "fundamentals" were mentioned occasionally by our colleagues on the bench and in Congress. John J. Rhodes, representative from Arizona, declared: "I would suggest that you go back to teaching conjugation, declensions, diagramming of sentences, and identification of the parts of speech." Robert Hale, representative from Maine, would like "drill in fundamentals of grammar."

Roscoe L. Barrow, Dean of the Law School of the University of Cincinnati, felt that "additional emphasis in high school and college on grammar . . . would greatly aid the pre-law student in preparing for his professional study." Leon H. Wallace, Dean of the School of Law, Indiana University, felt strongly about understanding the structure of the English language and its precise use.

EVALUATION AND SUMMARY

It is evident from these statements from outstanding representatives of several disciplines that instruction in grammar and the "fundamentals" appear to them as rather important aspects of our task as teachers of English. It is significant that far more such recommendations have come from men and women in industry and in civil service than from the college representatives. How much of this is due to nostalgia for one's high school and college days with recollection of subjects taught, or how much is due to actual studies in the relationship between knowledge of grammar and ability to speak and write effectively, it is difficult to say. The frequency of the appeal for greater emphasis on grammar from so many respondents indicates at least this obvious conclusion: to *them* grammar is very important, and its real or apparent neglect to be deplored.

Perhaps greater distribution of the Council's publication of the *Report of the Commission on the Curriculum* to nonteaching personnel would benefit all of us who are endeavoring to perform the huge task of meeting the needs of almost 50,000,000 Americans in English. Greater dissemination of information of actual practices in teaching grammar in the schools and colleges would allay some of the unfounded fears and misconceptions. More evidence of how much grammar should be taught, how and when it should be taught, and how to make the transfer from knowledge of rules to effective application in speech and writing should be publicized not only among our English teaching colleagues but to the informed public generally.

READING SKILLS AND LITERARY BACKGROUND

The history of American education is almost a history of the criticism of American education. The history of reading in America is likewise a history of the criticism of reading instruction. Flesch's *Why Johnny Can't Read* happened to obtain more publicity, but it had many forerunners and will undoubtedly have numerous successors.

Among the 79 college presidents who responded, 23 made some comment about reading which was critical of the skill or the tastes of students in reading. Typical of the criticisms were such statements as:

1. Greatest inadequacy (of the four aspects of language arts) was in reading. (Alabama, Arizona, Arkansas, Tennessee)
2. Students have not been required to do much reading outside of textbooks. (Earlham, Iowa)
3. Weakness in comprehending what is read. (American U., Carnegie, Southwestern, Xavier, Cincinnati, N. Carolina)
4. Less and less knowledge of classic and traditional literature. (Rhode Island, Tennessee, Princeton, Vanderbilt, Villa Madonna)
5. Lack of proper training in reading skills. (Baylor, Nevada, Northwestern)

Similar criticisms may be found in the letters from representatives of other professions. Just as there were many criticisms of reading skills and tastes in reading of recent graduates, there were likewise many recommendations for remedying these deficiencies. The second highest number of recommendations among the college presidents (or their representatives) pertained to reading and literature (26). Some of the recommendations were general, such as "more reading encouraged" (Alabama) or "encourage students to read widely" (Southwestern) or "encourage reading and discussion of challenging material" (Wisconsin).

With these recommendations, every member of the Council would agree. Among the more specific recommendations were:

1. *Better reading materials*
   . . . work for better reading materials in the secondary schools. At present I think many of them are still working with some of the so-called classics when they could accomplish a great deal more by reading books which have some

vital interest to teenagers. This doesn't mean that the reading has to be trash. It can be reading which stimulates ideas which can in turn serve as the basis for practice in composition. (Kelso, M.I.T.)

2. *More close reading*

... students in grammar and high school could profit greatly by more practice in close reading of materials of recognized quality. Rapid reading of second- or third-rate magazines and books may have a very real place in the high school curriculum. But nothing will take the place of disciplined reading in class of good works ... The National Council could officially endorse a fairly stable curriculum in English, with emphasis upon class reading of good books —I think it could be a great service to the cause of better preparation of both terminal and college-bound students. (Sensabaugh, Stanford)

In a similar vein Dr. Estrich for Ohio State writes:

While our poorer students have usually read practically nothing, and sometimes can't read, our real problem for the average student is simply that, first, he hasn't read enough and that, second, he hasn't read enough stuff that makes an intellectual demand upon him. ... It doesn't matter whether one picks out informative prose, fiction, plays, or poetry. The students have had too little experience in distinguishing what is major from what is subsidiary, in following a pattern of thought, in recognizing the way in which a body of material is organized, in following logical, or emotional, or rhetorical lines. These weaknesses come out of sheer inexperience. The youngsters have not been required to do enough careful reading of reasonably adult material.

As a result, they don't know how. This again, of course, in so far as it is peculiarly an English problem, is as much due to the overwork of the teacher as to anything else.

3. *Emphasize the position of literature in the lives of the students*
   Some typical expressions of this recommendation:

   I can only voice my hope that NCTE will continue to insist as it has been insisting on the central portion of literature in our lives. (Cronin, Fordham)

   . . . can affirm and reaffirm the central and crucially important place of literature in the high school course. (Bailey, Nebraska)

4. *Reading literary works of high quality*
   Such recommendations came from Princeton, Oberlin, Iowa State, U. of Connecticut, Regis, Swarthmore, Yale.

5. *Training students to read exposition* (Texas)
   With all of these recommendations the Council has long been in agreement, as its various statements in the volumes of the Commission on the English Curriculum and other publications well testify.

RECOMMENDATIONS ON READING FROM BUSINESS EXECUTIVES

Twelve of the executives in business made recommendations to the Council to improve the reading competence of our students. They ran the gamut from the long-desired goal of every English teacher—"devise ways to instill a lifetime reading habit among students at the earliest possible age" (Yale and Towne) to "the more people read, the better they write" (Motorola).

Categorizing the several recommendations:

1. Concentrate on reading comprehension. (American Tobacco, Campbell Soup)
2. More thorough reading . . . training (Chubb and Company)
3. . . . promote reading as a habit and a skill to the end that it becomes an enjoyment. (Equitable Trust, Socony Mobil Company)
4. Have more required reading. (Goodyear Tire and Rubber)
5. Stimulate students to read more material on current events, as well as basic literature. (Pfizer)
6. . . . young people who have had a wide background of reading tend to be better communicators. (International Paper Foundation)
7. . . . by study of the best literature . . . the development of a writing style which expresses clearly, accurately and vividly the intended message. (Liberty Mutual)

Civil service administrators had one recommendation each for reading and literature. The Director of Operations of 3700 Military Training Wing ATC, recommended "increase skill in reading for speed and comprehension." The Director of the Bureau of Programs and Standards of the U.S. Civil Service Commission was in favor of "requiring a higher proportion of students, no matter what their technical interest, to take courses in literature —or anything which required wide reading."

Among the replies collected by E. H. Morse, Jr., Director, Accounting and Auditing Policy Staff of the U.S. General Accounting Office, several contained recommendations on reading:

> I believe that college students, and graduates, should be urged to read recognized masters of the English language more often than they now do, whether those masters be poets, novelists or writers of nonfiction.

Encourage students to read good books and other material. The fact should be stressed that reading not only improves the mind and vocabulary but also gives an appreciation of good composition and a feeling for good word usage and sentence structure. Here too the point should be stressed that good English is a tool for self-advancement. English teachers should realize that they have something to offer just as important in a materialistic way as that offered in technical courses that stress "know how," methods and procedures.

. . . step up required reading, place emphasis on ingraining the reading habit.

I suggest that students be required to do more reading of good literature.

Encourage and develop good reading habits. Reading good books is one of the best methods by which a person can expand his vocabulary.

To require, within the existing curriculum, extensive outside reading on the part of both high school and college students.

Since Mr. Morse elicited his replies from 100 individuals in the Washington office and 19 regional offices, it is reasonable to assume that the comments above pertaining to reading represent thinking in various parts of the country.

RECOMMENDATIONS FROM MAGAZINE EDITORS PERTAINING TO READING IMPROVEMENT

Seven of the magazine editors replied with reference to reading, in more detail than their confreres in business or in civil service. From Kay Thomas, Managing Editor of *Charm:*

I think that all students of English should be encouraged to read more—good books, classics as well as the best modern books. I believe in long reading lists during the school year and summer vacation, with mandatory reports, both oral and written. Perhaps some system of credit could be inaugurated to encourage more reading—for those students who settle for the minimum work.

John Fisher, Editor of *Harper's,* spoke in strong terms:

Adoption of curricula which will demonstrate to high school students that books can be exciting, interesting, and useful, rather than deadly bores. A first step might be to eliminate from the required reading lists such old chestnuts as *Ivanhoe*—a third-rate historical novel which is still required (or so I understand) in many American high schools today, in spite of the fact that it probably has alienated more children from reading than any work in history.

Finally, there is the strong comment by Alice Morris, Literary Editor of *Harper's Bazaar:*

As the mother of two children who have attended both private and public schools, I have been struck by the poor imaginative and literary quality of the "readers" used in the first four or five years of learning to read. . . . the method—one of repetition of new words . . . seemed perfectly intelligent. However, the characters and subject matter were so banal, so lacking in imagination, excitement and literary stimulation that I cannot see how these books could accomplish what should be a primary aim: to make the child think of reading as tremendous fun, as opening the door into strange and wonderful worlds outside his own immediate experience.

We could all agree with Marjorie L. Burns, Copy Editor of *Cosmopolitan,* who would "teach students to be critical readers by instructing them in elementary logic and helping them develop sensitivity to diction, tone, and intent in writing. We need shrewd and wary language consumers as much as we need skilled producers."

Editors of newspapers made 6 recommendations for improvement of reading. Again, these varied from such generalities as "stressing the value of reading good books for pleasure" from the *Buffalo Evening News* and "increase emphasis on English literature" from the *Houston Chronicle,* to such an extended comment as that by D. F. Caswell, Education Editor of the *Los Angeles Examiner.*

This field certainly is no worse than in my school days of 25 years ago, and it probably is better. The bad effects of trashy TV and comic books, never any worse than vaudeville and dime novels, have been at least offset by some very good TV and paperbacks, widely accessible. Men like Dr. Frank Baxter have shown TV audiences that Shakespeare and Dickens can be exciting, exalting and great fun when taught by good showmen, and showmanship always was the main tool of the teacher of literature, long before TV, whether we admit it or not.

A touching comment by (the late) Seymour Berkson, publisher of the *New York Journal-American,* has added poignancy because of the personal reference:

One of the best avenues toward mastery of the English language is familiarity with the great works that have been written in that language. One of the tragic consequences of modern life in America, with the invasion of television, etc., is the deterioration of reading habits among youngsters and the difficulty teachers have in stimulating and inspiring our young folks to taste the joys of literature.

As the father of a teenager, I know that I went through a long period of struggle with my own son, who is now 19, in an effort to inspire him to read the beautiful works that were available in our library at home. He was a youngster in his formative years, was subjected to the initial attraction of TV. We had many difficulties on that score but strangely enough, during his second year at Lawrenceville prep school, it was an English teacher there who managed to capture his imagination to such an extent that suddenly he began to sit up all night devouring the wonderful works that he had been guided to discover. He developed, from that point on, a real proficiency in his English to such an extent that he graduated with top honors in both poetry and essay writing. He is today headed for a writing career and his mastery of English is nothing short of unusual for his age.

W. E. Christenson, president and editor of the *Omaha World-Herald,* has the impression that a good many young people who "want to write" have not done enough reading, and thus have not acquired a proper feeling for the language or a decent respect for it. Finally, Edward J. Meeman, editor of the *Memphis Press-Scimitar,* would require more of students. In his judgment, this is a responsibility of parents as well as teachers.

From the three educational editors who made recommendations on this aspect of English, there were three different emphases. William W. Brickman, editor of *School and Society,* wants "more exposure to foreign (comparative) literature." George G. Mallinson, editor of *School Science and Mathematics,* thinks "a great deal more emphasis should be placed on . . . the analysis of modern literature—in both high school and college English. In my own judgment, much of the classical literature perused by students both in high school and college is a waste of time."

Finally, E. I. F. Williams, editor of *Educational Forum,* makes a strong plea for worthy materials:

> In the teaching of literature I think the tendency is rather strong to use materials which have little rank as literature just because they appeal to the child's or teacher's fleeting interest in current magazines. I believe that the interest of children reflects the character and quality of the teacher. So far as the age group allows, I think it would improve our English teaching were the subject matter in literature selected on the basis of enduring rather than ephemeral values.

OTHER MISCELLANEOUS RECOMMENDATIONS

Two deans of law schools responded on this point. Daniel P. Ward, Dean of the De Paul University Law School, wanted "requirements for extensive outside reading." Roger Howell, Dean of the University of Maryland Law School, suggested an "increase in the amount of required work in literature." Robert Hale, Congressman from Portland, Maine, suggested more reading of good books.

Since not all the respondents felt that our students were less prepared in reading skills and literary appreciation, it would be only fair to quote their reasons. From Dr. Becker, Head of the Department of English at Swarthmore, comes the opinion that:

Present entrants into Swarthmore are certainly more widely read in modern literature than they were 10 years ago.

Dr. Hughes, Chairman of Freshman English, University of Vermont, feels that:

Students have read more widely in various fields and have a more general breadth of knowledge.

President O. C. Aderhold of the University of Georgia thought that:

Their general knowledge of literature seems improved.

Similar improvement was noted by Dr. Hankins, Head of the English Department of the University of Maine.

IMPROVEMENT NOTED IN READING SKILLS AND LITERATURE

1. Their (recent students) general knowledge of literature seems improved. (Aderhold, Georgia)
2. Present entrants into Swarthmore are certainly more widely

read in modern literature than they were 10 years ago. (Becker, Head, Department of English, Swarthmore)

3. Students have read more widely in various fields and have a more general breadth of knowledge. (Hughes, Chairman of Freshman English, University of Vermont)

4. Possibly some improvement in appreciation of literature. (Hankins, Head, Department of English, University of Maine)

5. Over the past 10 years there has been improvement in the quality of the reading skills our students bring to college. (Streeter, University of Chicago)

6. There was general agreement that Barnard students of this day seem better prepared in English than the students of 5 to 10 years ago. (Robertson, Head, Department of English, Barnard)

7. The general feeling seems to be that students who are coming to Boston University are now somewhat better prepared in all areas of English than they were 5 to 10 years ago. (Winslow, Head, Department of English, Boston University)

ANALYSIS AND INTERPRETATION

From almost all types of respondents came many expressions of opinion about the importance of literature in the lives of all of us, and of the desirability of improving the skills in reading at both the secondary and college level. The National Council has long been interested in improving the reading skills in schools above the eighth grade, as well as in the primary grades. Hardly a meeting in the past 15 or 20 years has failed to include these topics on the annual programs. Such portfolios as *They Will Read Literature* and *What We Know About High School Reading* reflect the Council's constant advocacy of strong reading programs on the secondary level, both for skill improvement and appreciation.

The many book lists, which have included thousands of recommended books, for the past three decades have guided countless English teachers, librarians, and members of boards of education.

Likewise in the advocacy of newer reading materials that are challenging both in their content and difficulty, the Council has long anticipated some of the recommendations of our friends in nonteaching professions.

Perhaps more improvement in reading tastes has taken place than the average person realizes, as the chapter in this report based on reports from librarians and publishers would seem to indicate.

TEACHER PREPARATION AND CERTIFICATION

The Council has long been deeply interested in the preparation and certification of English teachers. Its Committee on Preparation and Certification has made significant contributions to various publications dealing with this subject; its members have recently (at the 14th Conference of Teacher Education and Professional Standards in 1959) achieved nation-wide publicity, have spoken up vigorously before various accrediting bodies in behalf of better standards of preparation at the training institutions. Furthermore, Volume V of the *Report of the Commission on the Curriculum* will be devoted entirely to teacher preparation at all levels of English education.

For all these reasons, teachers of English and teacher-trainers will find the recommendations by the respondents of this report of more than passing interest. As might be expected, a large number of college personnel had some comment to make on the improvement of teacher training. Eighteen suggestions were made on this topic, six on teacher certification, and two on recruitment. This is the second largest number of all recommendations coming from the colleges, and testifies to the importance attached to teacher preparation as one way to strengthen the English program nationally.

As was to be expected from such a group of respondents, there was much emphasis on strengthening the subject-matter courses as opposed to the education courses. Such suggestions came from all kinds of institutions and from all parts of the country.

1. More stress in college on basic courses and less on methodology. (Bonham, Dean, Alabama)

2. The training of students who are going into English teaching needs careful review. A truly functional program which emphasizes reading, writing, speaking, and listening, should supplant the usual series of courses in education taken only to meet the demands of teacher certification. (Clark, Head, Department of English, American University)

3. Reduced requirements in education for high school certification. Five semester hours of practice teaching plus six semester hours of theory is more than enough. (Faulkner, Head, Department of English, Arkansas)

4. Many members of the Department feel that liberal arts education for future teachers of English should be stressed, rather than courses in methodology. (Winslow, Head, Department of English, Boston University)

5. Improve the training of teachers in their subject matter. (Ogilvy, Head, Department of English, Colorado University)

6. . . . many teachers in the secondary schools are themselves inadequately prepared . . . Too many teachers are certified for work which does not excel the level of the college sophomore survey course. Many teachers colleges do not have adequate offering of high level period and genre courses, and their students count as work in their special field, courses in education. We must all work to keep the

hours of education required for permanent certification to a maximum of 18 and we need to plump increasingly for the M.A. in English. (Novarr, Director, Freshman English, Cornell)

7. . . . college students preparing to teach English in high schools should, perhaps, have their course requirements in English increased. A course in linguistics might be especially valuable to them. (Perkins, President, University of Delaware)

8. Dunn, Head of the Department of English, Drake University, comments: The Iowa Council of Teachers of English . . . is exerting very strong pressure upon the colleges in Iowa to increase the requirements of teacher training in subject matter to 30 hours.

9. The council can help instruction in English by championing . . . better college training in subject matter. (Dean, Head, Department of English, University of Connecticut)

10. . . . NCTE can be of best service to us by doing all possible to encourage and support by every means available the better preparation of prospective teachers of English on the secondary levels. It might, for example, tactfully continue the evaluation of college programs for English teachers with secondary teaching needs very particularly in mind. Our English Department seems convinced of the need for more training in language fundamentals and more attention to practical problems that are likely to be encountered by teachers in our secondary schools. (Martin, President, Emory)

11. . . . continuing to emphasize the necessity of high school English teachers receiving a strong undergraduate major in English. This should include work in the English language, composition, and British and American literature. (Steffens, Executive Dean, University of Idaho)

12. By bending its efforts to the sponsorship of adequate standards of preparation and proficiency for teachers . . . the National Council can assist markedly in upgrading the profession. (Rice, Head, Department of English, University of Michigan)

13. The Council should emphasize to all teacher training colleges and universities and to the high school teachers themselves that they improve, deepen, and strengthen instruction in the subject matter of English language and literature. Instruction in the methodology of English teaching need not be given any more emphasis than at present. (Hovde, President, Purdue)

14. . . . by insisting that they be specifically trained in subject matter. (Simmons, Head, Department of English, University of Rhode Island)

15. The Council can continue to be the most helpful in emphasizing the importance of the subject matter content of English courses at all levels. Unless a teacher knows very thoroughly literature written in English and the English language, and unless he is enthusiastic about this material, he cannot be a very effective instrument in training children and young people. (Ehvensperger, Head, Department of English, State University of South Dakota)

It is quite obvious from these 15 quotations that future teachers of English should have a thorough training in the backgrounds of the subject they will teach. To be perfectly fair to the teacher-training institutions it would have been desirable to receive comments from their representatives, indicating how many courses in education they deem necessary for competence in meeting the needs of today's children and youth.

TEACHER CERTIFICATION

Closely related to the preparation of English teachers is the matter of certification. In this area there were 6 recommendations, as follows:

1. Increased requirements in subject-matter fields for certification. Advanced composition and grammar should be required, and journalism courses should not count toward certification. (Faulkner, Head, Department of English, Arkansas)

2. Secondly, I think that we must turn our attention to getting at the teachers who are not primarily English teachers. English teaching is the football of people who are preparing teachers' loads. Principals in Iowa seem to hire home ec teachers, coaches, foreign language teachers first; then they spread the English courses among the people whom they have already hired. (Crosby, formerly Writing Supervisor, State University of Iowa)

3. . . . increased subject-matter requirements for certification of high school teachers. (Kitzhaber, former Director, Freshman English, University of Kansas)

4. Continue the excellent work of the Committee in behalf of studies and investigations leading to the improvement of the preparation and certification of teachers of English. (Emberger, Director of Composition, University of Louisville)

5. By bending its efforts to the sponsorship of . . . better methods of certification the National Council can assist markedly in upgrading the profession. (Rice, Head, Department of English, University of Michigan)

6. The Council might well have a thorough look at current "certification" requirements under which prospective public school teachers take an excessive number of education courses and recommend that prospective teachers of Eng-

lish be required to extend their training in the subject matter they are planning to teach. (Hovde, President, Purdue)

The two comments on teacher recruitment expressed the desire with which all of us would agree that every effort be made to recruit the best possible candidates.

RECOMMENDATIONS BY BUSINESS EXECUTIVES

Even among the business executives, there was a deprecation of excessive preoccupation with methodology as evidenced by the reply from the representative of the American Fore Insurance Companies:

Unfortunately, meaningless methodology, as prerequisite for a license to teach, has precedence over basic knowledge of subject matter as the fundamental qualification for teaching.

From DuPont came the suggestion that "There is opportunity for establishing a better balance in teacher preparation between method and subject content, which would give us improvement over anything we have had in the past."

Finally, Eastman Kodak expressed the thought that "any efforts made in the better preparation of English teachers at all levels will be thoroughly applauded by industrial management."

As to the place of educational courses, American Fore Insurance would "suggest that educational courses be eliminated and replaced by additional courses in English grammar, literature and composition in the college curriculum as prerequisites for candidates for teachers of English."

RECOMMENDATIONS BY CIVIL SERVICE PERSONNEL AND OTHER GROUPS

There were no recommendations on teacher preparation from any of the civil service administrators. There were two interesting comments from the magazine editors. Herbert R. Mayes, Editor of *Good Housekeeping,* was rather strong in his recommendation:

"I have come across few teachers who can speak the English language correctly or who are familiar with the rudiments of grammar. I have been shocked constantly by the extraordinary inability of most of the teachers I have met to speak and write English properly. In addition to my personal meetings with teachers, I can tell you that several years ago I conducted a short story contest that was limited to teachers of English in American colleges and universities. Several thousand manuscripts were submitted. I believe it was at that time that my hair turned white. So my recommendation, if any, would be to teach English to our teachers in order that they might better be able to teach it to their students."

John Fisher, editor of *Harper's,* advocates "the appointment of English teachers who have some skill in and affection for the English language—whether or not they may have taken all the technical courses in education required by most teachers colleges."

A plea for more subject matter also came from Edward J. Meeman, Editor, *Memphis Press-Scimitar,* who urged that we "give up the requirement that teachers study 'education' which none of my own excellent high school teachers had studied—but require them to know their subjects."

Royce Howes, Associate Editor, *Detroit Free-Press,* stated that "Chief emphasis . . . should be placed on better preparation of English teachers—as English teachers."

Adequate preparation in the area of English was also advocated by George B. Schick, Editor, *Journal of Developmental Reading.* He would like to "get down to the level of the PTA, room mothers, and interested parents and provide these groups with solid facts, cogent arguments, and inspiration to enable them to *demand* that certificating agencies recognize fully the requirement of adequate preparation in his own area for every qualified teacher."

T. M. Stinett, Editor of the *Journal of Teacher Education,* would "press for certification and preparation requirements which would assure broadly educated English teachers."

Inks Franklin, Editor, *School and Community,* made two suggestions:

"Other things being equal, better students are produced by better teachers. This then leads to the making of two suggestions: First, those who desire to prepare to be teachers of English should receive more careful screening before being permitted to enter courses leading to a certificate to teach in this field; secondly, we would hope that those who teach our future teachers of English at the college level might be better prepared to do this job through the use of a few well selected educational courses."

Frank E. Maloney, Acting Dean, School of Law, University of Florida, was another proponent of increased emphasis on subject matter. He urged the Council to "use its influence to change the methods of training teachers. Currently the accent seems to be on teaching teachers how to teach, rather than on giving them proper knowledge of their subjects."

George McGovern, member of the House of Representatives from South Dakota, felt that stepping up the qualifications of our teachers on all levels was the key to the problem of improving the English program. "Good teaching," he stated, "has always been the heart of education. It is regrettable that inadequte salaries and the condescending attitude toward the teaching profession on the part of many communities has hampered our efforts to maintain a consistently high quality of teaching standards."

SUMMARY AND INTERPRETATION

The many quotations of this section seem to argue for:

1. Stronger preparation in subject matter of English both in literature and language.
2. A re-evaluation of the proper place of courses in education that will be helpful in preparing teachers to meet the needs of today's children.
3. Greater degree of selectivity of personnel to be trained.
4. Adequate training in the basic skills, so that teachers might be exemplars for their students in the areas they teach.
5. Less employment of non-English trained personnel to teach English.
6. A re-evaluation of certification requirements, especially with respect to the proportion of courses in subject matter and courses in education.

An examination of the recent statements of the Committee on Preparation and Certification of English Teachers of the Council would demonstrate agreement with the recommendations made by the respondents of this report. However, most of the respondents probably were unaware that in most secondary programs for preparing teachers of English, only 10% to 15% of the total hours required are in education, with two or three times as much in English.

The shape of English to come, both as to its content and methodology, always fascinates the scholar. While it would be foolhardy to predict with any degree of certainty anything in this uncertain world, the many facts and opinions in *Attitudes Toward English Teaching* point to some valid conclusions. For the purpose of clarity and emphasis, these are arranged in categories.

I. Emphasis on English as the Basic Subject in the Curriculum

Almost every document in recent years that has discussed education in any way has referred to some extent to the importance of English and to the greater emphasis that should be placed upon it at all levels of instruction. These include such statements as the Rockefeller Brothers Report, *The Pursuit of Excellence,* the Conant Reports on the junior and senior high schools, the Jewett study of courses of study in English Language Arts for the U.S. Office of Education, and many other statements. Even such critics of current educational practice as Admiral H. G. Rickover and Professor Alfred Bestor have asked for greater emphasis on English at all levels. A cursory reading of the many expressions of business executives as given in this book will demonstrate the high regard that our business leaders have for English both for personal growth and development and economic success. The various programs being carried out in technical institutions for enlarging the place of the humanities in the training programs for future scientists, engineers, and technicians all emphasize the need for a strong English language and literature ingredient in the training of these technical and scientific leaders. Perhaps the best summary of the point of view is expressed by Professor W. W. Watson, Chairman of the Physics Department of Yale University:

"I feel that the most important subject in the entire course of study in the elementary and college preparatory years is the English language. What can be more important than to handle our own workaday language with facility, no matter what the lifework, business or profession? I have some younger physics colleagues who obviously write with difficulty. They are promising scientists who love to work in the laboratory but they are laggards in writing papers that describe their results. But what good are research reports unless they are properly described in a well-written report?

"Also, it is most important that a scientist or engineer be able to get on his feet and speak clearly about his work. Some practice in public speaking, debating, or dramatics should be a part of every student's course.

"I am pleased to note that one of President Conant's main recommendations is that all school students should study English every year, and that half this work should be in composition." [1]

II. Emphasis on Articulation of English Content and Methodology at All Levels

Teachers at all levels realize more and more that the entire English program would be immeasurably strengthened by a closer articulation. When courses of study appear today, they are more often appearing as Grade 1 to 12 documents rather than English for Primary Grades, Middle Grades, Junior High School, or Senior High School. The teachers and supervisors preparing such courses of study are usually representatives from all levels of instruction, frequently including consultants from the liberal arts colleges and teacher education institutions. In this manner, the whole spectrum of the student's English needs can be examined by experts from all levels, and provisions can be made for a well-articulated program.

In addition to articulation in curriculum construction, there are other interesting experiments going on, which may well influence English instruction throughout the country. For example, the Conference on Basic Issues in the Teaching of English, sponsored in 1958 by the Modern Language Association, the College English Association, the American Studies Association, and the National Council of Teachers of English, demonstrates close articulation on a horizontal as well as a vertical basis. The publi-

---

[1] Quoted by John F. Schereschewsky, Director, Rumsey Hall School, at the 33rd Annual Meeting of the Secondary Education Board, New York City, March 6, 1959, and reprinted with his and Dr. Watson's permission.

cation in 1959 that resulted from these conferences, *Basic Issues in the Teaching of English,* has been circulated to tens of thousands of English teachers in every section of the country, to be followed by serious discussion and plans for action.

Furthermore, various experiments are going on between colleges and school systems in which secondary school teachers and college instructors exchange classes. In this way firsthand evidence is obtained about the problems of teaching on the secondary level which will lead to greater understanding of the needs of college students. In some instances summer institutes are being conducted to which secondary and college instructors are invited. Exchange of opinions leads often to common solutions of basic problems. When Thomas Hale Hamilton was inaugurated as President of the State University of New York, he pinpointed the problem well in his statement:

"A major and too infrequently noted weakness in our education is its segmentation—segmentation which manifests itself horizontally by the unnatural splitting of knowledge into smaller and smaller compartments, and vertically by an insistence that the domains of elementary, secondary and higher education have boundaries as inviolate as those of sovereign states. Yet nothing could be more false or better designed to weaken the total impact of the educational enterprise.

". . . Truly, let an elementary school any place be wounded and some place, some time, a college will bleed."

III. Greater Individualization of Instruction

America was founded on the concept of the value and dignity of the individual. More and more teachers and administrators are expressing concern for methods of individualizing instruction, despite the growing enrollments in schools and colleges. Among the means that are being employed are the following:

1. Multiple-track courses that would achieve a modicum of homogeneity of native potentialities, interests, and needs with subsequent programs to meet these needs.

2. Reduction of class size to permit more attention to each member of the class. The Conant recommendations of 25 students per class with a maximum of 100 to a teacher is gradually being adopted by individual schools and school systems which can afford it.

3. Individualized reading and writing programs, with special attention to books, methodology, and evaluation.

4. A rich program of extracurricular activities such as publications, dramatic performances, and similar enriching experiences for the individually gifted child.

5. Adequate supply of textbooks and other instructional materials to serve all the students.

6. Preparation in teacher-training institutions that will enable future teachers to recognize individual differences and modify their teaching in different situations.

7. Experimentation in evaluative procedures so that the student who may be "different from the crowd" may not be lost or neglected.

Here again, attention to individual differences is not particularly new in the history of education. Confucius apparently was similarly concerned, for he wrote:

"There are four common errors in education which the teacher must beware of. Some students try to learn too much or too many subjects, some learn too little or too few subjects, some learn things too easily and some are too easily discouraged. These four things show that individuals differ in their mental endowments and only through a knowledge of the different mental endowments can the teacher correct their mistakes. A teacher is but a man who tries to bring out the good and remedy the weaknesses of his students."

IV. Greater Emphasis on Written Expression

As was indicated in previous pages, most of the recommendations for improving English instruction were in the area of written composition. Recent reports, like those of Dr. Conant, have likewise stressed its importance and the need for more corrected written work. This is a problem which must be met by concerted action of all who are concerned with education. The taxpayers must be willing to grant adequate budgets so that class size will be realistic enough to permit a secondary school teacher to correct an acceptable number of papers frequently enough to achieve improvement. Administrators must provide sufficient time in a teacher's day to permit conferences with students for guiding their work. Study halls and cafeterias can just as well be manned by mature but untrained adults, who would then release English teachers to perform duties for which they are especially equipped. Administrators could help also by insisting that teachers in all subject areas do their part by insisting that students submit legible, carefully organized papers, free from gross errors. Teachers of areas other than English must become aware of their obligation to insist on high standards in the written work submitted to them. This may necessitate joint meetings of several departments to decide upon minimum standards of legibility, correct form, and organization which would be required of written work in all subject areas.

English teachers will have to assume the major burden of improvement of written composition by discovering more effective ways of motivating their assignments, by presentation of the principles of good and effective writing, and by judicious and frequent evaluation of their students' papers. A word like "illiterate" written in violent red ink across the first paper of the term will contribute little to the urge for self-improvement or the way toward self-improvement of any child. Nor will such an assignment as "For Monday—write a composition of 1,000 words on ——" go far to produce verbal gems of purest ray serene. There are many things we now know about motivation, preparation, anticipation of probable errors, and effective evaluation which English teachers must and should apply if they are to carry their share of the burden of the concerted attack on improving written composition.

Parents, too, have a contribution to make. They should realize that writing is perhaps the most difficult of the language arts to acquire and that it is as difficult for their child to produce a well-organized and gracefully written composition as it is for a highly paid professional writer to produce his latest short story or article. They should know that good writing requires concentration, freedom from distraction, frequent revision, and considerable time. They should have enough pride and interest in their child's work to see that it is done neatly; to give it the courtesy of an occasional reading; to be willing to discuss with their child the preliminary phases before the child begins to write; and to examine the evaluative comments from the teacher.

Finally, the student must be willing to do his part in the concerted effort. After all, no amount of tax outlay, good instruction, well-lit classrooms, and other favorable circumstances will contribute much to writing improvement without a corresponding desire on his part to improve. He must develop pride in his work, a sense of integrity in employing sources, courtesy to his teacher who acts as a highly skilled but lowly paid editor and critic of his effusions. When students will have developed the same enthusiasm for excelling in written expression as they now show in excelling in sports, in personal dress, or in social living, a great part of the battle will have been won.

As the many comments on the economic and personal values of excellence in English indicate, elsewhere in this volume, teachers must constantly hold these truths to be self-evident. When highly paid business executives and leaders in many other fields of endeavor emphasize time and time again that excellence in English is almost indispensable to excellence in any pursuit, then students should take to heart the wisdom of our leaders and resolve that they will develop now the attitudes and skills in the mother tongue that will lead to their success.

Thus the schools of the future will not have to rely upon the harassed, almost blinded, overburdened English teacher alone to carry on the fight for better written work. Many persons working in concert and with mutual understanding will do a much better job.

V. Reading and Literature

Despite various polls and the outcries of critics, the opinions from so many librarians, booksellers, college store managers, and publishers seem to indicate that our secondary and college students are reading much more and much better materials than is generally agreed. (See Chapters 10 through 14 of this book.) Even in the matter of skills in reading, our students, despite the presence of large numbers with deficiencies, seem to be doing as well in comparative tests as their counterparts of 10, 20, 30, and more years ago.[2] Nevertheless, there is no doubt that there is considerable room for improvement. Among the trends which offer hope for even greater achievement in the years ahead are these:

1. Inclusion in courses for training senior high school teachers of methodology and content for developmental and corrective reading programs. With our educational system committed to providing a high school education for almost every American

[2] See "English Meets the Challenge," *English Journal*, February 1960, pp. 70–71.

youth, we must be prepared on the secondary level to diagnose and develop reading skills. Secondary English teachers cannot afford to say that reading should be taught in the elementary grades and that those in the high schools can't bother with it.

2. Insistence upon some degree of reading skill before sending students to the next educational level. School systems which have adhered to the principle of 100% chronological promotion have changed their policies in recent years. The many bitter criticisms expressed throughout the pages of this book show the dissatisfaction that is found when students are permitted to enter high school and even college without attaining the reading skills requisite for success at these levels.

On the college level, many institutions are abandoning their "open door" policy of admitting everybody with a high school diploma from the state. Students who cannot achieve a certain minimum of excellence in English on entrance examinations are never permitted to enter. Those who cannot maintain themselves on a certain level are quickly "bounced out." Thus the tendency will undoubtedly be for more and more selective admissions into college and more insistence upon maintenance of standards while in college.

3. As to the content and amount of reading, there has been well nigh a revolution in reading habits at all levels, thanks to the availability of the thousands of paperbacks everywhere. As the replies from the bookstore managers and librarians indicate (Chapters 12, 13, 14) students are now purchasing quality books in inexpensive paperback editions in the millions of copies. Teachers can now provide far greater flexibility in their instruction, and students' interests can be satisfied at far less expense than in the days before paperbacks. Such studies as those made by the Committee on Paperbacks of the National Council of Teachers of English show the extent to which countless schools and individual teachers are utilizing the paperbacks. Some pub-

lishers of literature anthologies are also investigating the possibilities of publishing supplementary paperback volumes for enrichment and individualization.

4. The great new market for children's books and books for young adults by established writers, like the Landmark Series, and the publication of such books as Nancy Larrick's *A Parent's Guide to Children's Reading* and *A Teacher's Guide to Children's Reading* will undoubtedly contribute to greater knowledge of books among the younger generation. This knowledge and pleasure in reading books will, in turn, contribute to a greater understanding of literature in the college years.

VI. The Mass Media of Communication

Promising as are the developments in book publishing for the future of America's readership, the developments in the mass media are likewise important. Since the advent of television, millions of American children have entered school with vocabularies, speech patterns, and knowledge of the world which are far superior to those accomplishments of students of earlier generations. The motion pictures and the recording industry have likewise made significant impacts upon the skills and attitudes of our students. From time to time, various studies have been made to channelize more effectively the experiences our children and youth have. In this area the National Council of Teachers of English has established committees to study the uses of recordings, paperbacks, commercial television and educational television, and several useful documents have already appeared, plus a magazine, *Studies in the Mass Media.*

Closely allied to a study of the use of the mass media is the study of teaching machines. As the 1960's begin, there is not enough evidence one way or the other to form valid opinions as to their effectiveness. Yet they may have much to offer in the years ahead when larger enrollments unaccompanied by a corresponding increase in teacher supply will force schools and colleges to make use of some of these devices.

Neither the mass media of communication nor the teaching machines can replace the English teacher; but they can become valuable adjuncts to the instructional program if properly employed. In years to come, much experimentation will be necessary to determine how they can be used most effectively.

VII. Language Study

Many of the comments about the deficiencies in English instruction center around the presumed lack of knowledge of grammar. Occasionally hope is expressed for greater knowledge of linguistics or for the "linguistic approach." The years ahead will see a greater clarification of the role of grammatical knowledge in effective speaking and writing. Likewise there will be a diffusion downward through the teacher-training systems of the newer understandings of structural linguistics; so that future teachers of English will have a greater awareness of how language develops and operates in many cultures.

It is not a question of whether or not to teach grammar, but which grammatical concepts and at what levels to teach them. Much experimentation is needed on the best ways to transfer a knowledge of grammar into more cogent and graceful speaking and writing. Too many students can answer every question on a test in grammar and still write incoherent sentences and badly organized paragraphs.

In the area of linguistic study, it is gradually being realized that a teacher who understands how various languages operate can understand better how the language which he teaches operates. At ease in the understanding of the true structure of his language, it is presumed that he will not make impossible demands upon his students or waste their time with study of useless forms and paradigms that contribute very little to language growth.

VIII. Teacher Preparation

The finest courses of study, the most up-to-date school plants, the most expensive books and machines may not necessarily produce the best prepared students in English. The adequately prepared and devoted teacher is still the central element in the English program. To study this problem, the National Council of Teachers of English has for several years had a Committee on Teacher Preparation and Certification which has inquired into the teacher education programs throughout the country and fought for better preparation of English teachers.

Occupying a crucial role in the education of the child and youth, the English teacher must have a deep understanding of how children learn, how language skills are best taught, as well as a rich background in literature, both American and British, of the past and present. Not only must he know the facts about these literatures—and those of other countries as well—but he must be able to inspire his students to develop the same love for literature that he possesses. This is no easy task, and cannot be accomplished by the home economics teacher who needs an extra class to fill out her program, or by the health education teacher hired mainly for his prowess as a basketball coach, but who is also given a program in English. Even for the adequately prepared teacher of English to develop the attitudes and skills and to impart content is a tremendous undertaking.

One of the 5 volumes of the *Report of the Commission on the Curriculum* of the National Council of Teachers of English is to be devoted entirely to the preparation of English teachers on all levels—elementary, secondary, and collegiate. There will be found the most complete discussion in print of successful teacher education programs based upon an intensive study of courses in many institutions and the available research.

Index